SEEKING A NEW VOICE

Autobiographical Perspectives

BARRY MERCHANT

SEEKING A NEW VOICE

Autobiographical Perspectives

March 2014

To Mary

Best Wishes

Barry Merchant.

MEMOIRS
Cirencester

Published by Memoirs

25 Market Place, Cirencester, Gloucestershire, GL7 2NX
info@memoirsbooks.co.uk www.memoirspublishing.com

Seeking a New Voice: Autobiographical Perspectives

All Rights Reserved. Copyright © 2013 Barry Merchant

No part of this book may be reproduced or transmitted in any form or by any means, graphic, electronic, or mechanical, including photocopying, recording, taping or by any information storage or retrieval system, without the permission in writing from the copyright holder.

The right of Barry Merchant to be identified as the author of this work has been asserted in accordance with the Copyright, Designs and Patents Act 1988 sections 77 and 78.

The views expressed in this work are solely those of the author and do not necessarily reflect the views of the publisher, and the publisher hereby disclaims any responsibility for them.

ISBN: 978-1909544543

DEDICATION

I would like to dedicate this book to the memory of my parents: Joe and Minnie Merchant (Nee Corbett).

ACKNOWLEDGEMENTS

I would like to thank my partner Lis Bird, and my friend Tony Green for their help, encouragement and editing during the writing of this book. I would also like to thank my friend Lawrence Darani who gave me his time and energy so that I could discuss various important personal things about my life.

Thanks also to Wayne, Lucy, Jeff and Daniel for their kindness and my dear friend Sanghadeva who has given me such support over the past 20 years and to my former therapists Clive Eiles and Mark Craven. Last but not least my sincere thanks to Diadem Books for their professional support during the whole process of editing through to publication of this book - thank you all.

PROLOGUE

For as long as I can remember there had always been lots of children living in what is now the former family home. I had twelve siblings, six older and six younger than I. Mayhem had been a way of life, shouting, screaming, bellowing and all sorts of noises. If something didn't happen in the Bradbury household then it didn't exist. Fights among brothers were a daily occurrence and usually had to be broken up by my mother, an unsung heroine who kept everyone fed and clothed, and yet asked for very little in her own life. The early morning rant at some of my siblings to get out of bed and clothe themselves, have breakfast and get on their way to school most school mornings was the frustrated voice of my mother coming from downstairs. Sometimes she had no choice but to walk up the stairs and sound an almighty boom at them to 'get out of bed or you will go to school with half a mouth'. There was a reference to some sort of immediate physical threat if they did not obey. Two or three of these repeated were usually sufficient to get them out of bed, into appropriate clothes and downstairs for their breakfast and out to school all within ten minutes. Mind you, most of the younger siblings, including me, had given my mother a hard time of things over the years, but she could look after herself both physically and verbally!

CHAPTER ONE

THE BACKGROUNDS OF MY GRANDPARENTS AND PARENTS

I decided that if I were to write about the Bradbury, paternal, side of my family, including both sets of grandparents, then I would have to find out information about their lives. Who were these people, what did they do for a living and where did they all come from? I soon realised that I knew very little about my grandparents and would have to become some sort of amateur detective if I were to get to know them. With this in mind, I started my family research into the background of my paternal grandmother Roffe (1887-?). She was born in Millbrook, Bedfordshire to William and Elizabeth Roffe (née Neal) and was the eldest of five children. I took the train to Millbrook station and walked two miles along a busy country road, passing arable and pastureland into the small village. Walking along the road with a blue sky above me, I thought about my grandmother who way back in the late 19th century/early 20th century as a young woman had all those years ago walked the same road to the station on her way to London. As a young working class and unworldly woman, she had left the security of her home to seek her fortune in the big wide world. I had this mental picture of her dressed in Victorian clothes with a hat on and holding her worldly possessions in two small bags.

Apparently she had found a job working as a maid in a large house not far from Brixton. In those days Brixton was made up of very wealthy and powerful people, where domestic help was in great demand and very cheap to hire. She worked long hours for little pay and had a half day per week to herself. I don't know how and where she met my grandfather. In those days young working-class women did not frequent public houses, cafés, gambling joints, brothels and the like. Maybe they met in the local church or at a bible class, which in those days would have been run by middle class women possibly from the Temperance Movement. In that religious era of God and Country, there were many Christian groups who were prepared to do anything to save the working classes from the evils of alcohol and sex. According to family anecdotes, my maternal grandmother was liked by all, was a very quiet old soul who became deaf later on in her life.

In Millbrook village I found the local church, St Michael and All Angels. Looking around the graveyard I saw several headstones with the name of Roffe on them. One headstone in particular was dedicated to one Jacob Roffe (1796-1878), the inscription stating 'this memorial is erected by friends in token of their gratitude and esteem'. He had lived the life of a committed Christian and the Bible was his daily study. When I entered the church I realised there was some sort of Thanksgiving Day going on with a few people arranging different fruits and vegetables on colourful tables. After a few minutes an elderly man came up to me and introduced himself as the Churchwarden. I explained why I was in the church and asked how I could best seek out Roffe family information. I could not believe my ears when he explained to me that this 'church held the original parish registers dating back from the late sixteenth century'. With a huge grin he told me to follow him to the back of the church where he unlocked a door into a small dusty room full of iconography adorning the walls. From his pocket he brought out a very large old-fashioned key and said to me, 'This key dates back to the sixteenth century and a lot of my former incumbents have had to look after it, just as I am, doing their Churchwarden duties.'

He then used the old key to open an old safe and from inside he pulled out several dusty, worn books—the original parish registers. 'There you are, young man,' he said kindly, 'I will put them on the table over there and you can read to your heart's content.' I was so pleased that I said to him, 'I thank you very much for your kindness; I didn't think it would be this straightforward'—and sat down at the table eager to research the Roffe side of my family. As he was leaving to join the others in the church he nearly sang at me, 'And a good cup of tea, I'm sure you would like!' So there I was, left with a number of various spiritual beings looking down at me from the walls and conscious that I was intruding in their long inhabited home. It was an interesting three hours that I spent there locating the births, marriages and deaths of my various forebears including my father and paternal grandmother. My grandmother married my grandfather in June 1911 at St Paul's Church, Brixton. Due to the First World War bombing of London, Grandmother Roffe, who was pregnant with my father, returned to

Millbrook to give birth to my Father in 1914. He was christened Ernest Frederick James but was known to everyone thereafter as Joe.

Most of the male line of the Roffe family were farmers or farm workers and had farmed the arable and pastureland around the area that I had walked from Millbrook Station that day. Other occupations that were carried out by the Roffe family were shoemaker, lace maker and thatcher. From the various research carried out it appears that the earlier families were better off than the later ones. Before I made my way back to the station, I had a brief look round the village. There were several large detached houses and other cottage type houses, one pub/restaurant and a farm. As I proceeded to walk to the station to catch my train, I looked back at the village and contemplated on what kind of people my forebears were and what their dreams and aspirations were for what must have been a tough life. I pondered on the quality of life they had in comparison with the relatively secure and materialistic way of life we have today. As far as I could ascertain, very little is left of the Roffe family; my only contact from the past were the years I spent with my late father who didn't say a great deal about them.

My paternal grandfather, William James Bradbury (1880-?), was born in Newnham Street, which in those days was in the registration district of Marylebone. His parents were James and Mary Bradbury (née Hutchinson). I did visit the brightly painted house three years ago and it appeared to be owned now by one middle class family, which was not the case when my grandfather lived there, when the house would have been occupied by several working-class families. The whole area appeared to be very prosperous. James' father had the occupation as Dairyman, the same occupation that his son went on to work at. My research concerned this side of the family before they moved to London, probably to find work; I traced them back to Oxfordshire and before that to Gloucestershire. From reading some of the 19th century censuses, I gathered that my forebears worked as shoemaker, publican and farmer among others. There was even one John Bradbury who registered himself as a gentleman—no doubt I have his genes! For some considerable time I had assumed that the name Bradbury was Huguenot in origin and a few years ago I carried out research to find if this was the case. I therefore became a fellow of the Huguenot Society in London and started the research at their huge database but soon realised after a few hours that I was out of my depth and that I would have to employ an experienced researcher. After many hours and covering a very great deal of ground, the researcher concluded that although there is no doubt that some Bradbury's (the original spelling) were Huguenots, he found no evidence that any of them had gone as far as Gloucestershire.

Apparently my paternal grandfather was a difficult man to get on with and when not working spent most of his time on his own. (As a loner, I wonder if I have also inherited his genes.) He kept a pigeon loft some hundred yards down Ferndale Road, Brixton where he lived most of his life. I visited the house, which in my grandfather's time would have been occupied by several working-class families and was now occupied by one family. He had built the pigeon loft in his spare time, carrying the timber, bricks, felt and other materials that he needed from

Brixton market to the council owned site. He was very stubborn and independent, so my father recalls. Being an only child they did not for some reason get on very well and it was due to this unhappy way of life that my Father falsified his age and signed up for the British Army. It appears that his father did not know he had done this.

My paternal grandfather was also interested in horse and greyhound racing and regularly used to attend Wandsworth greyhound meetings, and when not working he used to travel to the occasional horse race meeting. It is important to remember that on all social occasions he would always be on his own. The only time my father remembered them being together outside the house was when they attended the funeral of his mother's aunt and also when they were invited to a party by his employer. My grandparents did not attend the wedding when my parents got married. There were a few times when my father was young that he recalled his father took him to the theatre in Brixton and elsewhere. That was at a time when the only entertainment available for most people was live theatre and stand-up comics such as Little Titch and Max Miller who were top of the bill. I don't know what eventually happened to my grandfather, where he lived or what he did with the rest of his life. All I remember was that he died sometime in the 1970's; my parents and one sibling were the only people who attended his burial. As with my grandmother's family, my late father is all that reminds me of my grandfather's background.

My father (1914-1997) had grown up in Ferndale Road, Brixton as an only child with his working-class father and mother. After returning at the age of four from Millbrook where he was born during the war, my father, like so many working class children around that time, had a hard time due to relative poverty. World War One had nearly bankrupted Britain so there was little wealth to be had. His parents were decent people and they worked hard for each other, as most other parents from that background did. You had to get on with it and make do. I don't know of the various schools that my father attended; in those days every boy and girl went to the same local school and church and always in the area where they lived, not like today where children attend schools miles from their homes. All the children in my father's time knew each other intimately; they played football in the streets, hopscotch on the pavement and met in the local park for the Mayor's yearly grand fête. Change happened very slowly in the days after the war. For a treat parents would take their children to one of the many music halls that were around in South London and afterwards eat a plate of cockles or whelks.

As mentioned before, when my father was about sixteen years old he falsified his age to join the British Army. After training he was sent to India and he apparently experienced a difficult time there. Like a lot of young men from his working class background, he wanted to get away from his family and see the world. Most of those young men, including my father, had no money, so the only choice left to them was to enlist in one of the armed services. My father also told me that a good friend of his had died in India but he didn't say what had happened. I will always remember my father's face when in the 1970's some of my siblings and I brought home an Indian takeaway. His experience in India of eating bad meat with curry was a terrible one and something that never left his mind. Indeed, occasionally he would walk out of the room when our curries were too smelly for him. When he returned to civilian life in London, his father, who was a manager at one of the United Dairies depots in London, got him a job that eventually led to passing his Heavy Goods Vehicle licence, and driving a large articulated lorry delivering milk. With a grin on his face, my father told me that his one enjoyment while driving his lorry was to park in some out of the way place and to help himself to a ladle of fresh cream from one of the on-board urns.

After leaving the United Dairies, he went on to open up a second-hand car business in South London. It is not known how he started up this business, whether it was money he had saved himself, or if it was his father who had given him the money or perhaps he had inherited or won on the football pools or horseracing. Wherever the money came from he did for a little while venture into the sometimes murky world of selling second-hand cars. It was while he had this business that he met my mother who would walk past his garage on a daily basis. She did so because she worked at Whites Button Factory in Battersea, which was about a mile from my father's car business. According to my mother, when she walked past his garage, my father would nearly always whistle and say to her 'Mornin' darlin', 'ow are you?' and 'Fancy a drink sweetheart?' There was one occasion, my father recalled, when my mother shouted at him from a passing bus, 'Stick your cars up yer arse!' Not surprising, as my mother was outspoken throughout her life. Eventually my mother agreed to meet my father and go out with him for a local drink.

My mother (1916-2004) was born into a working-class family from Battersea. She was one of six children, three girls and three boys, and she was the second eldest. She was christened Minnie Louise Florence and grew up in a strong supportive family. Her mother and father had always worked hard for the family. Times were tough for the household, yet they got by on hard graft and honesty. I recall my mother telling me several times, 'You can get to the bottom of a thief but never a liar.' Like most young girls from her background, she worked at several unskilled jobs around the Battersea area. The longest job she had was when she worked for Whites Button Factory, which wasn't far from her house. To save spending money on bus fares she would walk. After working there for a while as a machine operator she was promoted to supervisor. She told me in later life that she enjoyed working at Whites Factory and as she knew most of the girls they could have a good laugh and singsong. Also young guys worked there, and they were always up for a joke or two especially in the lunchtime canteen. Occasionally my mother told me she 'would meet up with some of the factory girls after work for a drink and a fag'. With tongue in cheek she laughed when remembering times with her factory friends, when 'Lil, Rose and me got drunk in the West End in a posh restaurant and were told to leave the place otherwise they would phone for the police'. My mother would say, 'They were great times them were!' People from my parents' and grandparents' background were always held back in life due to their class and education. Life was so predictable; where you were born was where you would stay, and you had to get on with it. As my late parents used to say to me, not unkindly, 'Life is a lot better for you people today— you can get on and be educated and become successful.'

My parents married in April 1935 at the Registry Office, which was in the registration district of Battersea.

The one grandparent that I did spend some time with was my Nanny Corbett, as we all called her. She was born Elizabeth Mary Jane Holland (1893-1976) in Bermondsey to William Holland and Minnie Louisa Stowe who shared a staunch working-class background, being rooted in the London Docks. Although she was getting on in years when I first got to know her, I found Nanny Corbett to be a kind and happy person with a strong reassuring Cockney accent. She had four sisters and one brother. Her father and grandfather both worked in the London Docks as labourers and I remember Nanny Corbett telling me that there were several other males in her family who also worked there. She was an integral part of the good and hard times when she lived with her husband and children in Battersea. Many times she explained about parties at home when neighbours would just come for a beer and song; there were no formal invitations in those days. Even the local police officer would come in, take his helmet off and sit down on a chair with a beer. Hard, usually unskilled, work was central for survival in working-class families where everyone did their bit. When she lived in London Nanny Corbett had several cleaning jobs so that she could buy food for her family. One such job was in the West End and she had to start at 6 a.m. You can imagine her getting out of bed before 5 a.m., making breakfast for her husband and then running for the bus to take her into central London. If you were late for work more than once there was always someone willing and ready to take your job.

After her husband died in 1950, she moved from the house

she had lived in for many years and was given a new council flat where she lived on her own for the first time in her life. With a lot of her family and friends around to support her, Nanny Corbett settled very quickly. She did tell me on one of the many times I visited her that living on her own was the best time of her life. Although she was getting on in years, she had found a cleaning job at the local doctor's house in Runton. Nanny Corbett had made many friends and enjoyed going out to visit various places she had not been to before. There were trips to the coast by coach and rail and she really enjoyed visiting the local pub for a glass of stout with her close friend Mrs Noble. My Mother used to visit Nanny Corbett on a regular basis and my parents would often invite her round to the house for lunch or to a restaurant. Of the four grandparents it was Nanny Corbett that I have fond memories of and how she epitomises the good qualities and decency that human beings have. What came first to her was the well-being of her family and she grafted, as did my grandfather and my parents, to provide for them. What used to make us all laugh was when Nanny Corbett would say, 'I love that American pop singer Elsie Presley!' She was a good sort, as they say.

I don't recall ever meeting my maternal grandfather, but my mother insists that I did on one occasion as I walked to his house with the gift of a banana for him! Albert George Otway Corbett (1889-1950), was born in Battersea, London and worked as a railway porter for most of his life on several London stations. His parents were Albert and Caroline Bundle. My grandfather married Elizabeth Mary Jane Holland, my maternal grandmother, on 29th October 1912. Of the scant information I could find, among his male forebears had been a locomotive engine driver, painter and general labourer. At the age of 61 years he died of lung cancer and was buried in the graveyard of St Mary the Virgin in Runton Village. My parents and maternal grandmother are also buried in the same graveyard.

From the various anecdotes that I have collected along the way, my grandfather was a decent father and trusted friend. My mother told me of the many occasions that her father used to take the family to London Zoo and treat them to candy floss and toffee apples. There were good times at Christmas and birthday parties when several uncles and aunts used to visit the home. My mother used to be able to play the piano and her father, mother and the whole family would sing songs for hours. A 'good old knees up' as my mother fondly used to call it. When my mother and her siblings were young, grandfather used to take them all to the Cinema, a new and exciting venture in those days. There they would watch their heroes like Fred Astaire and Ginger Rogers, Charlie Chaplin, the Keystone Cops and Roy Rogers among many others.

Like most of us lesser mortals, my grandfather used to enjoy a good drink, especially at parties. Apparently when he went to parties and whether he was drunk or sober he would always refuse to sleep in another person's bed. My grandparents and even some of his children would have to walk miles sometimes to reach their home. It nearly always caused bitter rows between my grandparents. Another activity that irritated his wife was his gambling on the horses and greyhounds. Being a rank and file trade unionist, my grandfather used to buy the *Daily Mirror*, from where he would pick his winners or (probably losers). As he was a drinker and smoker all his life it is not surprising that the Grim Reaper got him at a relatively early time in life. One thing my mother did recall with pride was her dad's pub singing. Around the Battersea area Albert Corbett was well known for his singing of the old favourites, especially after a few pints of beer. He loved nothing more than getting up in a crowded pub and roar, 'It's only because I'm a Londoner', 'Roll out the barrel', 'Oh you Beautiful Doll', and his favourite, 'Doing the Lambeth walk'. He would sing a medley of the old London tunes and of course people would accompany him. Afterwards the local fish seller would come in the pub selling jellied eels, muscles, cockles and whelks. All that finished when my maternal grandparents, my parents and several of Mother's siblings, all moved from Battersea to Runton in Surrey. Between the two World Wars huge swathes of land was being developed for housing between Wimbledon in London and Epsom in Surrey. Most of the development was for private housing, but a small percentage had to be allocated to those people who could not afford to buy their own house. Due to the unhealthy housing they were living in, my parents made a successful application for social housing and at the time Runton was considered countryside.

My parents were very young and inexperienced when they arrived in Runton with the intention of spending the rest of their lives there. They had been given a three-bedroom semi-detached house with a long garden for the children to play in. When most of the children were young my father made a small pond for several ducks and chickens and it was good fun playing with them. He also planted several fruit trees, which included two damson trees. My siblings and I used to shake the trees so fruit would fall to the ground and we would eat them. Can you visualise several young children all holding their stomachs waiting for the toilet? Beyond the garden was a small wood with the River Wandle running through it where we played a lot of the time. Also at the back of the house were council allotments which later on in his life my father would rent—two plots—and he produced an abundance of vegetables over the years. The council had many good quality schools including a grammar school which is not surprising for Runton had a middleclass way of life. The housing estate we lived on was mainly all private semi-detached houses with well-maintained gardens and a family car. At the back of all the houses where we lived was a green belt that stretched for miles, eventually finishing at Tolworth. On these newly conceived green belts my siblings and I would play and cycle with other children we had met at school.

This was a new beginning for both of my parents and something they had dreamed about for most of their short marriage. In London things had not been particularly successful during their short lives on this earth, but things could now change with commitment, hard work and a little luck. My Dad's second-hand car business had not been a rip-roaring success; he just about made a living each week to keep the wolf from the door. If he was honest about being self-employed, he would have said, as he did later on in his life, 'I would have made more money and had less responsibility if I grafted for an employer.' Also, as my mother had been confined to semi-skilled/unskilled work not far from where she had been born and brought up, her opportunities were very limited. I am not being disrespectful to my mother's family but they would agree that with hindsight your prospects in life are better in Surrey than they were on a large Council Estate in Battersea. So with very little money in their pockets, no job and a few pieces of old furniture, they were going to take their chances in Runton.

Things settled down for all the family. My grandfather of course kept his job with British Rail as a porter working on Clapham Junction station where he had been for a number of years. He was very popular with both colleagues and customers alike; he nearly always had a joke or smile for most people. Occasionally he would give them a London Cockney tune over the loudspeaker system where customers would sing along with him until his boss heard about it. His boss was a chap named Bob Stokes who lived locally in Battersea Rise and had started as a porter himself at the age of fifteen and worked his way up to station foreman. Bob was married with three sons and his wife Sybil had worked nearby in a working-men's café, as they called them in those days. My grandfather and Bob, when they weren't working, used to from time to time go racing to Epsom, Sandown and Hurst Park. As my Mother used to tell me many times when I grew up, 'Your grandfather used to go racing and most of the bloody time would lose his money, so don't waste your time going to those poxy places!' I'm afraid her comments fell on deaf ears! But what was important for my grandfather and his colleagues was the camaraderie that racing, football pools and a few beers brought. During the Second World War Clapham Junction took several large hits from German bombing and two of my grandfather's colleagues were killed. Both of them had been close colleagues and good friends. My mother explained to me and some of my siblings that 'he (our grandfather) and colleagues had collected money for the bereaved families and took it round to them along with food'. What a remarkable gesture, considering the time!

It had only taken my father a few days before he found a lorry driving job in nearby Epsom. It was for a small local family business that had been operating for some thirty years and in the main delivered coal and coke to the nearby psychiatric hospitals. I think there were only two other employees working for the family business and my father got to know both drivers well. He was a gregarious sort of chap and got on well with most people including his new employer. Being an only child I found my father to be a kind and generous man who usually thought of others. I remember when I was young one of his colleagues called Bert coming round our house on several occasions for tea and dropping off various things for my father that could well have fallen off the back of a lorry.

One story my father told me and my siblings on several occasions was to do with a patient who resided in one of the local psychiatric hospitals. On this particular occasion he drove, as he usually did, on to the hospital weigh bridge with his intended full load of coal when a young male came up to him and asked whether he would help him escape from the hospital. With no questions asked, my father told him to go down to the boiler house, where he unloaded the coal, and, 'if you want to jump into the back of the empty lorry, I will drop you off nearby Epsom town'. That is exactly what my father did and nothing more was heard of the young man.

Another time my father gave some work to a psychiatric patient who lived in another local hospital. His name was Phillip; he was about fifty years of age, was born in London and apparently had been educated at Cambridge University. He had been in the hospital for about twenty years, no one ever visited him, and, he had become lost in the bureaucratic psychiatric system. My father drove Philip to our house explaining to him the various vegetables that he wanted planted in the back garden. When he returned a few hours later my father realised that most of the plants had been planted upside down. Gardening, it appeared, was certainly not on the syllabus at Cambridge; but to be fair to the chap, he was by that time probably institutionalised. In time my father also became friendly with some of the porters that operated the weigh bridges in the hospitals. One porter in particular was a chap named David Fox; many years later I would go to school with his son Howard and visit a Soho strip club together. Incidentally, when Mr Fox retired he moved to live with Howard in Australia who had emigrated there.

Both my father and mother were both slowly but surely putting down roots and getting to know various local people. Her parents and siblings would visit on a regular basis and generally support each other. Nanny Corbett had found a local cleaning job and when another came vacant in the same place informed my mother who applied and got the job. She did not work there for long however, because she had become pregnant with her first child and the first of thirteen children she would conceive over the years. In 1936 at the tender age of nineteen years she gave birth to Martin in Camberwell Hospital, an old Victorian Hospital; he was born a good weight, strong and healthy.

Being the first child he was the centre of attention; lots of clothes and toys were bought for him by all his extended family. My mother told me that after several months all the family wanted her to visit them with little Martin who by this time had started to walk and was developing his own personality. My mother started taking her child to the GP practice to get him weighed and to the local mother and child clinic where she subsequently met two young mothers with whom in time she would become friendly.

Over the years I would visit these two women with my mother and play with their children in the attractive garden of their private house. One of the reasons I enjoyed visiting this house was the food I was given to eat. The lady of the household, Brenda Bethel, would cook all the children mouth-watering eggs and bacon with chips. Other times she cooked beans on toast with lots of tomato ketchup and egg sandwiches. This sort of food was something I did not get to eat at home or at school. My parents could not afford to buy luxury food due to their income. With the utmost respect for my parents who worked very hard to provide for the family, we would usually have bread and jam followed by orange squash. These children went to the local state infant school I recall but later on they went to a fee paying private school. No doubt their parents had aspirations for them and I don't ever remember seeing them again. One incident has stayed firmly in my mind over the years and that is on several occasions I gave this exaggerated speech in front of her family and remember Brenda Bethel saying to my mother, 'Doesn't he speak well.' That exaggerated speech could have meant my increasing unconscious sense of inferiority or insecurity was growing.

In 1937 my mother gave birth to her second child, a girl, named Jennifer. She was born in Epsom District Hospital, a typical modern urban hospital, strong and healthy. She attended all the local schools and did very well both in sports and academics. Due to various problems she had with my mother, Jennifer moved to live with her female friend in Kent. As I was very young at the time, about 6 years of age, I am not aware what happened to Jennifer when she left home to make her way in the world. It wasn't until many years later when I visited her home that she explained to me what happened and how her life had developed. This also applies to several other older siblings. As I was born in 1947, I am unable to make any in depth comment about my first six siblings when they were young and not a great deal is known about them later on. It will only be possible to comment about them as my story unfolds, where I will be in a position to discuss rather scant information. But I do not know what my parents or siblings did with their lives most of the time. All I wish to do is to be as honest and open about my life as much as possible.

With the Second World War fast approaching in 1939, my mother gave birth to a third child, a son called James, in Epsom District Hospital. Similar to the other two children, James was born strong and healthy. It appears that he was an average pupil but was good at most sports, playing for the school and district soccer teams and was also a competent boxer. During the war my father was in the home guard in a place called Northbrook, where most of this work was carried out in the evening. During the day he continued to make vital coal and coke deliveries to the local hospitals. In addition and for the remainder of the war he delivered coal and coke to Army barracks in East

Surrey. Also it was during these evenings, under the cover of darkness, that the German planes would drop their bombs on London and other important areas of the South East of England.

Within the years that followed my mother gave birth to three more healthy children, two sons and a daughter. David was born in 1941, Robert in 1942 and Margaret in 1945 and all three of them were born in Epsom District Hospital. With so many children to cook and feed my mother was not able to earn money working. My father continued to drive his lorry delivering coal and coke to more hospitals in Surrey as his employer's family business grew. He certainly needed the money to provide for his growing family.

CHAPTER TWO

MY BIRTH, ELECTROCUTION, SEXUAL ABUSE AND SCHOOL DAYS

I was born in January 1947 in Epsom District Hospital, and according to my mother, was healthy and rapidly put on weight. The first significant experience that I can recall happened to me when I was about three years of age and it was to probably have a major impact subsequently on my life. Most of the traumatic incident is vague, but I do remember being in the back bedroom of our house and touching the wall-mounted electric fire when all of a sudden I starting shaking uncontrollably until my mother held me in her arms close to her chest. Even in the reassuring arms of my mother my little vulnerable body was in alternating spasms from very stiff to near lifeless existence. I had been accidentally electrocuted by 240 volts by the live wires that were hanging from the electric fire. Everything else is blank; suffice to say I do not remember going to see the doctor or having any other kind of therapy or treatment to help me overcome this traumatic accident. My parents never said anything about the incident for the rest of their lives. But I must assume that my father had over the years experienced a considerable amount of guilt for allowing me to play in a room exposed to an electric fire in such a dangerous condition.

The reason I point out the guilt factor is because of the way my parents, my dad in particular, used to treat me somewhat favourably compared to my siblings when I lived at home. I would like to clarify my position by saying that when I was treated 'favourably' it is with benefit of hindsight. At the time I was very young and would not have had the insight to understand what was happening to me. It began to dawn on me as the years went by, that I could demand things from my father that my other siblings could not. For example, when I was about three years of age my father took me and three of my siblings to London Zoo. I refused to walk all afternoon, so my father had to carry me. I demanded ice creams and he bought them without buying them for my siblings. Other times he would give me money to buy sweets and comics when others went without. When I used to come home from school with a list of things I wanted, he would buy them for me—things such as sports plimsolls, books, soccer boots, money for school trips and outings, and so on and so forth. I now realise all this favouritism that was heaped on me as a young boy and continued into my early twenties was very unhealthy for me, and it is possible that it could have held me back from developing both emotionally and intellectually. Furthermore, the major trauma I experienced when I was young could have made it very difficult for a healthy attachment to develop between my mother and me.

By the time I was five years old and had started infant school, two more children had been born, making it nine children at that stage. In June 1948 Sidney was born and in 1951 Susan; both of them were healthy and had attended the same hospital that we all had (except for Martin). At the infant school in West Lane, a handsome looking Victorian building, I was doing quite well and within two weeks I had found my first girlfriend called Christine Bungard. I shall never forget this name as nearly all my siblings, even the older ones, called me Bungard whenever they saw me and especially in the house my nickname was reinforced at every opportunity! I played in the class football team, rounders team and was chosen to act in a play called *Humpty Dumpty* in front of teachers, pupils and parents. When the play had finished the Head teacher, Miss Smith, gave a brief talk to the audience about how good and skilful we all were. She then encouraged us to bow in front of everyone, who by this time were taking photographs of the ragbag actors.

Miss Smith was short, slim and popular around the school where she would walk round the playground and orchard smiling and saying hello to everyone. She reminded me of that quintessential middleclass English spinster who really enjoyed helping her fellow man. My parents were there to see me perform and I was proud at what I had achieved. That night when I arrived home my siblings and parents all congratulated me; I also remember feeling on top of the world even when they continued to call me Bungard.

One incident that happened to me which was of great embarrassment was when I fell over in the playground, after it had been raining, and had soaked the back of my short trousers. One of the female teachers, they were all female teachers, saw me fall and noticed the state of my trousers so she took me to the first aid room where I was told to take off my sodden trousers. She said to me, 'Come along Barry, don't be shy and take off those wet trousers and pants so we can dry you.' All I could do was to look at the teacher in extreme panic trying to think that the only person ever to do that was my mother. Eventually she coaxed them off, dried me and gave me a dry pair of trousers to wear. That incident has stayed in my mind for the rest of my life.

By this time Sidney (Sid to everyone) had started at the same infant school. The class teacher, Miss Soames, a young fair-headed slim woman of about 25 years, delegated me to look after Sid who at this stage was rather apprehensive of the noise and conformity that was happening to him. All I can assume is that I must have gone through a similar experience myself, insofar as leaving one's mother for the time is painful for most children. Nonetheless he settled in well and was soon rampaging around the playground shouting and screaming at everyone in sight. However, his classroom teacher told my parents on more than one occasion that Sid's work in the classroom was good though from time to time he needed to be reminded where he was and what he should be concentrating on. Sid and I, and other boys who were in our gang, often used to meet after lunch in the orchard where we played five a side football pretending we were playing for Chelsea. Great stuff!

One naughty activity we engaged in was walking round the playground or orchard pinching girls' bottoms which was received by them with scorn. On one occasion one of the gang, Reggie, who was a bit of a tearaway, quietly walked up to the back of a girl and tried to pull her knickers down. Not surprisingly she complained to her class teacher who in turn brought Reggie up in front of the Head Teacher who told him to apologise to the girl concerned and if it happened again he would be in big trouble. When it was time to move on to the junior school, unfortunately Reggie moved away from Runton as his parents had both found work in the West Country and I did not see him again. He was a good friend, tall, slim and well-spoken and at the time he always had a crew cut hairstyle. I often wondered what became of him in the mainstream of society; perhaps he became a successful businessman or doctor or even a senior police officer. If you read these words, Reggie, let me know how you are.

At around the age of seven years I became more aware of things generally and in particular my place within the group. It is odd really how these things kind of creep up on you. Maybe the logical explanation was that at school, learning and interacting with many others for the first time, provided the conditions for my young brain to grow and develop. There was one incident that I found to be particularly painful and which has once again stayed in my head throughout my life. We were sitting in the classroom one morning when the teacher, Miss Soames, informed us that 'Terry (a pupil in my class) now has a new baby sister. His mother has given birth to a baby girl called Anne only yesterday and we should congratulate him.' We all, including Miss Soames, clapped for at least a minute. At this stage I had an overwhelming experience that I would recall many years later, of a sense of inferiority welling up inside me that I wanted to hide away from everyone. What caused the intense feelings, I assume, was that only the day before my mother had also given birth to a healthy son called Wayne. At that moment I thought, why didn't Miss Soames announce the birth of my brother to the class, and why had they not given me an almighty applause? In that split second I realised that somehow I was different to the others; whether that was real or imagined I cannot recall or explain. I felt sure that the teacher must have known about the birth of my baby brother, and if she had not known about the birth, then why not ask like she did with Terry? I remember sitting at my classroom desk feeling that I was not wanted by anyone. Whatever the explanation was for the awful feelings I had experienced, things would not be quite the same again. With the benefit of hindsight, I wondered whether the trauma of being accidentally electrocuted was, even at this stage, affecting me. I realised that at this stage, aged seven years, I was experiencing intense anxiety in certain situations. This would get much worse when, later on, I started to develop severe anxiety, which I would find disabling throughout the first forty years or so of my life. This was exacerbated by other conditions, which I shall refer to later.

Another thing that I was acutely aware of throughout my infant and junior school days at West Lane was the stigma of receiving free school meals. In the two schools I had attended we had to line up early Monday morning to pay for lunches for the week; when it came to my turn I had to state that my food was free, due to my father's income, in front of all the other children. My growing sensitivity even at this stage was distorting, I felt, the way I was trying to understand the world around me. For example, even at the age of seven I felt that people did not like me as I was preoccupied with thoughts of being found out or humiliated over matters I did not understand. For one so young and vulnerable, I thought much later, it must have been so difficult to have been burdened with such intense feelings.

Round about this time there was also some enjoyable things happening within the family. Both my parents had worked very hard to save enough money to buy our first car which was a blue Ford (EGN 805) so they could at last take the children out. I vividly remember most Saturday evenings during May to October several children helping my mother to make the mountain of sandwiches and gallons of squash we would all consume the next day. My mother was always the first to insist that she 'wanted to get the children out of the house and get some fresh air into them'. Most Sundays during the seasons my siblings and I would be out of bed very early in the morning to get ready for the day's outing in our new car, highly polished by one of us working to a weekly rota. What a sight it must have been in the middleclass area where we lived, at least five, maybe six, children shouting and giggling among ourselves, holding the food, various bats and balls, and all trying to squeeze into a small car.

The neighbours must have given a sigh of relief to know the Bradburys would be out of town for a few hours, especially when they heard the booming sound of my mother's voice echoing around the streets. I soon realised that to have some control of her near environment, my mother would have to be a relatively controlling and dominant person over an ever-growing family; otherwise things would quickly get out of hand. A lesser mortal than my mother would have ended up in a psychiatric hospital, but to her great credit I never once in my life saw her take any prescribed medication. However, there were times when she could have benefited from short term medication to support her through the difficult periods. But as she so eloquently used to say, 'They can stick that stuff up their arse!'—and it is important to remember that from her background they did not trust people from the middle classes.

Be that as it may, my parents with the children in mind on our Sunday outings took us to many different places around Surrey and Kent. We went to Boxhill on numerous occasions, an interesting place where we could run down the steep hill to the River Mole to try and catch the unsuspecting fish with our cheap 6d nets. Failing that method we would throw small stones or branches into the river hoping to stun the fish instead or on occasions obliterate them. When our parents were not around we would have a tremendous laugh climbing the tall trees, paddle in the water and as we got older, Sid and I would smoke our cheap park drive fags or, failing that, kerbside twists (dog ends). On one occasion Sid and I met two working-class girls around our age also playing in the River Mole splashing each other. We asked them into the nearby bushes for a fag and both of us tried to touch their breasts but they refused, saying they had to go home.

Wherever we had our sandwiches to eat, it was like watching monkeys fighting amongst themselves at the zoo rather than a civilised family outing. Mother would dish out the sandwiches followed by equal amounts of squash to each child. After about a minute's silence, one of us would accidentally on purpose knock over someone's squash and all hell would then break loose. Someone would kick over another sibling's drink and he/she would throw the others sandwich down the hill. Fighting and shouting would ensue with my mother trying to bring sanity to the group. Even as a youngster, I can still visualise the other normal families there on the hill laughing at the sight in front of them, assuming we had been let out for the day from some Institution.

On another occasion my father drove us to Brighton for the day, arriving early in the afternoon hot sun with the car full of mountains of sandwiches that my mother had made the night before, ably assisted by rampaging kids. After my father had parked the car nearby, my mother was followed by six young Bradburys holding buckets and spades as they descended onto the stony cold beach where we kicked, pushed and shouted at each other. The people already sitting quietly enjoying themselves on the beach must have been horrified at the sight of the Bradbury clan arriving when we started kicking over the immaculately built sandcastles built by others. After ten minutes my father arrived holding two deckchairs he had rented for a few hours for him and my mother. Then all of a sudden there was an almighty roar: 'You, put this fucking deckchair up for me, I can't do it!'—from my mother shouting at the top of her voice to my father, whereupon it appeared that all the people sitting on the beach turned round at the same time, startled by the commotion. Although I was no more than ten years of age at the time, I still remember how embarrassed I was to be associated with my mother who, as the years went by, would further humiliate my father in various public places.

As well as visiting many other places for the day, Worthing,

Lancing and Richmond Park among others, my parents started taking the family away for one week, and then much later when they had more money, for two weeks' holidays. Even though my father drove for a living he was keen to drive his family to various places outside London. During one of the earlier holidays in Margate we rented a two-bedroom brightly coloured bungalow on a private estate with a delightful garden with a large well maintained lawn and borders full of roses, lavender and rosemary. After a relatively long journey—even roads in those days were usually full—we arrived in the afternoon with all the kids on board the car shouting and screaming at each other, and no doubt, I made as much noise as anyone else. The local retired elderly residents must have thought that Chipperfield Circus or the inmates from the lunatic asylum had just arrived. They probably wondered what they had done during their long lives to deserve this intrusion!

My mother took three of my siblings and me shopping to the local store to buy the food for the family meal. Before we left she emphasised to my brother David that he must look after the food that was cooking on the gas stove. With his stammer, David nervously said he would 'keep an eye' on the food. My mother angrily retorted, 'Keep *both* fucking eyes on it!' At the store Sid and I stole two apples, a Mars bar and Bounty which not even my mother, with her eagle eyes, noticed. Out of the shop, we all trundled back to our abode, each of us holding a large bag full of potatoes, greens or mince, which was our staple diet for the holiday.

When we all walked through the back door into the bungalow we were greeted by the horror of seeing mincemeat all over the walls and ceiling of the attractive pale blue kitchen. Then mother shouted at David, 'What the fuck have you done', as he tried his utmost, badly stammering, trying to explain what had happened. It appears that he went out into the garden for ten minutes to hang out the children's clothes to air them, and when he returned to the kitchen there was meat everywhere. My exasperated mother once again shouted at David, 'I told you to stay in here and keep an eye on the fucking mince, didn't I', going red in the face with rage. 'Right,' she said most clearly, 'you three', pointing at David, Bob and me, 'go and buy a plastic bucket, sponge and a packet of cleaning fluid from Masons convenient store up the road and don't be long'—handing a pound note to Bob. On our return we all thoroughly washed down the walls, ceiling, floor and cooker so that no stains could be seen. By this time father had returned from the local garage where he had the car tyres pumped up after our relatively long and tiring journey from Runton in Surrey. When he walked into the kitchen, he could see and smell that the kitchen had been cleaned and asked with a smile on his face, 'What has been going on here?' Mother explained, still rather animated by the incident, and all my father could say rather philosophically was, 'Never mind kids, that's life. Let's go and buy some chips!' It turned out to be a good holiday for everyone with my parents taking us to the local castles and National Trust gardens. The only minor problem during this time was when Sid couldn't find a toilet at Howard Castle and had to have a wee, rather indiscreetly, on one of the flower beds where he succeeded flattening some of the Trust's prize petunias.

On another holiday in Ramsgate we lost young Wayne—he

was only about five years old—for a few hours until the local police located him in Butlins holiday camp. It appears that he went wandering on the beach, not far from the house where we were staying for a week, on his own and got lost. Instead of asking someone for the correct directions back to the beach—'Don't talk to strangers!' Mother had always insisted—he kept walking and walking, eventually ending up at the main gates of the local holiday camp. After observing Wayne for a few minutes the holiday camp security officer asked him if he was lost from his parents, and if so, he reassured him that he would find them. It appeared that Wayne was not upset by the experience.

Two miles or so back along the beach, where all the family were from the holiday camp, my parents had notified the police and coastguard about Wayne's disappearance. It transpired that Butlins had phoned the police of the whereabouts of Wayne and we would have to collect him from there ourselves. My father delegated me to collect my brother and saw me onto the local bus, requesting the conductor to put me off at Butlins. When I arrived at the main gate the security officer sent me to the restaurant where I found my brother, with a large grin all over his face, digging into a large plate of fish and chips. I wasn't so lucky; all they gave me was a cup of tea and a jam bun. Afterwards we took the bus back to where we were staying, and as Wayne only had a flimsy bathing costume on, I gave him my thick jumper to wear. What an insult! We were all so relieved that he had been found safe and that no harm had come to him even though my father clumped him round the head for straying up the beach. I remember years later about this incident when at the time my mother had thought he might have been 'washed out to sea by large waves'. There was never a dull moment when the Bradburys were around.

Early one Sunday morning my father had a great idea, so he thought, to drive down to Portsmouth to visit Lord Nelson's flagship, *The Victory*. With all the children, sandwiches, drink, bats, balls and everything else except the kitchen sink, we drove forth from Runton, no doubt to the great relief of the neighbours, arriving about three hours later. After eating our food, a show on its own, we set out to find Nelson's great ship, now visited by many thousands of tourists every year. Eventually we found the ship in dry dock. 'Look mum, there's Nelson's cannon,' I said enthusiastically to my mother. 'Fuck his cannon!' was her response to an innocent young child's enjoyment at the first sight of an old artefact.

Back at West Lane school it was time for me, being now eight years of age, to take a big step and join the all-boys junior school, which was literally next door to the infant school. During the past three years I had been surrounded by female teachers and at least half the class were female; now I was going to be in the presence, apart from one female teacher, of males. As I was physically and emotionally growing up, that meant, among other things, I had to be more responsible for myself and demonstrate to a certain level that I was now fit for more mature society. When that dreaded Monday came and I walked, unlike the way I entered the infants' school, on my own with a new uniform and books to present myself at Runton junior school. The school was a charming Victorian brick building which could not cater for more than one hundred and fifty pupils. I remember parading in the playground along with about thirty other young boys of a similar age. Standing before us was a military like figure that I instantly recognised as the Headmaster, Mr Frost, who had given me and several other pupils from the infant school a tour of the school some two months before. At that time we were shown into his classroom where my older brother Robert was a pupil, and in front of everyone shouted to him in a loud voice, 'Your younger brother needs a haircut, Bradbury!' I had wished the ground would open up to hide me from everyone who was looking at me; humiliation, it seemed, was stalking me!

As things settled down, I began to develop friendships among the twenty-five boys in my class. The classroom teacher, Mr Still, was a reassuring person who used to tell us jokes about his army days fighting in Europe during the Second World War. He would pull up his right trouser leg to show us his war wound, a largish scar just below his knobbly ultra-white knee. Tall and slim with a mound of brown hair, Mr Still was born in Wales and moved to London to find a teaching job when he was in his early twenties. He was proud of Welsh singing and rugby and would always try to buy a ticket to watch England play Wales at Twickenham. As time went on I started to really enjoy going to his History lessons, to learn about how the Victorians had controlled a great empire consisting of a third of the world's population. It was due to Mr Still's enthusiastic lessons on the Industrial Revolution that I became interested in how working-class men made a living under sometimes terrible conditions down mines, in shipyards and in factories. His interest in such matters probably came from first hand experiences of his forebears, who had worked down the coal mines.

Around about this time my eldest sibling Martin had been called up by the government to do his two years national service. He had joined the East Surrey regiment for his training and after a few months was stationed somewhere in West Germany. He came home every few months to visit the family and usually brought home with him a soldier friend. When Martin used to be asleep in bed, I used to nick a pack of Flash American cigarettes from his army suitcase, which was full of cigarettes, sexy magazines, letters from girlfriends and rock and roll records of the Everly Brothers.

For a while I was very popular in my class when I showed several of my friends, as we congregated in the male toilets, the Flash American cigarettes. All you could see as we coughed and spluttered trying to smoke the strong American cigarettes was the smoke billowing out of the toilets like Battersea power station. When the fags were all smoked it was to be expected that my popularity would not last. At the time one important thing I was aware of was how proud I was of my oldest sibling Martin who looked so smart and attractive in his army uniform offset by short cut dark brown curly hair. All the army friends, many of them Cockneys, that he brought home called him 'Curl'. Another vivid cherished memory I have of Martin was the light blue Teddy Boy suit with drainpipe trousers he used to wear which typified the young at the time. While still in the army, he used to date a young woman, Nancy, who hailed from Dublin and worked as a nurse in one of the nearby psychiatric hospitals. I liked Nancy very much and she nearly always use to buy us children large bags of sweets and comics such as the *Beano* and *Dandy*. She was short, attractive, had long blonde hair and was always laughing. Nancy used to call round our home for Martin at least once a week, have a meal with us and when leaving to go out for the night socialising they would both look immaculately dressed in their hip clothes.

While on the subject of clothes, I remember discussing with my friend Roger one Friday after school about visiting the local cinema next day. As he was an only child, his parents could afford to buy him lots of clothes. He suggested that we wear our best clothes to look cool next day at the cinema. Unbeknown to my mother, I had to sneak out of the house early next morning with a clean school shirt and trousers hidden in a bag. I walked to the woods at the back of my house to change into the clothes I had managed to covertly carry out of the house. I had to put my dirty clothes in the bag which I had to carry around with me for several hours until I returned home. When Roger asked why I was carrying a bag of clothes I explained that my mother was donating them to charity. Isn't it incredible that at ten years of age I didn't have the confidence to ask my mother whether I could wear my cleaner clothes to the cinema instead having to covertly dress into different clothes hidden behind a nearby tree! Even at that early stage of my life I must have been very frightened of my mother.

In the junior school I continued to make steady progress among my classmates. My academic development was about average with the usual end of term report stating that 'I could do better', 'Barry is easily distracted', 'he is easily led' and 'if only he would listen sometimes'. No doubt all valid comments from my teacher at a time, when I was trying to make friendships and develop some kind of identity for myself in an ever-growing and challenging environment of young males. Furthermore, I felt uneasy about whether people really enjoyed being in my company, and this growing doubt made me feel anxious.

One individual, however, that I did feel quite secure with was Peter Upton. He did not go to the local infant school but joined the junior school first year, having moved to Runton from Dorset with his Family. Peter and I got on very well from the outset. I remember first seeing him in the first year classroom sitting on the top of his desk smoking a large cigarette laughing his head off. 'Hello,' he said, 'I'm Pete, hope there are no teachers around.' I remember saying to him, 'You want to be careful, Taffy might catch you.' Even in those earliest days when I first met Peter he really did not appear to be frightened of teachers or pupils or anything else. He seemed not to take life that seriously although he was very good at drawing and painting particular landscapes but later his interest in the subject waned. It was only two years later when he got to know me, and other boys, that he went on to enjoy several other activities, especially football. Pete had something that I didn't have—confidence.

It was about a year later that my older brother James joined the Royal Marines, something he had always wanted to achieve. My parents gave a large party in his honour, which was attended by most of his siblings, his friends, girlfriend, and Martin was there with Nancy. I remember my father giving a speech about how proud he was that his son was going to train and work with the elite Marines. My father also said, 'My son James is leaving this household tomorrow and he will be sorely missed by all.'

It was unfortunate that he didn't share that sentiment years later when they fell out. The party went on until the small hours, when most people went to bed or left to go home, leaving James with his girlfriend at the time, Brenda, and my parents talking. He wanted to spend an intimate hour or so with those nearest to him as he would be leaving the home that morning, so he wanted to express his gratitude to them. My mother said that brief time before he left was 'very moving' and that they appreciated that their son 'was growing up and undertaking something very difficult'. When we crawled out of bed later that morning we realised that James would have arrived by this time at the Dorset naval base of Porchester. That meant that my two eldest brothers were now working for Queen and Country.

In the second and third years at the junior school, I began to excel at sports in particular playing for the school soccer team. A week before the school soccer trials, an important time for those players budding to be another Stanley Matthews or Tom Finney, the school's second and third year classes went for a coach trip to Hampton Court. As nearly always happens on these occasions, boys and girls would split up into small groups depending on sexual or other motivations at the time. Peter and a small group, including myself, went off to hide in the maze so that not one of the three teachers would see us lighting up to smoke one of our cheap 'coffin nail' cigarettes, as we called them at the time. In the maze Peter, John, Bill, Bryan, John and I were all blazing away with the cigarettes in our mouths, when all of a sudden one of the teachers called Mr Tate put his head round the entrance to the maze. 'What do you think you lot are doing?' he said. He went on in a rather aggressive tone, 'You can see the smoke billowing out from here a mile away', and he added, 'I am not surprised that you, Upton and Bradbury, are among this gang! Put those cigarettes out at once and follow me out of this maze to where I can deal with you all.' We all sheepishly followed the teacher, watched by several of our innocent classmates sitting on the lawn laughing their heads off, to where there were three wooden seats. Mr Tate instructed us to sit down, upon which he read us the Riot Act, promising he would report this serious incident to the headmaster as soon as we arrived back at the school. After he had finished scolding us, he said, 'Do not let me see any of you smoking again today or any other time. Now go and enjoy yourselves, be diligent and see how many different flowers and trees you can name in the grounds here for tomorrow's class discussion.' We knew where we would like to put the flowers. 'And as for you, Upton and Bradbury in particular,' he said with scorn, 'I expect both of you to provide me with a variety of different tree and plant names for tomorrow, and if this is not forthcoming then beware!' Well, we were left in no uncertain frame of mind what was required of us next day at school.

Back at school the following day the gang of us had been very busy writing down, preparing ourselves, not just for the nature programme with Mr Tate, but what we were going to say to the Headmaster after school had finished that afternoon. Mr Tate in his usual abrasive manner hauled the five of us up in front of the class not only to make sure we had done our homework from yesterday's outing but also to chastise us for smoking. Little did he know that most of the other pupils sitting down also smoked, and that the only crime in their eyes was getting caught! All five of us had to read to the class about our nature watch findings from the day before, mindful that most of the information we regurgitated had come from other classmates or from textbooks.

Satisfied with the work we had produced, Mr Tate sent us to the Headmaster's office for being caught smoking in Hampton Court. We walked tentatively up to the Headmaster's office and knocked. 'Come in!' he shouted like some sergeant major bellowing to underlings. Peter went in first followed by me and then the others. 'Sit down, all of you, and listen to what I have to say.' He went on about school pride, the importance of individual responsibility when visiting other public places and that we were now old enough to know right from wrong. 'I will give all of you one last opportunity—don't let the school, me or yourselves down. Furthermore,' he said, in his military style voice, 'go forth from here and be successful. I have heard from the sports master that most of you are good at soccer or athletics; well, let's see how good you all are.' With our tails between our legs he ushered us out of his office. We could not believe our luck—he had not caned us or imposed any restrictions upon us. I remember Peter saying of the Headmaster afterwards, 'I thought we would have been expelled or at least that he would write to our parents about our smoking.' The Headmaster was in essence a good person who thought that young people in particular deserved to be given opportunities in life which helped develop their self-esteem.

Although in future we continued to smoke more discreetly, we had put the incident behind us and we were now concentrating on the soccer trials. The sports master, Mr

Davies, had assembled about twenty boys who he thought had potential in the playground, as the rain pelted down, to see who was good enough to represent the school at soccer. Mr Davies was a good teacher who was liked by most of the boys in my class, including myself. He had been at the school for about six years, and for three of those years he had taught geography. With a small moustache and slim build he looked very much like Field Marshal Montgomery. When Mr Davies took early morning playground assembly some of the boys used to call out 'Monty', but he never said anything about it. One of the good qualities he had was to allow individual boys to express themselves both physically and intellectually on and off the soccer field. He would say sternly that 'it is important that boys are given the opportunity to develop their unique skills so that they represent the school with pride'. For the next few weeks we would meet up with Mr Davies in the afternoons for soccer trials which were held nearby on council soccer pitches. Thinking we were famous soccer players, the teacher taught us how to pass, trap and chest down a ball among the many other skills he thought we should have when playing soccer at all levels. When the soccer trials finished at around 4 p.m., Peter, I and others would skulk off for a smoke behind the changing rooms.

The final day of the soccer trials where coming to an end; this would be the day when Mr Davies would choose the soccer team to represent the junior school. With great anticipation, after training that day he gathered us around him and announced the successful twelve boys. Yes, both Peter and I had been chosen for the team! What a great honour, and I wondered what my parents and friends would have to say. After discussing the implications of being chosen for the football team with my parents, I then realised what representing the school meant. It would entail among other things travelling by coach to play other schools. It meant that I could wear with pride the old established red and black soccer shirts of West Lane Junior School. We would be mentioned in the school magazine, I hoped, for our great endeavours in bringing the Local Schools' cup back to West Lane. The last time we had won the cup was six years previously, so it was vitally important that this would be our year for success. It also meant that we might see some young females for the first time, our school being single sex, since we left the infant school some three years ago. But no matter what I had achieved, I would still continue to be nicknamed Bungard by my siblings.

It was 1953 and King George VI had died of cancer. He was succeeded on the throne by his eldest daughter the beautiful Elizabeth, who married the charming and attractive Philip Mountbatten, who was of Greek origin. The Bradbury household, similar to millions of other working-class households, were in front of the television for hours watching their new Queen telling the country that she would perform her duty. True to her word, the Queen some sixty years later continues her great service for the British people.

My younger brother Sid had by this time been at West Lane Junior School for nearly one academic year. He had done quite well in the infant's school, both academically and in school sports. My parents had visited the school to discuss Sid's work with both his class and head teacher. When my father asked the class teacher about his disposition and attitude to learning and co-operation, it appeared that Sid did at times become angry when told to do something. Today I would put that down to a healthy scepticism. All the sports that were played at the infants he did very well but on more than one occasion he failed to hand in his homework and some of the work that was handed in was not very good. Sid's class report sounded very similar to my own report which was that I preferred to put most of my energy time into sports instead of concentrating more of my time on academic work.

At the junior school Sid had settled in quite well, had made friends and his approach to academic work was encouraging. In accordance with most school banter, it was put about that Sid was supposed to be some sort of hard man, so keeping out of his way was the order of the day. There is always someone who is going to make trouble and ask you for a fight! This happened to Sid when he had been at the school for only four weeks, when a boy from the second year told him to be in the playground at one o'clock where he would sort him out. Apparently the reason for the boy offering Sid a fight was because Sid had looked at him in the lunch canteen the day before. The two boys met in the playground, encircled by many boys shouting and yelling, when the boy hit Sid in the face twice making his nose bleed. With that Sid informed me smiling, 'I went mad, punched and kicked the other boy several times, when one of the teachers jumped in between us to stop the fight.' He grabbed both the boys by the scruff of their necks and took them straight to the Headmaster's office. Both of them were made by the Headmaster to clean the playground of rubbish every day for two weeks after school had finished. This, he told them, 'will teach both of you a lesson not to fight in school again.' Not so our Sid.

It was round about this time that two younger siblings, Susan and Wayne, were attending the infants' school in West Lane. Susan had been there for a year and Wayne had just started; both, it appeared, were doing well. But as there were always so many children in our house it was difficult most of the time to have a conversation with anyone due to the constant noise and bickering. One tried to get some peace and quiet in the large bedroom at the back of the house, the room where I had been electrocuted, on your own for a little while but that space was at a premium in our household. As you can imagine, masturbation was impossible most of the time. If one wanted to do that you either went into our father's old shed just outside the back door, or if you wanted to make sure no one was looking, then you went to the woods at the back of the house. Several boys slept in this large bedroom. Each had one drawer for personal items. As I grew it gave me some respite to write and read on my own for longer periods but sooner or later one of the younger children would invade your precious space. During winter, autumn, raining and cold days when you couldn't go out, all you could do was grind your teeth and expect the inevitable mayhem. Later on in life space became a most precious commodity for me.

My parents had bought another car, a large blue Ford Consul, as my father began to earn more money from driving his lorry delivering coal and coke to the local hospitals. The inside of the car, with leather seats and large dashboard, was very comfortable indeed when compared to our first car and with a growing family they needed more space to fit them all in. My father gave me the weekly job of cleaning the car for two shillings which was well worth it, as this motor was quite big, taking me at least three hours to finish it. Sometimes I thought I was cleaning an Army tank! I remember the first time that I actually tried to clean the Ford Consul with a large tin of polish that my father bought for me. I applied the polish to the car and waited for it to dry but it wouldn't, so left it overnight only to find in the morning thick grease all over it. My father was horrified at the state of the car and asked for an explanation as to what I had done. It transpired that he had bought an industrial cleaner that was used for cleaning large ovens. That caused an almighty row between my parents, my mother accusing my father of trying to ruin their new car before she had paid for it. As with our first car, my mother always insisted that she had bought the car, and all other subsequent cars, by religiously saving up all the family allowance she received from the State. It was always very difficult to explain to her that father was bringing home a wage packet every week to provide for us all. Nonetheless my mother was quite an amazing person; she had lots of energy and with her family in mind nearly always tried her best for us. That also applies to my father who worked hard every day of his life to provide the basics for his ever-growing family. Another good quality he had was that he was never out of work during the fifty-eight years of his working life.

The football season had commenced at West Lane Junior School with our first match to be played away at Longshore Junior School, Stoneleigh, some six miles away. On the day all the players, thirteen in all, and Mr Davies the sports teacher, assembled outside the school to board the green and white Bedford coach that drove us to our first football match anticipating victory. We ran out onto the pitch dressed in our new red and black outfit to the jeers of about one hundred Longshore supporters, including many young sexy girls, shouting for their team. That strong support certainly did the trick as we were very soundly beaten six goals to nil. There was doom and gloom back in the changing room after the match where Mr Davies said we had played well enough but beaten on the day by a fitter and stronger team. I well remember him saying that day, 'We have to train much harder and smoke a lot less if you are determined to have a successful season.' Mr Davies knew that we were smoking behind his back and attributed that to our abysmal display on the football field.

The following weeks leading up to the Christmas holidays saw Longshore football team play five more matches, winning three and losing two. We had played six matches where we won three and lost three. 'On the whole we showed more resolve in the way we approached each match, that was obvious,' according to Mr Davies, who had a trained eye in these matters having played semi-professional as a young man for Enfield Town. We had scored about sixteen goals during the six Football games, which was quite good going for a team that had not been together for very long. Peter Upton had scored five of those goals where throughout the entire five matches he had applied himself very well indeed, being fast, strong with a keen eye for goals This was some sort of a transformation for him bearing in mind that about only two years before he did not participate in sports, contented to work on his art. Nobby James, himself a good right winger, had also scored five goals and I scored three. At that time Nobby had an older brother called Roger who had a football trial with Crystal Palace, then in old Division Two of the football League which no longer exists. I didn't know the outcome of his trial but Nobby was a skilful and speedy player of short stature and slim build but he always made his presence felt. Over a hundred yards he ran like a greyhound seeking out a bitch on heat, no doubt the fastest player in a football team of mainly donkeys.

Christmas break was fast approaching when we would have three weeks holiday away from school and we would be able to play with friends and generally enjoy ourselves. We all said our goodbyes to our school friends, class teachers and hoping when we returned in the New Year the school football team, and later on in the year the sports team, would be successful. During holidays we used to play quite a lot in the Chessington Road Council owned playing fields where several football teams from the nearby Council Estate, Gibraltar Crescent, used to come over for many hours of rough tough matches. It was a great laugh playing with other working class boys my age, clothed similarly to me and my siblings, in hand-me-down clothes sometimes twice the size of the kids wearing them. Most of them would have pudding bowl haircuts and snotty running noses or candles, as my father used to nickname them.

On one occasion we were playing in a clump of trees on the edge of the playing fields when all of a sudden a young black girl jumped over the fence of St Ebbas psychiatric hospital nearby and ran into the trees, where I was climbing, to hide from the nursing staff who could be heard calling her name: 'Where are you Alison? Come back at once, you naughty girl!' The girl ran up to me and asked rather shyly, 'Please hide me from the nursing staff at once because I don't like any of them.' I took her into a large bush hoping that they would not find her hiding there. For a few minutes we were both kneeling on the ground only inches from each other's faces when I realised I was becoming sexually aroused by the first black woman to have been so close to me. In those days of the 1950's Surrey life, the only time I saw non-white people was on the television, in newspapers or sports books.

During my schooling days at Hurst Road I remember that out of about several hundred pupils only one person, an Indian male, was non-white. Within a few minutes the nurse had arrived to escort Alison back to the hospital through a small locked gate built into the security fence for staff. How things have changed in fifty years when the only few non-white people around Epsom in those days would have worked at one of the five psychiatric hospitals, but now I have noticed many different races living outside cities in smaller towns or even villages all over South-eastern England.

In my household we were all busy preparing for Christmas Day. Two days before my parents had driven to Kingston, where they usually shopped every Saturday, to buy a massive turkey to feed the hungry Bradbury children. Most of the turkeys they bought were so big that their muscles resembled those of the heavyweight boxer Frank Bruno! This time of year used to remind me of the Biblical story of feeding the five thousand. My parents also bought many presents for the children, sweets, fruit, nuts and decorations for the Christmas tree. Christmas Eve was always a time when the children found it hard to go to bed at the usual time due to all the commotion going on anticipating what presents our parents had bought us. Next day, being Christmas day, we were all out of bed early around eight to stampede downstairs to find our presents and open them to see what was inside. With a bit of luck during the mêlée you could even open someone else's present, but woe betide if you were caught!

My parents had bought me my first Timex wristwatch, which was something I had been craving for a long time. In those days when you bought a watch, even an inexpensive one, you had it for life, as no batteries or any other gadgets were needed to keep it ticking. I immediately placed the watch round my wrist as I was so proud to have one to call my own, but something happened when I was playing games in the evening with my family that even today I find inexplicable. I was sitting on the floor when all of a sudden I ripped the watch from my wrist, breaking the strap, and then I broke the glass and watch hands by throwing it against the wall. Some of my siblings asked why I had broken the watch but my parents said nothing at all. Very impulsive behaviour for one so young and behaviour that would, at times, dominate my life. Perhaps I was jealous that my mother or father where not paying attention to me. This incident, and many others, was a missed opportunity, maybe for my parents to have taken me to the doctor for investigations into my behaviour with a view to long-term therapy. Clearly at such a young age my behaviour was at times abnormal, yet my parents failed to act on my behalf.

Other childhood incidents that should have caused my parents concern was when I used to defiantly swear at them while playing in the garden on my own or with other siblings. On some of those occasions my father used to clump me round the head, but that used to make me even more belligerent.

My elder sister, Margaret, was most happy as she had received a beautiful red dress with matching jumper and as she was in the secondary modern school, Hurst Road, she would look most attractive among her peers. As we were all sports people in the Bradbury household, it was not surprising that my elder brother, Bob, also at Hurst Road, was given a new pair of Stanley Matthews football boots. He went on to use them for a whole season while playing for the school and district teams, eventually passing them down to me so that I used them for quite a while at West Lane. Stanley Matthews was our hero in the 1950s and 60s as was the case for most working class boys at the time. He played on the right wing for Stoke City, Blackpool and England and went on to play football well over the age of fifty. Later on when I supported Chelsea, I travelled to Bloomfield Road, the home ground of Blackpool football club, to watch my idol terrorise the young Chelsea team with his skilful magic.

With the Christmas period over we returned to school, which no doubt pleased my mother to get us all out of the house and return her life to some normality. My school classroom had been painted an eye-catching lilac colour which caused our teacher to remark, 'Boys, I do hope that these wonderful colours inspire all of you to great things this coming term and beyond these walls.' We had a new teacher for geography called Mr Bryant who hailed from Cape Town, South Africa. He was about thirty years of age, tall, well-built and had just arrived in England with his wife and two children. According to school gossip, he was a colourful character having played football for Cape Town Nomads for three seasons as their goalkeeper with an excellent record for having let in the least number of goals in one season. When in his geography classes he had the attitude that young people should be able to express themselves whenever possible to the extent that he gave pupils the opportunity to stand in front of the class to explain whatever we liked. Most of us found expressing ourselves sitting at our desks very difficult, yet alone in front of our class. He had realised that most of us came from working-class backgrounds that did not lend itself to any of us being intelligent or confident enough to speak coherently for ourselves. He had of course planted very small seeds in our minds that one day would hopefully bloom into fruition.

The football season continued after the Christmas break with the team doing quite well, winning two and losing two matches, until we came up against the eventual winners of the league title away from home, Hook Road Rangers. As the game was played in the afternoon, all the team had their lunch and then assembled outside school where the newish blue Bedford coach, owned incidentally by a father of a younger school pupil called Simon Peach, drove us to our biggest mauling of the season. We had about fifty pupils supporting us from West Lane but they had nearly the whole school shouting them on which included many sexy young girls with long hair and wearing short skirts. After just five minutes of play, I tripped up their big burly ginger-haired centre forward in the penalty area and he scored from the awarded penalty. Thereafter every time I touched the ball there was loud booing and hoots of derision aimed at me, most vocally from the girls, which made me pray for the whistle to be blown to end the game. In the second half they completely ran all over us scoring another six goals winning the game by eight goals to nil. In the changing room afterwards we were all very quiet and really dumbstruck by such a drubbing that had been inflicted upon us by a superior team. What would the headmaster, class teacher, class pupils, my parents and siblings say when they heard of our public humiliation at the hands of Hook Road Rangers? One person who didn't really give a damn was Peter Upton who within ten minutes of the game ending had gone round to the back of the changing room and was smoking one of his father's Senior Service cigarettes. In no time at all Peter got a message to me and the others, including two players from the victorious team, that fags were available to everyone. We weren't that concerned, I remember, of the whereabouts of Mr Davies as we had given our best during a one-sided match.

The only consolation we had to look forward to now was success at the school's sports day that would be held in Alexander Sports Stadium in Epsom where at least six local schools would compete against each other. Mr Davies would choose who he thought were the fastest athletes to represent the school, but first of all we would have to hold trials in the playground where we would race against each other to select the fastest ten pupils with five standing as reserves. After the various races concluded the sports master chose his team of ten boys that included my close buddies Peter, Nobby, John and me. Academics we certainly weren't but hopeful athletes we aspired to be. Another person chosen from our class for the athletics team was a rather fat pupil called Henry who was a real scream. (He moved away from the school after one year.) We would always look forward to history lessons with Miss Copeland, not because we were interested in Nelson or Churchill, but because Henry used to sit directly in front of her in class and drop a pencil deliberately onto the floor so that he could look up her skirt. When Miss Copeland was speaking to us, sometimes the whole class would be in hysterics knowing that at the same time we knew Henry was under the table with his mind on other matters.

At assembly that morning the Headmaster spoke enthusiastically about how well we had competed during the football season and went on to say he wanted all the school to support our athletes during the school sports day in the afternoon. As the sports stadium was four miles away several coaches were arranged to drive as many pupils as possible to the sports arena. Others would have to make their way there under their own steam, knowing that the Headmaster had given everyone the afternoon free of lessons to attend; some took advantage of the occasion to buy bottles of cider to drink up on Epsom Downs.

When we arrived at the Stadium the place was packed with coaches that had brought youngsters in from local areas, the centre of attraction being young athletes most of whom were wearing a number pinned to their sports vest. My mother was there with two of my younger siblings who were already running unofficially up and down the athletics track in their bare feet. She came up to me, gave me some sandwiches, squash and reminded me, thereby adding to my anxiety, that in previous athletics meetings my siblings, especially James and Bob, had done well in winning several races.

I was scheduled to run in the usual competitive one hundred and two hundred yard sprints; also, I competed in the handball team competition, though we had very little training for this at school. In the one hundred yards heat I finished fourth and was eliminated. The race was won by a bloke from a local school who was at least six inches taller than most of us. It was a similar story in the two hundred yards sprint heat where I finished third and was eliminated once again from the finals. The same boy not only won this race but went on to win both the one hundred and two hundred yards finals in record time. He not only had the height of a giraffe but also had the speed and stride of a gazelle. It is not surprising, therefore, that everybody from his mother to school teachers called him Lofty.

The whole team, excluding Dave Watson and Philip Smith who both won their respective heats but not the finals, had not done very well. When it came to the handball competition, I and my four other colleagues including Nobby thought we had a reasonable chance of winning the cup. We assembled on the grass with seven other teams we would compete against. After the semi-finals Melvin, Chris and I had all dropped the ball at least once and we were eliminated from the event with our school ending up without any medals at all. My parents and siblings did not say much about not winning any medals when I arrived home, the only comment being, 'Hard luck, Bungard!'

In no time at all, it seemed, the time had come for most of the final year at West Lane to move on to the senior school, Hurst Road Secondary Modern. I was now eleven years of age and that meant for all of us, whether moving to Hurst Road or elsewhere, we would be starting at the bottom again just as we had done in the two previous schools. It also meant that there would be girls in our class for the first time since we left our infant schools and it also meant more competition and responsibility was expected of us.

Hurst Road Secondary Modern School was a handsome looking pre-Second World War brick building that could accommodate at least five hundred pupils. The school provided two large soccer pitches, a cricket pitch and a large tarmacadam play area for general use including netball, rounders and five a side football. There was also a large productive garden that provided for us underachievers a weekly two-hour opportunity to plant flowers or vegetables, supported by a knowledgeable gardening teacher. The football pitches would provide for me over the next few years a great opportunity to develop my soccer skills, play for the school team and give me some sort of personal kudos.

On the academic side of school activities, there was an incentive for people to achieve whereby they could move up into the grammar stream class. But as for duffers like me who failed their eleven plus, I languished in the bottom class for the duration. Predictably that meant for most of us, not reading the classics or studying Darwinism, but re-enforcing the class status quo leading to unskilled work and low rank.

As we stood to attention in the playground during our first assembly I realised that Peter, Nobby, Bob, Tony, Melvin, Chris and I were among the pupils who had made the move from West Lane to Hurst Road. The others, who had not moved to Hurst Lane, had moved, for various reasons, to senior schools around the county, or further afield. In front of us was a pleasant looking woman of around fifty years of age, with brown greying hair, of medium build and wearing a two-piece brown suit. Her name was Mrs Salter and she taught English, and would be my form teacher for the next three years. She explained to all the new boys and girls congregated together in the playground, about eighty altogether, where the classrooms, toilets and other relevant information was to be found. All my six friends that had moved to the senior school would also be in her class, which was reassuring.

When the formalities had been completed we were encouraged to have a walk round the school, when an older stocky pupil with greased hair and several metal badges on his school blazer approach me. ‘Hello Barry,’ he said smiling, ‘I am Chris Hassell, captain of Canterbury House and was wondering if you would like to play soccer for us?’ He went on, ‘I knew two of your brothers, James and Robert, and they were good soccer players.’ ‘Yes, all right,’ I said, rather enthusiastically thinking that I must be quite good at football if they wanted me to play for their team, and they must know that I played for the junior team at West Lane. Later on that day when I was walking down one of the long corridors, I read that there were four different sports houses in the school known by their colour: Canterbury house was blue, Exeter was red, Winchester was yellow and Salisbury green. Once you were allocated your colour house, you usually kept that for the duration of your schooling.

We all assembled around midday on the first day in our new classroom with Mrs Salter standing in front of us. 'Welcome boys and girls to your new classroom,' she said, 'I will be your form teacher for the next three years.' She told us to sit down and from a register in front of her she called out our names to see if we were present. I looked round me to try and understand all the new information that was bombarding my brain, which stopped when I noticed all the lovely sexy girls that were in the same room as me. For the first time in my life I was in a room with about fifteen well-dressed young girls, but I immediately thought, would they like me and how would I talk to them? With my sexual awareness growing around me, these were feelings that I had never experienced before in my previous two schools. I later recalled that we were told by the former Headmaster to become more responsible, independent and self-sufficient.

With those words of wisdom ringing in my ears, during the next few weeks I was slowly coming to terms with my new school, which at times seemed to overwhelm me. I looked forward to the lunchtime canteen where we could collect our lunch, meet other pupils and generally interact with others. Lunchtime also gave me the opportunity to walk both round the playground and the large playing fields. Around the perimeter of the field where huge oak, elm and silver birch trees growing, ideal on a hot sunny day, when you could sit underneath them for shade to observe the girls go by or chat amongst the lads about football.

I was amazed by the variety of older girls with big breasts, long or short hair, wearing short school dresses—some even having cosmetics on their faces, sitting down on the grass. I thought this is the kind of place for me, but not really understanding what I should be doing due to lack of confidence. Later on that day in the school corridor, I immediately became embarrassed when an attractive girl smiled at me. That girl, who was my age but in a higher class, I later fancied so much that I got the word to her via a mutual friend that I wanted to take her out. One day walking across the playground Brenda (that was her name) called me over to where she was standing with other girls to tell me that she did not want to date me. I was so overcome with humiliation that I dared not look at her for the next year or so without feeling pangs of inadequacy.

The one area where I felt competitive and self-assured was when I was playing football against other males. Chris Hassell had got together a large group of younger boys from the first and second years to carry out football trials to see who would play in the first game for Canterbury House. All my friends that had moved to Hurst Road with me were chosen to join other colour houses including Peter Upton who was in Exeter House. Incidentally, Peter could not believe his luck either when he saw all the young girls walking around the playground and playing fields. I trained with Canterbury House for four afternoons and two evenings when Chris Hassell eventually chose the first six boys, including me, to play six-a-side football in the playground later that week against Winchester House. Considering it was the first time we had played together, things went well. We won six goals to four, and I scored three of them. As there were four teams in the school inter-house league, we would go on to play each other about four times during the season.

I found academic work difficult which is not surprising considering the large learning leap we had to make from one school to another. Other than football and sports, my favourite lessons were composition, history and gardening. In fact, one composition I wrote was very good, according to the young female student teacher on placement, that when she returned to college, she said she would show her colleagues. In those days pupils from my background were not expected to achieve high academic ranks, which was grossly unfair, because if you failed your eleven plus exams you were entrenched in that low achiever group for the rest of your school life. Naturally all the classes were categorised by ability and achievement where good exam results would see an individual promoted to a higher class, the highest class being A and the lowest C. I was in form C and would remain there for the whole of my time at Hurst Road.

One well known pupil that attended Hurst Road School was the Led Zepplin guitarist Jimmy Page who hailed from nearby Epsom. I can remember him playing his guitar in the playground at lunchtimes being followed even in those days by many young attractive girls. In contrast to my lowly educational achievement, I would look forward very much to summer evenings when I would go cycling with Pete, Nobby, Melvin and Chris to Nonsuch Park, Epsom Common and Cheam Park among many others. As fit young men we would cycle for many miles before finding a shady spot off the beaten track to have a much needed smoke sometimes followed by a large bottle of Woodpecker cider. Nobby in particular used to collect empty beer bottles from his father's or grandfather's house, put them into a large box and make a few bob by returning them to the local off licence. Given the opportunity Nobby used to steal them from the back of the local shops, clean them and then return them to the same unsuspecting shop owner for cash.

Round about this time, due to the prompting of a Hurst Road pupil who was in a higher class than I, Alan Fox and I started to go train-spotting together. We would walk to Runton station—children in those days walked nearly everywhere—then take the train alternate weeks to Wimbledon or Clapham Junction station. This was the era of steam on British Railways. Standing on various platforms we used to write down the numbers of steam engines, electric trains and Pullman cars all day as they thundered through London railway stations en route to their destinations. As a young man Ian Allan, of ABC fame, worked for British Railways, based at Waterloo station in one of their information offices. Over the years he would receive so many train enquiries, by post and phone, that he realised what was needed were detailed books on locomotives and other motive power.

He published his own British Railways Locomotive books covering all the train regions in Britain which became so successful that he in time started his own business selling the now famous ABC Books. I still have in my possession one of his much cherished ABC books printed in the winter edition of 1961/2 priced 2/6d. Other times Alan and I would take the train to various London engine sheds where we had the wonderful opportunity to stand next to the steaming giants hissing and blowing out steam. On one occasion while visiting King's Cross engine shed I was thrilled to stand next to the powerful Mallard engine that once pulled the train that broke the world rail speed record for steam. These were great times travelling around on trains, writing down British Rail locomotive numbers until I got home excitedly to see if I had already marked them off in my ABC books or had it been a first sighting.

Most of the pupils from my form, including myself, really looked forward to the gardening lesson taken by a teacher called Mr Pratt who was quite an eccentric person. He would come into the garden, where we would meet him for the two hours lesson, smoking a cigarette and wearing large Wellington boots. When he would take them off at the end of the lesson he never had socks on his feet. He was, however, a decent person who liked nothing more than to demonstrate how to dig up clumps of flowers, prune roses or plant young seedlings. One can imagine with a name like Pratt the sort of ribbing and banter that we gave him. He was about fifty years of age, tall, fat, with a big stomach, a balding head and had worked at the school for some considerable time. It was put about in the school, as these things are, that he was in the Navy during the Second World War and that his ship was sunk in the Atlantic and he lost many of his comrades.

One occasion that I can vividly remember was when I was digging out some old plants ready to plant new ones. I slipped over a spade, falling spot onto his prized sunflower and destroying it. You can imagine how some of my form pupils started shouting and whistling at me when trying to bring it back to life with Mr Pratt looking on with a great deal of anxiety. I remember him with fond memories.

Another teacher, Mr Symes, who taught us metalwork was by far more of a disciplinarian that Mr Pratt but still had good qualities. Being an avid train spotter, I wrote to the senior engineer at Stratford engine sheds requesting that several young boys, including myself, could have a permit that would allow us to go and look at the new 'Deltic' English-Electric Diesel being built at their works. The engineer wrote back to me explaining that we were all too young to attend on our own, but if we could get a teacher who could arrange a visit it would be possible. I ran to school in excitement to show Mr Symes the letter that the Senior Engineer had sent me and he agreed that he would write to Stratford Engineering Works to formally request that he and his class could make a visit to look round the works. Two weeks later during the end of our metalwork class Mr Symes explained that he had received a letter from Stratford stating we had been allowed to visit their sheds on 6 May 1960. All the class arrived early at school with our sandwiches that day eager to board the Clarks coach that drove us to Stratford for a wonderful exciting day out where we were given a conducted tour by the Senior Engineer, Mr Simon Caulfield, of the new Diesel that was introduced in1961.

The subject of teachers' behaviour and how different it was when I was at school is highlighted by the following: In1962 I was standing outside Hurst Road School talking to a male friend called Trevor, who was at least 17 years of age, when one of the teachers who was driving out of the school suddenly braked, got out of the car to demand that my friend 'put that bloody fag out at once'. Trevor insisted he was old enough to smoke whereby the teacher started punching and slapping him around the head, then got back into his car and drove off. With the teacher clearly in the wrong, Trevor wrote to the Headmaster to complain about his colleague's behaviour but nothing more was heard of the incident. Fortunately today there are clear guidelines about the duty or care a teacher has when pupils are in their charge.

Later on that year, in June1962, Trevor and I cycled up to Epsom Downs during the Derby weekend when thousands used to visit the two large Fairs. In those days there was also another Fair on the Downs beyond the racetrack. While we were there a man of about forty years of age asked Trevor if he and I would like to work for him on his coconut shy stall. It transpired that Eddie who was a local gypsy or traveller lived in Epsom with his parents and they all travelled together with their stall during the season to various Fairs around Britain. We both worked for a few days collecting money, handing out balls so people could try to knock the screwed down coconuts off their perch and only once did I give a coconut to a winning punter. Several times the five of us would eat our lunch, sitting on the grass next to their large caravan and car, which consisted of tinned salmon or pilchards, salad and bread. When Eddie's father had finished his meal he would blow his nose with all the snot coming out right next to us on the grass. It was the dirtiest behaviour I had ever seen from a mature person yet the three of them were all the same, the most disgusting creatures that I have ever come across, not having the slightest awareness of any other person being in their company.

They appeared not to be short of money with a caravan full of expensive furniture, rugs, brass ornaments, yet they were dressed worse than tramps with skin that had not touched water for a considerable time. Eddie, who one could tell was after gay sex with his filthy innuendos and gestures, drove both a car and lorry but appeared to do very little work when we were there. It is not surprising therefore that many find them most loathsome and despicable people whose only modus operandi is to make as much money as possible regardless of how that is achieved. At the end of a week's working they had the audacity to ask Trevor and me if we would like to travel with them to the next Fair in Hastings. You could imagine trying to sleep in the caravan at night with Eddie trying his utmost to sexually abuse us with his filthy hands, in front of his consenting obnoxious parents.

Back at school, Canterbury House continued winning in the inter-house, six-a-side football matches. The sports master Mr Bloor was preparing to hold football trials for the school team which were eleven-a-side to play other school teams in the Epsom District. Mr Bloor had worked at Hurst Road for years, being a bit of an institution in his own right. As a young man he worked as a baker before going onto play for Derby County, and other teams, as a professional footballer. He was a tall, slim, agile man for his age with a strong sense of fair play. Those pupils he thought were worthy, I never did know how or why he chose me, were given the opportunity to look at his very interesting scrapbook that stemmed from his days of playing professional football.

When I turned up with my football boots, the boots

handed down from my brother Bob, I was among twenty other hopefuls all looking hungry for success. Mr Bloor came up to me and said in his heavy Yorkshire accent, ''Allo Bradbury, I am your sports teacher, and how are your brothers? Still playing soccer are they?' Being rather shy, I said, 'I don't know, Sir.' 'They were good competitive players, your brothers, I 'ope you are the same, Bradbury.' 'Yes Sir,' I replied, moving away from him so that I could get changed for the football trials and earn that place in the team where I desperately needed to do well.

I was expected at my age—I was now around twelve or thirteen years old—to earn some money of my own so that I could buy things my parents were unable to such as jeans, shoes, jumpers and visit my favourite football team, Chelsea. Around about this time I managed to get myself a morning and evening paper round working for Mr Brown, who owned a large shop half a mile from my home. For the first few weeks I borrowed Bob's bike to deliver the huge number of papers I had to deliver to earn my ten shillings for the week. After several weeks I had managed to save enough money to buy my own second-hand bike from a friend, Kevin Broom, who had probably stolen it himself. Every morning I had to get out of bed and especially during the cold winter months this was very difficult with no heating in the house. The only heating we ever had was an open coal fire, but my parents later on did buy two gas fires. Without washing, I would quickly put my clothes on and cycle to the shop to deliver the papers, mostly the *Financial Times*, destined for the middle-class professional people of East Runton, a ten minutes' cycle ride from the shop. Most of the houses that I delivered to were detached with large gardens, garage with the usual aggressive dog quietly waiting for you to deliver the paper when they would try to grab the paper or your hand or both. When I remembered where the nastiest dogs lived I would sometimes anticipate when they would try to grab the paper by really shoving it hard through the letterbox, hopefully trying to smash them in the jaw.

During this time I was also delivering the evening newspapers, the *Evening News*, *Star* and *Standard*, after school hours for a much smaller shop owner called Mr Burrows, who, along with his wife, were decent people. Mr and Mrs Burrows had moved to Runton some twenty years earlier from the West Country, where they were both born, got married, had one child (a daughter) and had owned a small successful public house in Barnstaple. Due to family bereavement they sold the public house and moved to London to buy the newspaper shop with a two-bedroomed flat above. Mr Burrows was a kind person with a strong softly spoken West Country accent. He was of average height and build with a full head of brown hair and nearly always had a cigarette in his mouth. I delivered less than half the amount of newspapers in the evening than I did in the morning but received a similar amount of money. This earned income allowed me to buy modern up-to-date clothes, shoes and more importantly, I could travel by public transport to support my team Chelsea Football Club.

When I left the morning paper round, (or was I sacked?), another financial opportunity occurred when I used to work with my father delivering heavy bags of coal on Saturday mornings. By this time the owner of the local family-run haulage business that my father had worked for twenty years had died, so he had found another local job delivering coal. We would both be out of bed at about six most Saturday mornings; my father would then drive his Foden lorry to the depot and we would load about five tons of coal together. Out on the road, I would climb on the lorry, turn the bags round ready for my father to carry them on his back to deliver to the customer. Most customers were kind and used to give my father and I a financial tip ranging from a shilling to half a crown. If the truth be known they probably felt sorry for me. After we had finished the coal round my father would drive me home at full speed so that I could wash myself in time to take the train to support Chelsea. Most of the time my washing was no more than a cat's lick as I used to have two large black marks round my eyes which resembled a circus clown!

Earning money from working with my father on most Saturdays and also earning money from the evening paper delivery round enabled me to attend more football matches, not just on a Saturday but also on weekdays as well. It further enabled me to travel to Chelsea away games for the first time, visiting teams such as Birmingham, Liverpool, Manchester and Cardiff. Douglas was an ardent Chelsea supporter, who was a few years older than most of us, was working full time so he could afford sometimes to supply us with bottles of light ale and packets of five Park Drive cigarettes. He was a great laugh when several of us used to travel together by train to various places in Britain, usually drinking, smoking, and if we were lucky, talking to various Chelsea footballers who used to travel first class on the same trains in those far away days.

On one memorable occasion the Chelsea full back, Peter Sillett, broke his leg playing in the away game at Wolverhampton Wanderers. Douglas and I, who were at the match, on our return to Euston Station waited for the next train to arrive which would be carrying our injured hero Peter Sillett with a plastered leg. When he was about to alight from the train with the aid of others a mature smart looking man wearing a dark suit with a light coloured trilby asked me if I was waiting for the battle scarred Chelsea captain. 'Yes,' I said rather wary of this formal looking chap smoking a cigarette. 'Would you like to say something about Peter Sillett, young man?' he asked me. 'Me and my mate Douglas have been to the match and have waited here to see how bad his leg is. Who are you anyway?' I asked the well-spoken man in front of me who was writing down things into a small book. 'I'm a journalist working for a London newspaper and I would like to take your photographs. If you give me your names it will be published in tomorrow's paper.'

Douglas and I told the two journalists (he had been joined by his colleague) how we took the train to watch Chelsea lose 2-1 to Wolverhampton Wanderers and upon arriving back at Euston had waited to see how badly injured Peter Sillett was. They hailed a taxi that drove the three of us (Douglas had gone home on his own by bus) to Waterloo station so that I could take the last train home to Runton. Next day, sure enough, there was a photograph of Douglas and me, with a small piece of text explaining what we had done, on the back of the *News of the World*. For the next few weeks I was stopped by various people enquiring into my short lived fame!

I would also work with my father during some of the school summer holidays, which gave me the opportunity to save more money for future activities. As I was growing up, or so I thought (I was in fact little more than thirteen years old with more money in my pocket), my independence and confidence grew to where I would meet other boys and older men in and around Chelsea Football Club. For Chelsea home games, we would take the underground train from Wimbledon to Fulham Broadway station, where there were always several men selling Chelsea programmes and newspapers. A Chelsea programme in particular was something I would always buy to add to my growing collection. Within five years or so I had collected many hundreds, and in some instances rare, football programmes, annuals and souvenirs that I had bought myself, or requested free of charge from various football clubs who sent them to me by post. Today such valuable programmes could make the fortunate owner a tidy few pounds.

Travelling back to Runton by train after one of the evening matches there was an incident that scared the life out of me, involving a middle-aged man who apparently was a patient in one of the local psychiatric hospitals. The train that I was on had just left Stoneleigh Station, a few minutes from my destination Runton, when the aforementioned man opened the train carriage door and a passenger stopped him from jumping out onto the railway lines to his death. Before the trained had stopped, not giving any thought to my own personal danger, I managed to pull the open door shut. When the train finally came into the station, police were waiting there for the suicidal man who was handcuffed and taken away into their custody, though not before one of the officers praised my brave action by closing the railway carriage door.

For three seasons while I was still at school, Chelsea F.C. used to train pre-season not fifteen minutes' cycle from my home. Many youngsters, including myself, would wait for the coach carrying the Chelsea team to drive into the training ground so that in my case, I would get the autograph of my idol Jimmy Greaves. On one occasion when alighting from the coach he gave me several large black and white photographs of himself playing football which he signed, 'Best wishes to Barry from Jimmy Greaves.' They were my most treasured article within my football memorabilia and whenever family or friends visited me it was always a great opportunity to show off my revered hero. Many young lads around at the time tried to entice the photographs from me by offering me large sums of money but I would not sell them. It is unfortunate, to put it mildly, that years later when I was working full time trying to earn my living that my younger siblings destroyed most of my football programmes and my most cherished possession, my Jimmy Greaves autographed photographs.

Incidentally, during the third pre-season, I met the new Chelsea F.C. manager Tommy Docherty down the training ground where we would head and pass the football to each other for about ten minutes during the players' break. During these football knockabouts he gave me words of encouragement like 'good ball son', 'well trapped son', and 'that's a good pass son', although I must be honest and add that due to his strong Glaswegian accent, understanding what he said was rather a hit and miss affair.

As already mentioned, some weeks I used to travel on my own to Chelsea F. C. where I loved to walk around observing all the various kinds of characters selling different things from hot dog rolls, to Dalton's peanuts and cooked chestnuts. Most of those Cockney men wore flat caps, large heavy army surplus coats, heavy boots with a roll up cigarette hanging from the side of their mouths. I never thought it odd that my parents would allow me to venture so far from home on my own but years later, in hindsight, I realised that a vulnerable young boy of thirteen years old wandering around on his own would be now considered neglect on the part of my parents.

For the past couple of years I had been travelling to various places on my own which I thought was normal, but once again I realised years later that there were so many children to care for at home that I probably wasn't missed by my parents. The lack of care and attention comes to mind whenever I think of those years when I would be out in the world, on my own and my parents not knowing where I was. Spending time on my own would continue as I became older; it seems that my parents just let me go where I pleased which even at this early age had set an unhealthy precedent for things to come.

One of the people that I had met at Chelsea F.C. was a long-time supporter called Derek who I had seen at home matches most weeks. A clique of about twenty Chelsea supporters used to stand on the halfway line and in time we got to know each other quite well as the weeks went by. Derek was one of those friendly supporters who used to laugh and joke with me and some of the others. He was about fifty years of age, of slim build and lived in Kingston

Upon Thames. With the insistence of Derek, I had made arrangements on one particular Saturday to meet him outside Fulham Broadway underground station, a fine Victorian building, next to one of the old dirty working men's café frequented in those days by tramps, psychiatric patients and the unemployed. While I was waiting for Derek to arrive at the café, known in those days as greasy spoons, loud music was playing by American artists Bill Haley, Gene Vincent and Buddy Holly. This was the era of rock and roll, drain pipe trousers and coffee bars.

Eventually Derek arrived well dressed, smiling as he gave me a hug and kissed my left cheek. He suggested that I might like to visit a restaurant along the Fulham Road called The Golden Fiddle for a meal. As I had never visited a restaurant before (the only place I had been to before that sold food was a tea stall inside the Chelsea ground), I jumped at the opportunity of being served at the table by well-dressed waiters. When we arrived at the Golden Fiddle, we were greeted by a young handsome looking Italian waiter who took our coats and showed us to our seats. Although Derek and I were on our own, the round table was big enough for four diners and was suitably covered with an attractive yellow cotton table cloth with shining green handled cutlery. Music was being played in the background, but as it was not pop music, I did not know at the time what the music was called, only realising years later that it was classical music.

The waiter arrived with the menu for us to order our meal but I did not have a clue what to eat as I didn't understand most of the names of the meals as they were written in Italian. Derek realised I did not understand the menu in front of me so ordered on my behalf saying to me that I would find the food delicious. When the large plates were brought to our table I couldn't believe my eyes as it was full of sausages, eggs, chops, bacon, peas and chips with several different sauces in a round metal container. 'It is called a mixed grill, Barry, I hope you will enjoy eating it,' Derek smiled. I had never before seen so much food on one plate, neither at school nor at home; I was overwhelmed that anything so scrumptious could be dished up for my consumption!

After we finished our meal together Derek and I walked along the packed streets of Fulham Road, where most people where wearing Chelsea colours of blue and white on their scarves, hats and gloves, and into the handsome Victorian Britannia Pub opposite the main football entrance. Above this pub, in a large room with ornate coving and a glass chandelier, was the Chelsea supporters club which is a far cry from the modern facilities they have today at the luxurious Chelsea Village some two hundred yards up the road. I had joined the supporters club with two of my friends from Runton about a year previously, on the day that Chelsea beat Manchester City at home by three goals to nil. ''Allo there Barry, you all right son?' said Terry Francis, the likeable pugnacious supporters club secretary. 'Yes, I am well, Tell, can I have a programme for today's match against Fulham?' Derek and I browsed around the half full room advertising football information, then left to buy terrace tickets to watch the match, which developed into a good game on a warm and breezy day with some of the usual crowd standing there on the half way line.

After another Chelsea success we made our way to the exit

when Derek suggested we have a coffee and sandwich in a small café up one of the side streets away from the crowds streaming out of the ground onto the Fulham Road. After we finished our Italian coffee, Derek said in his soft spoken voice, 'There is a very good film on down the Plaza in Fulham Palace Road. Shall we go there, Barry?' 'Yes, why not,' I said, so we walked the mile to the Cinema, bought the tickets and sat at the back in attractive green beige seats. This fine looking Edwardian Cinema was originally a theatre. I remember we watched a second rate cowboy film starring John Wayne and Stewart Grainger.

After a few minutes Derek put his hand on my thigh, slightly squeezed it asking me if I liked that kind of thing. He then put his hand onto my lap, undid my fly buttons and slid his hand inside gently holding, then rubbing my genitals. No one had done this to me before so I didn't know what to say to Derek who had by this time got my cock out and was rubbing it with his left hand. He looked round at me smiling and said 'You like that sort of thing, don't you love?' with his hand taking a much firmer hold on my genitals.

This sexual behaviour with a mature man was a complete and alien experience to me. At home I would masturbate on my own and at school we would indulge in horse play in the showers after a physical education class with Mr Bloor. I didn't know what to say or what to do, so when he said 'Shall we go, the film is not very good', I was relieved when we walked up to the fire exit thinking we would walk out onto the Fulham Palace Road. He stopped before the exit, pulled out his erect penis and said, 'How about that Barry, would you like to hold it?' Once again I didn't know what to say but then he said, looking at me more intensively, 'Would you like to hold or suck my prick, Barry?' Again I was confused as to what to say to him when he opened my fly buttons and pulled out my limp penis. He went down on both his knees and put my penis into his mouth. After a few minutes my penis was erect and I was enjoying the experience, although by now I had realised that I could hear people at the other side of the exit wall, but thinking what we were doing didn't seem right. I didn't realise at the time that the sexual activity we were participating in was called homosexuality and it was illegal. It was only as late as 1967 that homosexuality was decriminalised. At school my friends and I called such people 'bummers, queers, bumboys and shirtlifters', but nevertheless here was I doing exactly the same thing. That demonstrates how innocent we were in those days.

Two weeks later I made arrangements to meet Derek once again in the same café we had used prior to visiting the Plaza cinema. In the café I noticed he had not arrived so I ordered a tea and sat next to the window overlooking Orchard Way which appeared to have Edwardian terraced houses down both sides of the road. The Edwardians, I thought, years later where great innovators and on the whole left a better world to their successors. The café jukebox was playing rock and roll music being sung by Eddie Cochrane, Elvis Presley and Tommy Steel, a local lad from Bermondsey who went on to be a successful stage performer. The heavens opened up and lightning and thunder was so loud that I couldn't hear the sweet voice of Doris Day on the jukebox, as torrential rain ran down the gutters. Out of the downpour Derek came into the café soaked to the skin with water dripping from his hair, coat and shoes. 'Bloody rain,' he said, 'fancy a cup of tea, sweetheart?' He sat down at the small table I had reserved for him but he sounded a bit apprehensive as he went on to say his printing firm 'might be moving out of London to the South Coast next year, but nothing is final yet'. The owner of the café brought over two teas and toast for Derek who by this time had managed to get his wet jacket off so that he could dry his wet thinning hair and sallow round face. Years later it dawned on me that I could have unconsciously viewed Derek as acting as some sort of substitute parent for me, insofar as he was plugging that void in my life that had obviously been missing since I was a young child.

We left the café and walked over to the Chelsea F.C. turnstiles to buy a terrace ticket to see our great team play Bolton Wanderers who were very near to the bottom of Division One (the top league then in England). My hero Jimmy Greaves ran out holding a football, with a short crew cut hairstyle and with his shorts nearly hanging round his kneecaps he reminded me of a cartoon character. Once again I met some familiar faces on the halfway terraces, which included two lads, Brian and Rodger, who I recognised were from Runton. There was one chap, aged about fifty, who I had known for about two years and had the nickname of 'Mr Penalty', as he used to shout for a penalty every time there was any physical contact in the eighteen yard box. Chelsea won the match by three goals to nil, two goals scored by my hero Jimmy Greaves and a late penalty saved by the Chelsea goalkeeper, Reg Matthews, in a game made difficult by deep mud. I agreed to Derek's suggestion that we have something to eat in one of the newly opened Golden Egg restaurants owned by the former London heavyweight boxer Billy Walker and his brother, which was only a short bus ride to nearby Earls Court.

As the rain had by now stopped, we walked from the Golden Egg, which served a very good meal but the sort of food that I had not eaten before. In essence the Golden Egg meal consisted of two eggs, bacon, beans, sausage and buttered bread—by today's standards very ordinary fare, but in those days a feast for a working-class lad like me. In some respects I was fortunate to have been taken to the various eateries because I would never have been able to afford to dine in such places on my own. We walked past a club playing loud music which had flashing lights on the outside of the building where Derek said, smiling, 'Let's go in here for a beer, I think you will like it here.' We entered and walked down the steep stairs into a basement quite full of men and women dancing. We sat in an alcove, which had a small wooden table, green coloured lights in the ceiling and the walls painted in a garish pink. I requested an orange but Derek thought I needed something a little stronger so he bought us both a small beer each. This wasn't the first time I had drunk beer as my father used to buy bottles of stout to drink at home where I occasionally used to steal one; also, I had beer with Peter Upton and David Crossman, my class friends. When I was older my father used to buy me a small cider or stout during the times when I helped him deliver coal.

The beer that Derek had bought me certainly made me feel more confident, but to put things in context, in everyday life I don't think I was that assertive and nearly always tended to be at the back of the action especially with other people I did not know well. The next time Derek went to the bar to buy another beer, I suddenly realised that the women dancing with male partners were not women at all but were men dressed in women's clothes! At first I was quite amused but it eventually dawned on me that these males, who were known as Transvestites, or trannies as Derek called them, were perfectly serious about what they were doing. I was spellbound by the way they dressed, for they all looked so sexy in high heel shoes, tight fitting short dresses and long colourful wigs! During the evening I went to the toilet and observed three trannies sorting out their attire and adding make up to their already over indulged faces.

Halfway through the evening Derek asked me in his feminine yet persuasive manner if I would like to spend the night with him in one of the local hotels. Earls Court, he explained, has been a very popular hangout for homosexuals even before Victorian times—people such as Oscar Wilde, Ronald Kray, Quentin Crisp and Lord Boothby among many others, who used to make regular forays into the seedy night life that Earls Court has to offer. There used to be many loud gay bars ideal for those cruising, basement clubs where drugs of all descriptions could be had and pornographic shops selling sex that catered for all tastes in abundance.

Derek decided that we ought to stay in a gay-friendly hotel where we could 'stay till the morning without being hindered by other people who were unaware of this way of life'. Most of what Derek had to say about this gay world I was unfamiliar with except from reading the occasional newspaper article or looking at some hand drawn erotic figure on the subject. 'This gay world, such as Earls Court, had its own subculture of small unlicensed bars and clubs, places where a nod or a wink meant sex in the toilet or somewhere down the street in some bushes,' Derek further explained, sounding like he was experienced in such delicate matters. Derek chose a small hotel in Philbeach Gardens which had a light blue painted front, small well-kept garden and a beautiful foyer brightly lit by a large dark blue chandelier above. A rather large, well spoken English lady led us to our room on the ground floor at the back of the hotel overlooking a largish garden with borders and beds with a small water feature. The woman gave me a longish stare realising that I was rather young to be booking in with a mature man like Derek, but probably thought that the money was more important than moral misgivings. My first impressions of middle-class Earls Court with its expensive looking residential buildings were of wealthy people living separate lives from the masses that walked the streets only feet away from them.

I found out years later that a few doors away from this hotel a gender reassignment doctor was helping males to change their sexual orientation to female (thank God I never ended up there). We washed, took our clothes off, and got into bed together for the first time since we had met although I felt like going home but something stopped me from doing so. He was obviously experienced at this type of thing and asked if I would like a back massage which I really enjoyed. Derek starting kissing me on my face and neck which I didn't much like, so by request, he moved onto the rest of my body having oral sex with me, eventually masturbating over my genitals. In the morning we had breakfast, along with another ten residents, in the small back garden full of warm sunshine. Being self-conscious of what Derek and I had been doing together hours previously, I thought some of the residents were looking at me with scorn like a parent scolding a child for doing something wrong. After finishing our good breakfast we went back to our room one last time to collect our coats (all that we had booked in with, which probably explained the proprietor's understandable second glance at me). We walked to Earls Court station, then took the underground train back to the nearly deserted Wimbledon station, where we embraced, Derek took the train to Kingston and I went on to Runton. We met several times over the next two years visiting various small friendly gay hotels which I must say I enjoyed until I left school to start to earn my own living. After that meetings with Derek ceased except for one occasion.

As Chelsea supporters we were able to buy reduced priced coach tickets for the away game at Arsenal so I met Derek outside the Brittania Pub on the Fulham Road early on Saturday morning for our short journey north. The journey there was uneventful except for lots of traffic around the West End which made us late on our arrival at Highbury Stadium. Chelsea played like their namesakes, the pensioners, who lived only two miles away near the Kings Road. As the winter darkness started to descend, the five supporters' coaches made their way back to Chelsea after witnessing our team receive a four goal thrashing by a much superior Arsenal team. After dropping supporters off along the way, Derek and I were the only two left on our coach when he pulled my face down into his lap telling me twice to suck his exposed erect penis which I flatly refused to do. He apologised for what he had just done, then, using a more soft approach, started gently stroking my head and face, which was again on his lap, first with his hand then again with his erect penis. After a minute or so I stood up realising we had arrived back at Chelsea Football Club. Standing on the dark cold Fulham Road he apologised for what he had done by inviting me to dine at the nearby Italian restaurant we had visited some time ago; but I was most insistent that all I wanted was to make my way home on my own.

The football trials that Mr Bloor, our physical education teacher, had held at Hurst Road playing fields over four successive evenings had gone well for Nobby, Peter and I. He had put us through our paces stretching our bodies to a level not known by any of us previously. Consequently all three of us had been chosen to represent the school at football (the only pupils from our class). The first match was away from home to the well supported Stoneleigh Tigers who we beat by two goals to nil in a rather fiercely contested affair, with one of their players being sent off for constantly fouling Andrew Smith, our inside forward.

Mr Bloor was pleased by our performance so he did not make any team changes for the next match, which was at home against the hot favourites Cuddington, worthy champions for the last two seasons. The day itself was most memorable for not only exciting football on the pitch but for other activities off it. Cuddington arrived in three silver blue coaches holding their team and many vocal supporters wearing their football team colours of red and white. Before the football match several members of our team, including Peter Upton and I, had all been smoking in the toilets, when two of the opposition players walked in talking about the match to follow. Peter said rather arrogantly to both of them, 'Today you will get the biggest thrashing of your lives and make no mistake you shit arse!' The taller of the two retorted, 'Your team is rubbish, fucking useless and you have no chance.' With that Peter, Nobby, Bill and I piled into them landing blows on their faces and heads many times. They tried to fight back but were overpowered until they managed to run out of the toilet back to the changing rooms for safety.

As the two football teams lined up for the kick off, our team with the new blue and white colours, I could see that there supporters, which included many young girls wearing their own provocative clothes, outnumbered us by two to one. From the very outset dangerous tackling was being carried out by both teams, causing the referee to bring the two teams together on the pitch to warn all of us about our future conduct. The referee's warning fell on deaf ears, when our centre forward Johnny Wilshaw was brutally kicked down to the ground from behind by an opposing player, who was instantly sent off for dangerous play. At half time Mr Bloor read us the riot act telling us to concentrate on the football to win the game. The second half of the match was much cleaner, when late in the game their right winger scored the winner, which gave the two points to Cuddington. It was a tough game but we got some consolation afterwards when Pete, Dave and I managed to chat up three of the girls from Cuddington school by taking them over to our local park, Chatsworth, for cigarettes and beer.

Canterbury House became the school six-a-side champions for the three successive years I played in the team, being beaten on only four occasions within that time. When Chris Hassell left the school, after doing so much for others, he went on to become the secretary of Crystal Palace F.C. and thereafter secretary of Lancashire Cricket Club. It is not surprising therefore that we did well to be school champions with Chris behind us. However, when I was about 14 years of age I was dropped from the school football team for a while when a friend and I vandalised Chris Hassell's bicycle. Mr Bloor, quite rightly, took a dim view of that abysmal behaviour, telling us so in no uncertain terms.

At the end of the football season Chris Hassell, once again, arranged for a team, in which I was included, from Hurst Road to play in a five-a-side football tournament that was held at Epsom Baths. We won a few games but were eliminated in the quarter final stage by the eventual winners Leatherhead. In one of the games, where I scored a very good goal from twenty yards, someone from the crowd shouted 'When are you going to have a wash Bradbury?' so that everyone could hear the words above the cheering. Just because of my surname a few people thought they had the right to shout abuse at me whenever they liked. That kind of abuse is nearly always aimed at particular types of groups or individuals who others feel they have the right to stigmatise for no reason other than their own ignorance. People project their own thoughts and feelings onto others because for some reason or other they don't want to be responsible for it. For example, many times during my schooldays, and occasionally afterwards, people came up to me to make trouble by saying 'you are a Bradbury and you think you are hard'; 'when are you going to have a wash?'; 'when are you going to wash your clothes?'; or 'why don't you stop breeding like rabbits?' The incident at Epsom Baths further reinforced the growing realisation that I felt inferior to other people who I thought could do better than me in life. That inferiority was made worse over the years when middle-class women, who meant well, would say to me, 'It must be wonderful to have all those brothers and sisters to play with!' Wherever it came from I don't know, but I have always been very sensitive to what others said to me over the years.

The Headmaster, who went on to be mayor of Guildford, obviously knew the kind of background I came from, so he tried hard to find various ways of helping me to develop a healthier self-esteem. On one occasion at the school prize awards evening in front of parents, teachers and pupils, the Headmaster gave me the opportunity to collect from him two large football trophies won by Canterbury House. Even at this stage in my life, I could feel my anxiety rising as I walked up the stairs onto the stage to collect the two trophies for my fellow footballers. Everyone was clapping and cheering for me. I was so elated.

On another occasion the Headmaster gave me and a friend the responsibility for looking after the fish and clearing out the rubbish from the school pond. After several weeks of steady good work keeping the fish healthy we, for some unknown reason, threw a large rock into the six-foot square pond, killing several of the carp. When the Headmaster found out what we had done he immediately sent for us and gave us four lashings each of the cane. Why I did those things I don't really understand even today but I really appreciate how that decent Headmaster tried to help me grow up somewhat.

The school football team did not win the league during my time there but we had some epic battles against Cuddington, Stoneleigh and Riverview Schools where in one match I scored four goals. I was also selected for a trial for the Leatherhead and District Schools but failed to be selected notwithstanding the pre-match encouragement I had received from the coach: 'Play well today Bradbury and you are in the team!' Not being selected to play for the District Schools was disappointing but not surprising due to the lack of confidence I generally had around other people. It was even more disheartening because football at least gave me some enjoyment and status above my poor school reports which explained why I was usually in the bottom five during class exams nearly every year.

I think the influence of the Arts scene not long after the Second World War, when boundaries between class became less important, had a major impact on working-class culture. There were authors at the time called the 'Angry Young Men' who were writing books that would inspire working-class people to articulate in words their lost identity. Writers such as Kingsley Amis, John Braine, Alan Sillitoe, John Osborne, Alan Ayckbourn and others had encouraged those less fortunate into social action. Powerful television documentaries and films such as 'Kathy Come Home' had an effect on the social conscience of the country. The effect of the Arts merging with working-class culture in the late 1950s and early1960s brought about the emergence of popular culture, which for the first time gave many the chance to be educated at University. Since Harold Wilson, whose policy paved the way for the Open University, successive

British Government Education policy has been to give the opportunity for more working-class people to attend higher education.

I was only about 14 years of age at this time. It was while I continued my activities delivering my evening paper round for the likeable Mr Burrows that I first came in contact with a man called Dennis who drove a stationery van for a small local company in Runton. At that time he was about forty years of age, of average height, friendly with an outgoing personality that was mainly focused on one thing: young boys. One day as I was leaving Mr Burrows' shop to deliver my newspapers, Dennis was delivering stationery to an office across the road. With a smile he said 'hello' to me, followed by the equally convincing, 'I have not seen you around for some time, the last time was when you were cycling like mad up Cheam Road. I thought to myself that darling boy is going to do his self an injury one day if he persists in riding so fast!' He went on to ask me, smiling even more, 'Would you like a Coca Cola later on when you have finished your paper round?' Before I could reply he went on, 'Look, tell you what my dear, tell me the time you think you will finish your paper round and I will wait at the end for you and drive you back.' This he did, then drove us both to a newly opened burger bar in Epsom Town centre which had lovely coloured tables and chairs with soft music in the background. Before opening his car door, he placed his hand firmly on my thigh, saying with a large grin all over his bristly unshaven face, 'Let's have a good time, hey deary? It's lovely to see you.' He kissed me on the cheek, we closed the car doors and walked to the burger bar.
As this was a new self-service restaurant, the young used to flock here in droves. 'Have you been here before, Barry?'

Dennis asked me in his soft feminine voice, trying to engage my attention. 'No, I haven't,' I replied, 'but I've been to the Wimpy Bar down Fulford Road in Cheam Village.' Placed on our new red plastic tray were a beef burger, chips and a milkshake which I tucked into with relish, being the first food I had eaten since my midday meal at school six hours previously. We continued our superficial conversation between eating mouthfuls of enjoyable food. Dennis smiled once again, recognising how needy I was, and said, 'Would you like to come to my flat after we have finished our meal? Don't be frightened, my dear, I'll look after you.' After some thought I responded, 'Yes okay, but I can't be long as I have to finish my school homework.'

With that in mind we finished eating our meal and left the restaurant to walk to his old dirty Ford car parked round the corner. He drove us back to the house where he lived along with several others in a multi-occupied house. The premises was a detached rambling Edwardian house with original wooden windows and covered in ivy with a drive big enough to take his and several other cars. We walked into the depressive looking Hall that resembled the reception of an Institution with its dark brown coloured walls, carpets and only one working bulb in the ceiling. If there were any redeeming features then it must have been the print of one of John Constable's seascapes I noticed at the end of the Hall.

Inside, Dennis' bedsit was not that much different to the shabby Hall or his shabbier car. The walls and ceiling were quite dirty with newspapers strewn all over the floor. A rancid smell of stale semen clung rather oppressively over the whole environment. There was also a vivid photograph of a young handsome nude man hanging from the side of the wall that overlooked his grubby looking bed. It appeared that the large front windows had not been cleaned for some considerable time, probably due to his hidden world of sordid sex with young boys like me. Dennis began to take his well-worn clothes off until he was completely nude in front of me. Breathing heavily, he said to me while at the same time holding his penis, 'Shall I help you take off your clothes sweetie'—knowing that I felt apprehensive about being there. 'No thanks, I will do it myself,' I responded half-heartedly.

Eventually I took my clothes off which aroused Dennis, who then sat on the bed masturbating himself until I joined him—whereupon he started kissing my body intently moving down to my penis when I eventually climaxed into his mouth. Similar to the intense experiences that I had had with Derek after sex, I immediately felt overwhelming guilt well up inside as I started to dress myself. In my mind I thought of my family and friends at school, especially Pete and Nobby; what would they say if they found out that I had been having sex with mature men over the past eighteen months? They would, among other things, be shocked. But I must say that at some level I actually enjoyed the sex I had with Dennis, as I did with Derek; he didn't make me have sex with him and I did not protest although it amounted to sexual assault. We met occasionally over the next year or so after which our sexual liaisons finished, although I did see him from a distance many years later.

As things were in constant flux, change was also happening in the Bradbury household: my two brothers, Martin and

James, had long finished their national service in the Army, moved away and got married. Martin had married a young woman he had met while on holiday in Cornwall, deciding that they should live together in a small flat in Bognor Regis, where they managed a hotel nearby together. After leaving the Army James did some travelling around Western Europe with several former army colleagues for about a year before marrying a young woman he had met while working for himself as a builder. My other brother Bob, being four years older than me, had also left home to marry his childhood sweetheart Lucy in a local church ceremony in Epsom. Jennifer had left home when I was still a young pupil at West Lane Junior School. Apparently she had a tough time with mother, so it is not surprising that as a young woman she moved away. Margaret had left school, and like most of us, she had no qualifications; she went on to work in British Home Stores in Sutton, about five miles from home. With regards to David, his story is somewhat confusing but suffice to say one day he just walked out of the house after mother had beaten him up, not to be seen until years later working in a pub near London Bridge station. Later on there is more to be told about David's life.

The six younger siblings were all at local schools: Sid was in the senior school, Hurst Road where I was attending at the time, and he was a determined football player and boxer, winning several badges. One brief story about Sid and I was when we were at the senior school: we used to take it in turns to play with one David Hay, a pupil in Sid's class, at his home after school—the reason being David's mother used to cook a meal for whoever was with her son at the time. That way Sid and I usually had a good fried meal each once a fortnight. Susan and Wayne were both in West Lane junior school though I knew little about their progress. Gordon and George were attending the infant school next door. At this stage Lawrence was only four, still too young to attend school, but he did go to play school in Epsom.

By this time I was now fifteen years old and would soon be leaving Senior School to seek my fortune. I wasn't particularly intelligent or self-confident and had no qualifications, but I was determined to try and make something of my life, difficult as that might be. At least there was one attribute in my favour: I wasn't afraid of hard physical work as I had grafted to make some money from two newspaper rounds, and had worked with my father on coal delivery which at times was tough going. I spent more time on my own which I am sure didn't help my self-esteem or outlook, making me as time went by probably unemployable. I realised in years to come that it is important to remember that learning comes about by being in group situations. That realisation came about when I had thought of my poor early socialisation. The school employment officer had arranged for me to attend an interview for the position of apprentice butcher in a family run business in Stoneleigh, not far from the school of the same name that we beat at football. At the interview the owner of the butcher shop asked a rather stupid question: 'Do you enjoy eating sausages?' In time it would have given me great delight to have strangled him with three pounds of them. He gave me the job at five pounds a week and I started employment six weeks later.

Several of my friends at the senior school left without finding a job; however, both Pete and Nobby did find work at Woolworths working as porters supplying different floors with various goods that customers wanted but didn't need. One of my former class friends, Gordon Stewart, was one of the few of us thick heads that did get himself a good job as a technician with the Inland Revenue in Central London. However, I never did hear how he got on with the job, whether he made progress or left that job for new pastures. As the years went by, I never found out what became of most of the other former classmates.

Both my parents by this stage were well over forty-five years of age, still working very hard; there was no choice, as there were still younger children at home to be fed and clothed. Not surprisingly in my father's case, most of his time was consumed just working physically hard to make enough money, and my mother tried to make ends meet at home where seven children were still living. And of course ever since they had been married it had been a way of life to work hard to provide for their children. With a child being born nearly every two years there was very little time available for my parents to spend with any one child for long. It is not surprising therefore that my own socialisation came about by spending time with my older siblings, who would have showed me the basics but nothing more. Not the ideal training to prepare a young boy for a world that is competitive, that demands a great deal of drive and commitment if you want to succeed.

As I sat in the garden shed seeking refuge from shouting younger siblings, I suddenly realised that today was Saturday, the day my school friends and I would meet for the final time before we left school to work for a living. After finishing my newspaper round, mindful that as it was summer holidays and there was no football, I thought of going to Saturday morning cinema but of course I would cycle to Nonsuch Park and meet up with my fellow school buddies. Whatever happened I must get away from the mayhem that was going on outside in the garden. My younger siblings were shouting, throwing things at each other and one started crying. An angry Wayne shouted 'Piss off and leave me alone, you moron' to an excited Susan who had just clipped him round the ear for touching her new mountain bike.

Eventually I decided to jump on my old bike, made up from the scraps of many old bikes I found in the local authority tip, and headed for Nonsuch Park. Even in those days, more than fifty years ago, there were busy roads that you had to negotiate and it could be hazardous cycling with buses and large lorries around taking up the entire road. I had been by now going to Nonsuch Park for at least five years, at first with my older siblings and then with school friends. There were times throughout the years when the latter would visit me in the woods at the back of my home for a few fags together. My older brother Bob had first shown me how to smoke a cigarette. I had placed a Weights cigarette in my mouth and Bob lit it for me with his old smelly petrol lighter. He instructed me to 'puff the fucking cigarette' and I started to cough and heave—I felt downright terrible! Bob shouted at me, 'You won't never be a smoker, you prick!' In time I became used to them and started buying my own cigarettes, called Park Drive, in packets of five with a penny book of matches to light them.

There was a large old oak tree in Nonsuch Park, which was the secret meeting place for my friends and me. On the oak were lots of initials gouged out by me and my friends with various stolen pens or scout knives over the years. There were inscriptions dedicated to various girlfriends we had known, who had now moved on to different schools or had left the area to live elsewhere. One such girl I had a crush on was called Linda who I remember was tall for her age, attractive, slim and had long blonde hair neatly tied with different coloured ribbons. All the boys fancied her but I was the only pupil in our class to have kissed her, as I thought. Her father, who I had met on several occasions when I visited her home, appeared to be a really decent chap; he was tall himself, educated to university level and worked for the Government as a scientist. He was nearly always smiling and telling jokes of the bishop/actress kind. Behind his back we called him names such as 'perv, queer, bum bandit, faggot' among many others. On many occasions, with one eye closed, he used to say to me, 'Well, young man, you are growing up fast, what are you going to do with your life? Remember, life is a tough place where you need qualifications to get a good job.' I should have taken heed at this and would remember these words later on in my life when walking down a lonely countryside track, somewhere in Cornwall, looking for somewhere to shelter out of the torrential rain.

He was promoted to a senior scientific job somewhere in Scotland and of course his family, including Linda, moved with him. I never did see her again, often wondering what became of her.

Peter arrived at the old oak tree on his newly painted racing bike, one of many his father had bought for him over the years. He put his hand in his inside pocket and pulled out an unopened pack of twenty Senior Service cigarettes. Pete gave us all a cigarette each which we lit and started puffing for all we were worth, not knowing of course, nor did we care, of the various detrimental effects they could have on our health. In those days very little was known about the hazards of smoking, or anything else, come to that. Our lives were carefree and innocent. All we really thought about were fags, girls, bikes and football; but soon, for the first time, work would be on the agenda.

I had known Peter Upton for several years, starting from Runton Junior School. At the age of eleven we both, along with other mates at the time, made the move to Hurst Road Secondary Modern school. Educationally, Peter was similar to me and most of our mates, which was pretty thick, to be honest. We were mates in the junior school for three years and had always knocked around together as real Jack the Lads. We played truant together, stole sweets and cigarettes from the local shop, enjoyed playing knocking down ginger (knocking randomly on someone's front door and running away), were both Chelsea supporters and rode our bikes to many different places around the Runton area as though we owned the place. Peter lived near the senior school with his parents and family. They were decent ordinary working-class parents who did their best to provide for their children. Pete enjoyed sports, cinema, art and masturbating, and was well known for bringing sexy pictures of nude girls to school in the magazine *Picture Parade*. He told us they belonged to his father and used to steal them from his bedroom. He said, laughing, that he had stolen half a crown from his father's pocket to buy the cigarettes. 'I often nick from the old man,' he told me. 'He often comes home after a few beers half pissed and in the morning he can't recollect how much he spent in the pub.' This seemed the case as Pete nearly always had money to buy cigarettes, sweets or comics. He once told me, rubbing his hands together, 'Last night I nicked a ten bob note from the old chap's pocket as he lay asleep drunk.' That was Pete Upton, a real tearaway if I ever saw one but a real friend. Many others didn't like him due to his casual approach to life.

Being a warm summer day I said to the others, 'Shall we go for a bike ride to see if Nobby is in?' 'Yes,' Pete enthusiastically replied, 'While we are there we can steal some of his neighbour's apples from the shed where he stores them.' We were ready to cycle off on our bikes when John, another school friend, turned up on his light blue hand-painted bike. 'Watch the soccer last night on the telly, lads?' he asked, commenting, 'Fulham are the greatest and will win the League this season.' He said this without any doubt. I laughed, 'Fulham are a terrible side, you must be joking!' John shouted and took out of his pocket a bent scruffy looking small cigar. 'Got a light, Pete?' he asked. Peter lit his cigar from a small book of Bryant & May matches. John nearly coughed up his guts several times until Pete gave him a drink of his lemonade that helped to soothe his throat. 'Fuck that stupid cigar,' John said as he threw it away over someone's hedge and we made our way by bicycle to Nobby's house.

CHAPTER THREE

GROWING UP AND EARNING A LIVING

It was 1962, a warm and bright summer day, as I jumped on my bike aware that it was time for me to commence my apprentice butcher job in Stoneleigh with Mr Cattel, family butcher. Mr Cattel was about fifty years of age, tall with a slim build, and had a finger missing on his left hand which he told me he lost on the butcher's block. When I arrived Mr Cattel made me tea, introduced me to the staff of four, including his wife, showed me around the shop and said to me smiling, 'Well, I hope you get on here Barry, keep your nose clean, all right.' My wages were five pounds a week which excluded various scraps of bacon he gave me at the end of the week to take home, but when I realised that my colleagues were taking home large joints of meat each, it once again reinforced my lowly position.

In the mornings my job entailed making sausages, which meant feeding pork or beef mixed with some rusk and seasoning into a machine fixed to a table. At that stage I had to fit a skin made from cow belly which resembled a large French letter, over the nozzle, hold it down firmly and slowly pull the handle. My first attempt of making handmade sausages was a catastrophe as they resembled a large piece of salami. At another attempt one huge sausage came out the machine the size of a horse's erect penis! Once I got the hang of using the machine my sausages started to resemble, with a little bit of imagination, something you could eat if you were desperately hungry. After my sausage debacle, I moved on to boning and rolling various sizes of meat that Mr Cattel placed before me saying, 'Keep the knife tight to the bone so you do not leave any meat on it; afterwards cut your string accordingly so you can wrap it tight round the meat.' Many times I seriously thought I would have preferred to wrap the string around Mr Cattel's neck, throw it over the door and truss him up like a Matthew's Christmas turkey! With my apprentice butcher development going downhill rather rapidly, the one part of my job I did enjoy was when I rose to the occasion going out on the butcher's bike to deliver meat to the houses of local middle-class housewives, until I realised the boring lives those women must have lived when only the men were employed and they dutifully stayed at home. Stoneleigh and surrounding areas were made up of row after row of semi-detached houses with small tidy gardens where the females worked prior to their husbands arriving home from the office.

I had been working at Cattel's for about two months when the youngest employee apart from me, Brian Walters who had gone to school with my older brother James, invited me out to an evening race meeting at Kempton Park, six miles from Kingston. Brian, who lived locally, was a good chap, over six feet tall with a big muscular body. Apparently at Hurst Road School he was a good boxer, became school champion and eventually boxed for Surrey. We left the butcher's shop in Brian's car around four thirty to drive to the racetrack through the affluent Royal Borough of Kingston, arriving an hour later, having paid the entrance fee which included the paddock and race card.

The only time I had been to a race meeting was at the Epsom Derby as a child with my parents, years earlier, when I remember I didn't see a thing due to the many thousands of race goers. In an alien environment, there were tick tack men directing many sharp well-dressed bookmakers to shout out various horse race odds, male punters wearing binoculars and holding race cards. Brian had decided to buy us both a bottle of light ale so we could sit down on the paddock grass to see if we could back the next winner. We came to the conclusion, or rather Brian did, that we were determined to have five pound each, my entire week's wages, on the favourite which obligingly won by six lengths at even money, giving us ten pounds each. Well, I thought to myself after gulping down another light ale and being at this stage slightly drunk, racing is the game for me! I had no doubts about it, especially when Brian came up to request ten pounds to put on the favourite which couldn't be beaten. Two furlongs from the winning post the favourite was at least five lengths in front when all of a sudden the horse began to tire and three horses easily passed him, so that he was well beaten, finishing fourth.

After having three more drinks and two losing bets I eventually came to the conclusion that I was getting drunk and that horse racing, contrary to what I had previously thought, was *not* for the likes of me. When we safely arrived home I had to explain to my mother how I had lost all my week's wages, having squandered it on drinking and gambling with a colleague. She replied, 'I hope it teaches you a lesson that you won't forget! I told you about your grandfather, didn't I?' Unfortunately it didn't teach me a lesson; it was only the beginning of a gambling career that was to last into my early thirties.

Later on, having seen a newspaper advertisement in the *Evening News*, I enrolled for an evening settling course taught in the West End by the manager of City Turf Accountants. Due to the lack of confidence I attended only two sessions of the course before walking out and not returning. Throughout the years I would enthusiastically start a new job, course, training or whatever, then after several weeks, for some inexplicable reason, I would not turn up any more. During this time I successfully found a job as a board boy in the West End with Sam Burns and Terry Downs, the former world boxing champion, who had bought a number of Betting Shops around London. But that job didn't last very long either. As my mother said to me later on in my life, 'Unlike most of your siblings, you've had the opportunities, son.' Similarly, when I met my brother James for the first time in thirty years he reminded me that 'many years ago I gave you a reference for the Terry Downs job and I thought you would become a millionaire'.

It was not surprising therefore that after a year in the apprentice butcher job things came to an end. I had worked there knowing that sooner or later I would leave to find another job but had not thought that work would entail delivering coal. One of the main reasons for leaving was that my father had informed me there was a vacancy available for a coal man where he worked in Worcester Park. I joined Brown, Coal Merchants, under the illusion that I was going to earn big money, but the most I ever earned was about seventeen pounds in a week for what was very hard work indeed. We had to be out of bed at the latest 6 a.m., wash, dress and drive to the yard to collect the coal lorry and drive to Tolworth Station where we would load the coal by hand, shovelling it into eighty hundred weight bags each load three times a day. After the first load we would have a cooked breakfast, along with several other coal men in a nearby transport café where the only attractive person was the café owner's daughter.

In those days I observed that some of the coal men I was having breakfast with were around 40 years old, and wondered whether they would continue delivering coal for the rest of their lives. Most of them looked old before their time, no doubt due to years of hard physical work—but they probably had no choice. Incidentally, about three years later while I was working for a building subcontractor in Surbiton, who was paying me about forty pounds per day, good money in those days, I was able to get my father a job with the same person where he received more money for doing far less than delivering coal.

Loading and delivering three loads of coal a day, for five days a week, with one load of a Saturday, for over eighteen months became far too much physical work for me to handle. It must be remembered that I was only seventeen years of age when I first started working for Brown Coal Merchants. As the months went by I became more and more exhausted from the mechanical repetition of getting out of bed early, driving with father in the depths of winter to load stiff icy coal bags. These bags used to split open my hands to such an extent that on one occasion I had to seek medical treatment from my doctor. During the harsh winter of 1963, when it continually snowed for three months, I was working with my father trying to deliver coal bags while at the same time I was constantly trying to dig our lorry out of the snow. This way of living had a detrimental effect on my social life as sometimes I was so tired after a day's work I was unable to find the energy to go out with my friends. When I did go out to socialise in different places, I invariably fell asleep.

On one occasion I went to the local cinema with a friend only to fall asleep for the duration of the entire film. Another time I took a girlfriend to a local cinema and when I eventually woke up she had by that stage walked out no doubt disgusted by my behaviour. Many times my mother would remonstrate with my father that the work was too much for me. Eventually I couldn't take any more of the brutalising effect delivering coal was having upon my young body, and I told my father I was leaving the job immediately. Years later I was so disappointed when I considered that a mature person of 51 years of age was unable or unwilling to understand the terrible plight his teenage son was experiencing.

It is of legitimate concern, even to this day, that the constant physical force of carrying one hundred weight coal bags on my back over a period of nearly two years, with the added pressure on my neck, could explain the origin of my cervical dystonia. Furthermore, during those two years all the coal bags had to be loaded by hand and shovel by me. In essence that meant my father would hold an empty coal bag next to him while I lifted shovelfuls of coal into the bag, which took about four or five shovelfuls of coal to fill. As there is about eighty bags of coal to one full lorry of coal, that means approximately 375 shovels of coal per full lorry of coal. The point that I am laboriously trying to make is that my neck was being twisted sharply to my left (I used to shovel left-handed) each time I placed a shovel of coal in the bag. If you add up how many times I twisted my neck throughout the week, you might understand the immense sustained pressure that my sternomastoids, the muscles contracting in cervical dystonia, were under. But of course none of this information was known all those years ago; besides, my father must have been under constant pressure himself trying to feed six hungry mouths every day of the week. Hindsight is a wonderful thing!

After I left the coal delivery job I was unemployed for about three months bumming around with various people who had taken up the life as wanderers. This was the era of the Beatles, Rolling Stones and many other similar rock bands, who represented a kind of anti-establishment ethos. I grew my hair long, smoked cannabis and generally wanted to tap into this culture. My friend Howard, who lived not far from me in Runton and a few years later would emigrate to Australia, bought two tickets for us to see the Beatles at Wimbledon Palace in an attractive Edwardian building. This was my first live rock concert experience. I remember very clearly hundreds of young girls all storming to the front of the stage to throw their handbags, high heeled shoes and even their knickers over the security railings onto the stage. The Beatles sang most of their hit tunes including, 'Love me do', 'Please please me' and 'Mr Postman'.

On the return journey, taking the 93 bus from Wimbledon to Runton village, there was complete pandemonium, when most of the girls started singing various rock songs at the top of their voices until the driver said he would stop the bus to call the police if they didn't stop. As they were having so much fun their only response was to tell the driver to fuck off! Those were the times that appeared to say, 'mock the old order' or 'insult the old order' or 'you've all had your days, now it's our turn'.

With mischief on our minds one Wednesday morning, Howard and I decided to take the train and underground to Soho to have a look at the various coffee bars that had proliferated there. In those days, unfortunately, Soho was not like it is today. Many family restaurants offering well-cooked cuisine from around the world had to close due to the financial constraints of powerful business. Due to the way it had developed, Soho had this seedy image of gangs, prostitution and runaway teenagers, but it appears that culture has changed or gone underground. Soho still is a complex area that offers many interesting activities for visitors; these include the film industry, theatres and many restaurants.

Howard and I added to the decadence of the area when we decided to watch a striptease show in a dirty Wardour Street basement fit only for rodents. Along with about ten other middle-aged males (two were decidedly much older), we paid ten shillings to be entertained by the ladies of the night. One lady simulated a cigarette in front of her covered up genitals and another bent over a chair to reveal her enormous breasts that would have saved many Titanic survivors. After a few minutes I realised that one of the middle-aged men standing next to me was masturbating himself, no doubt brought about by the thrill of seeing the female entertainer's bare legs. Those large hairless legs reminded me of telegraph poles crashing about the small creaking stage. Imagine, as I did at the time, those legs round your neck squeezing the life out of you when at the height of passion. What some people do to attract the opposite sex!

Months later I became a regular visitor to the West End and Soho where, among other places, I usually visited the Marquee Club in Greek Street. The Marquee Club had a long history of entertainment. When I went there, various young rock bands were often playing. Most were usually high on drugs yet they performed fabulous music that lasted sometimes for several hours. For some unknown reason the club eventually moved just round the corner to Charing Cross Road. I would go there full of alcohol and drugs, usually cannabis or acid, determined to enjoy myself if that is possible when you are less than half conscious. In the various clubs that I frequented for several years it was more of a world of make believe, deluding yourself that you were having a great time. Most of the time I didn't know what I was saying or doing with others who were in a similar state to me, out of their heads on concoctions of drugs. You could meet people from vastly different backgrounds and cultures, which summed up the fuzzy mix of the class division that was around then. For example, on one occasion I got talking to three young girls who were from a children's home and were allowed out, so they told me, by giving sex or money to the workers. On another occasion I had a beer with a man who had gone to Eton Public School, had his own publishing business and owned several race horses that were trained in Newmarket. But of course they and many more could have been in a similar position to me, drifting rootless round the world not knowing the time of day. Perhaps the Who rock band summed up the changing times, especially for working-class kids, with their successful song 'Can't explain' that so aptly expressed their confusion about the world they lived in.

My former neighbour Graham West, who worked at the time as a fitter in West Park Mental Hospital in Epsom, acted as a referee for me so I could successfully get a job as a porter there for three months. West Park Hospital was one of five large Hospitals that were built in Epsom in the 19th century to afford the Victorian city living victims of poverty a more humane existence by offering fresh air, good food and regular healthy work, all underpinned by Christian values. What a culture shock the Hospital turned out to be for me when I considered, in the name of medical science, the appalling way individual humans were ill-treated. My job as a porter included driving to various wards, to deliver the meals, some of which were some distance from the main kitchens. To fit in with staff rotas, not patient choice, breakfast was delivered at 6 a.m., lunch at 11 a.m. and the evening meals or supper at 4 p.m. After their last meal of the day most patients would go to bed as there was nothing else for them to do although there was a social club where they could meet others or buy a cup of tea. Even in the forward looking 1960s, when I both worked and socialised in West Park Hospital, and also socialised in other Epsom psychiatric hospitals, I found them to be awful desolate places.

The patients themselves, many of whom had been there all their adult lives, were shocking to see as they had become institutionalised with very few people on the outside to support them. It was an everyday occurrence to see older patients slowly shuffling up and down the long corridors picking up cigarette ends, shouting at their inner voices to go away. One consolation was that there were a number of good, decent workers whom I personally knew that were genuinely kind and friendly towards these forgotten human beings. During my working time at West Park Hospital I met three decent male nurses who became my friends and all of them condemned the powerful psychiatric medication, especially Largactil that was given to patients in the name of therapeutic treatment. The nurses themselves explained to me that in many cases powerful anti-psychotic medication often exacerbated the existing illness of patients as a result of which they were unable, in some cases, even to get out of bed in the morning.

They and most of their colleagues where so pleased when the large Psychiatric Hospitals started to close their doors for ever when the introduction of Community Care started to help patients to be integrated back in to society where they belonged. However, that wasn't the end, but only the start, of their problems when we saw patients used as a commodity for private and voluntary residential homes to make money.

One evening my nursing friends and I drove to a large pub/restaurant in Stoneleigh Broadway for a meal highly recommended by the local newspaper. We parked the car and were walking to the pub entrance when we became involved, for some unknown reason, in an altercation with a small group of males, when one of them hit me, apparently, knocking me to the ground where I hit my head on the pavement. My friends explained that the heavy fall onto the pavement had knocked me unconscious whereupon I was taken into the pub for assistance and given smelling salts. All I remember was being assisted to my friend's car and that he drove me home and I managed to walk unaided indoors. I did not receive any subsequent treatment or medication for the heavy blow to my head and I don't know, therefore, if there have been any long-term detrimental effects to my brain. Once again I have to consider the possibility that the heavy blow to my head, falling to the ground and being subsequently unconscious for many minutes, could have caused the trauma that brought about dystonia. The next day, as if nothing had happened, I continued with the portering job at West Park Hospital.

When I left the porter job at West Park Hospital my life was once again irregular and unpredictable to such a degree that I went walking in the West Country to get away from the drug culture, both prescribed and non-prescribed drugs, which I had inadvertently become a part of. Down in Padstow I was able to give some thought about my life such as employment, college courses and drugs, and how I could change things for the better. But not a lot happened in Padstow while I was there except getting drunk with a local college girl who was studying psycho-pharmacology at the Institute of Psychiatry in London, a place that later on where I would become a patient, then a student. Padstow was full of hippies who appeared to have taken Timothy Leary's advice about dropping out but in essence the place, like a lot of Cornwall at the time, was a menagerie of youngsters all strutting their stuff. I travelled first back to central London, which was a terrible decision, then down to Epsom to seek some help and guidance if not from family, then from friends. I started visiting the local snooker hall on a regular basis, which again was not what I wanted or needed as the place was full of tramps, the unemployed and gamblers.

It was in the snooker hall one day, standing at the tea bar, that I met an Irishman from Dublin called Jimmy Hughes who was kind enough to say to me, 'Have a tea and roll on me.' I got into conversation with Jim who informed me in his strong Irish accent that his older brother Patsy was a stable lad for the Epsom trainer Ron Smyth. Jim, Patsy, Colin and Sean, were all brothers that had come over together from Dublin about two years before to find 'any sort of the crack called employment', as Jim belligerently put it. Jim was well dressed, clean and prepared for work, but so far he had applied unsuccessfully for so many jobs that it had started to make him depressed. It appeared that the brothers, apart from Patsy who had found digs with his employer, were sleeping rough, or as Jimmy called it, 'the fecking skipper'.

The three Hughes brothers and I started sleeping rough in an old disused horse stable that was rented at the time by the racehorse trainer Dave Haney. Those stables, along with many others, were on land that belonged to the Rosebery family estate, which amounted to thousands of acres of prime land stolen from the nation by his forebears long ago. After another bout of heavy drinking around the many pubs of Epsom, we staggered back to our horse stable hotel holding several bottles of cider for a nightcap. After a good drinking session we all fell asleep oblivious to the world.

While we were sleeping that morning, with all the Hughes brothers farting like bellows, there was a loud bang from someone outside of our stable. It awoke Jim who went outside where he found an old Irish friend of the family, called Larry the Louse, drunk on the ground having fallen over several metal buckets full of water. Larry had two bottles of cider, four bags of cold chips and several pairs of dirty socks in his pocket and he looked a most desperate sight indeed. After Jim had brought him into the stable with all of us now awake, Larry in his broad drunken Dublin accent said to Jim, 'I rode a winner today Jimmy my son. Have a fecking beer my son.' Jim responded angrily, 'Larry you prick, you couldn't ride a clothes horse.' After eating his cold sodden vinegar soaked chips, Larry took off his jacket and trousers to reveal dirty black pants and skin that hadn't seen water for six months. 'By the way Jimmy, could yer inform yer poor ole Larry here where can I find the Monastery of Labour?' I wasn't sure whether he was looking for a religious teacher or a job. He was away with the fairies in ten minutes.

Jim eventually found work locally as a building worker on a large private building site and his other two brothers moved to North London to live with an uncle. Larry the Louse just disappeared like he usually did, and I said goodbye to the rest of them after aimlessly walking around on my own to different places until I moved to Brighton for a while.

I must tell the brief yet hilarious story about the time when Jimmy and I travelled by train from Waterloo to stay for a few days in sunny well-heeled Bournemouth. We didn't have much money between us; the ten pounds we did have had been spent drinking in a local run down pub, so Jim had the idea that he would tap the local Catholic priest for a few pounds. We took the local bus to a place called Peterlee, some five miles from the Town centre, where we asked for the address of Father Angus. On foot we approached the large detached well decorated Georgian house, covered in shining green ivy, whereupon Jim opened the metal front gate, walked up to the house and pressed a large buzzer to the right of the green wooden door. Anticipation was high. The door was opened by a middle-aged male wearing a black suit. 'Good morning gentlemen, how can I help you?' he said in an educated Irish voice. 'Good morning Farder,' Jimmy said hesitantly, 'please forgive us for taking up your invaluable time, Farder, but I have had all me money stolen in a hotel in Bournemouth so we have been sleeping rough Farder and I was wondering if you could help me out so me friend and I may find lodgings until we can find local work.' Just before the priest could respond Jimmy further added, 'They even took me rosary beads, Farder, so they did.' Looking at Jimmy, the priest, smiling said, 'Of course I will help, my dear man, wait here—I will be back in a few minutes.'

The priest returned to the front door with a nearly new five-pound note in his hand, saying to both of us, 'This five-pound note will help you; be careful and may God be with you.' 'May God be with you too, Farder,' Jimmy most solemnly recited to the good priest. Jimmy was a good actor, I thought, and a lying bastard—he should have been performing on the London stage in a starring role all of his own. 'Many hundreds of Irish men do that kind of thing every day around the countryside when they get short of money so they do,' said a cheerful Jimmy lifting his third pint in succession. He added, 'The Catholic Church is very wealthy; to be sure they won't miss a few pounds from their donation plates.'

Before moving to Brighton something rather enjoyable happened to me that put some rosy cheeks on my face that would linger there for a few weeks. My brother Bob and a few friends had made a phone enquiry about an advertisement that was placed in the local newspaper requesting a part-time gardener. Bob contacted the person concerned, visiting her home at midday and after negotiating an hourly rate was employed for six hours a week maintaining the large garden. The lady of the house was called Lucy Green who was a middle class, middle-aged woman who was married at the time to a successful newspaper businessman. In appearance she was well groomed, had blonde hair, and was of average height and weight. One day Bob was called in to the house for a tea whereupon she said to my brother, 'I am going upstairs to my bed—would you like to follow me?' Bob could not believe his luck and at once followed Lucy into her bedroom to have sex with her. These liaisons continued for some time until several friends of Bob's also started having sex with her on a regular basis, but in different locations. There was another man, a friend of Bob's, who had taken over the gardening from my brother, who did very little gardening but spent most of the time in her master bedroom planting his seeds in Lucy's attractive body.

Some time after my brother phoned me to ask if I could drive his car to pick up Lucy as her car had broken down, then drive her to his house. This I did, dropping her off round the corner from Bob's house; then the two of us walked brazenly past some of the neighbours into his house. After having sex with Lucy upstairs in his bedroom, Bob then encouraged me to 'fill my boots' with this sexy looking woman. As I entered the small dark green bedroom smelling of semen, Lucy was standing there with nothing on looking just like some Greek Goddess, and she told me to lie on the bed. Smiling, she said to me, 'Would you like a lolly, sweetheart?' I thought to myself what an odd thing to ask if I wanted an ice cream lying on the bed with nothing on but a stiff penis. I had nothing to lose so I said to her in anticipation, 'Yes please'—whereupon she gave me oral sex for the first time in my life. She then mounted me and it was all over in seconds as I exploded inside her. The few girlfriends I had had hitherto had all been young, immature, and lacking sexual experience, but Lucy was something else; in those few minutes she had shown me what real sex was all about. Unfortunately I never saw her again; apparently she had moved away to live in another part of the country, but her lasting legacy was that she would always be known as the Pumpkin, due to her shapely kissable bottom.

In Brighton I soon found the place to be very cosmopolitan where, if you wanted, you could meet up with anyone who would supply most things legal or illegal. Here was a counter culture that had developed out of the late1950's 'angry young men era', from working-class revolution that demanded a change in consciousness to transform the vision of a modern Britain. During this energetic time of change we witnessed the growth of birth control technology, whereby women had a right to control their biology supported by the radical elements of feminism, which were determined to make permanent political change in a society based on equality. Also in this timeframe we came to experience the decriminalisation of homosexuality in Britain which at the same time in the USA was still considered to be a mental illness. It is important, I say, that a significant minority of people over the age of eighteen are legally entitled to have enjoyable consensual gay sexual relationships. From the early days, Kemp Town in east Brighton has been an area where people have lived recognising their difference and supporting others to do the same.

I moved into a small bedsit not far from the sea front or working lanes community as I frequented the many pubs, dives, cafés and the emerging number of various spiritual places that were opening up around the ferment of change that was happening in Brighton. The bedsit I had was delightfully painted, with pale blue ceiling and lemon coloured walls, within a large Victorian house occupied by different people that included students, beatniks, roamers, anarchists, poets and many others who were unclassifiable. If you had walked past this house or most other houses in central Brighton at the time you would probably have smelt the odour of cannabis, overheard strange Indian music and watched people with long hair wearing coloured smocks doing yoga in the front garden. While I lived here, I became friendly with a bloke called Mitra, who was Indian, who had travelled thousands of miles overland to eventually reach his destination, Brighton, where he studied fine art in the local college. He was from an untouchable caste background, which made life for his family in India very difficult insofar as they were given all the most demeaning work such as emptying latrines or washing the feet of rich merchants.

Mitra and I walked on the South Downs together for miles, starting at Devil's Dyke car park, down to Amberley and beyond. On one occasion on the South Downs Way we walked seventeen miles from Eastbourne to Southeast station, a marvellous experience, passing some wonderful scenery, including many wild flowers such as orchids that attracted pollinating bees and butterflies. As Mitra was a practising Buddhist he used to meditate at least twice a day in his little bedroom that had a shrine in the corner with a metal figure of a Buddha sitting on a lotus flower, contemplating the suffering of Brighton residents.

He used to say to me most sincerely, 'It would be most wonderful if Buddha could have visited Brighton to give prayers to the many thousands seeking refuge. I was born an untouchable but will die a much higher being.' This was something he would constantly say, not necessarily for my ears but to reassure himself that he was doing the right thing. Mitra was the most wonderful human being that I ever had the privilege to meet and I sometimes think the enlightened asked him to spend time with me so he could support me through this difficult period of my life.

The first time I ever flew in a plane was with Mitra. We decided that we would like to walk on the Island of Jersey, well known for its lush green coast path covered with wild flowers. Also on the Island there were many small coves that one could visit, these being ideal for meditation or solitude. We arranged for a cab to take us to Brighton station, travelling on from there to Clapham Junction and then by train down to Weymouth, where we found a small family hotel to stay for the night. Around this time of the season Weymouth appeared to be most popular with tourists as most of the long sandy beach was full with screaming, laughing children digging up the sand with their buckets and spades, and energetic dogs running in to the sea to retrieve a ball thrown by the owner.

Mitra was fascinated by the Punch and Judy beach show where he started shouting, along with the children, at Mr Punch for being so nasty to his wife. He loved children, having three younger siblings himself, and enjoyed being in their company feeling he was one of them. In essence Mitra had a young child inside of him that he sensitively nurtured daily to love the world regardless of all limitations.

Weymouth seafront is made up of many small multi-coloured family-owned terraced houses offering B&B accommodation, along with several handsome hotels, and pretty council owned flower beds planted with summer bedding plants. Up early next morning—Mitra never did adjust to a cooked breakfast—we took a rather slow ferry, due to hazardous rocks, to St Helier in Jersey, disembarking six hours later, tired, yet enthusiastic to find out about the Island. Our short enjoyable break in Jersey started when we found a local B&B accommodation owned by the only speed cop, sergeant Peter Gaul, on the Island whose family, as he informed us, first came to Jersey from north west France 75 years ago to find work labouring on a farm.

We made a brief visit to the capital, St Helier, on only two occasions, first to have an evening meal in a very good restaurant and second to collect a prescription for Mitra whose stomach gave him problems ever since his arrival from India due to the Western diet. During the warm summer season the pubs open early in the morning to cater for the French people in particular, who have the chance to eat before sweating in the fields for many hours picking the ripe red tomatoes that are eventually exported. Incidentally, I observed the pickers eating for breakfast their own baked bread rolls, soft French cheese and onions picked fresh from the earth, instead of the traditional fried breakfast.

On the final day we took a cab to the airport to buy two single tickets from British Airways before the plane took off on our maiden flight to Heathrow Airport, landing an hour later in glorious sunshine after which we took a fast train back to decadent Brighton. As some sort of homecoming there was a large International music carnival making its way past the impressive Victorian clock tower, eventually finishing down in front of the west pier.

One of the main reasons I enjoyed my time in Brighton was the open atmosphere. What attracted me was the courage of various people who assumed responsibility for a different way of life in which they opposed the oppressive anti-family regime, instead setting up a new bohemian lifestyle.

However, the drugs, sex and rock and roll way of life did not last, due to the lack of a clear vision for a future lifestyle based on growth and development as those individuals aged. But it most certainly did help some people to move on to a more wholesome spiritual existence.

It was around this time that I moved back to London to move in with my family for about six months. My parents were both well and looking forward to their forthcoming holiday in Cornwall along with their son Bob and his wife Linda. For the first time in my mother's life she didn't have very young children to look after which meant more time to pursue her own personal interests. My father was still working at the building job that I helped him to obtain some time ago and since then had been taken on full time by the main contractor. At this stage he was earning by far the highest amount of money he had done during the whole of his life which really pleased me because it meant my parents would have the opportunity to have a far greater choice for the first time in their lives.

There had been changes within the household; my sister Margaret had got herself married to a man from Woking, having met him six months earlier on a holiday in Rome, and they were now living together in a small flat in Guildford. Other siblings, Sid and Wayne, had also moved out of the family home, living together in an independent lifestyle by renting a house in Croydon. Apart from the other four siblings who were still living at home, namely Susan, Gordon, George and Lawrence, all the older siblings lived elsewhere. I had not been around the home for some time so I did not know much about my siblings' everyday lives.

One day out of impulse I bought myself a black Ford Prefect from a car showroom in Epsom determined to show my family and others that I could find a job to turn things round from a rather haphazard past three years. I started going out more now that I had the support of a car to take me to various places in Epsom, Sutton and Croydon where, with a bit of luck, I thought, I might be able to find myself a girlfriend to spend time with. In Epsom it appeared there were not any decent dance clubs or discos where you could go to meet someone. On some occasions I left my car at home as I sometimes felt uneasy on my own without a few beers inside me and I did not want to take the risk of being stopped by the police for drink-driving.

All the local places I visited on my own I found to be quite parochial so I decided to spend more time again round the West End, including my well known haunt, Soho. I visited many different pubs and clubs then but it reminded me of past experiences which I did not want to repeat. During the next three months I visited many different pubs in the West End but I did not meet anyone I liked, so I continued on my own, which at times I found to be reassuring. It is easy to meet people, many of them, in central London pubs in particular, but you are asking for big trouble as most of them will try to fleece you of your money or anything else they can lay their hands on. Things can get worse if those conmen or crooks ask you back to their home for a drink, when they will rob you of everything you possess.

CHAPTER FOUR

LIVING WITH DYSTONIA, LONG TERM ADDICTION TO VALIUM, PRISON AND ALIENATION FROM MAINSTREAM LIFE

One rainy afternoon I was driving my car home when all of a sudden my neck went stiff, similar to a stiff neck, pointing to the right. I wasn't unduly concerned at the time as I kept driving with my left hand holding my head in place with the other. My neck was still in spasms as I entered the doctor's surgery two days later when my GP explained that I had contracted spasmodic torticollis, or cervical dystonia as it is now referred to. He prescribed a month's supply of valium to reduce the spasms but at the time I didn't really understand what all this medical jargon meant. Other than the visiting school doctor who inspected our heads for lice, I had not seen a doctor before but of course I should have done on at least one occasion when I was electrocuted. The GP also said he would arrange an appointment for me to see a psychiatrist at Westminster Hospital within the next three weeks.

On the day of the appointment I travelled up from Epsom to Waterloo, from which it was a short bus journey to the hospital where I awaited my fate. I had not been to this area of London before; in fact, I had never been to a Hospital before except for my birth, so I was not sure of myself and at the same time I felt overpowered by the tall buildings in Horseferry Road which had an air of authority about them.

The psychiatrist was a tall, slim, middle-aged white man who walked with a pronounced limp. He called my name to go into his office, offered me a seat and then sat down at his desk to ask me the first unusual question: 'Do you grunt like a pig, Mr Bradbury?' Rather puzzled by the question, I just looked at him. 'No,' I said. In his rather posh accent he then asked me another question: 'Do you feel inferior to other people?' Once again I said no. If I had not been so nervous I would have said yes to the second question, but after the appointment I was angry with myself for not doing so. After less than ten minutes in front of Dr Dally I asked him, 'What is the matter with me?' He solemnly responded, 'Torticollis.' That was it—the interview was over and he said he would be writing to my doctor about my condition, which at the time was considered not uncommon, with the emphasis on the psychological rather than the neurological. I returned home to visit my GP the next day when once again he gave me another prescription for a month's supply of valium: three10mg pills per day. Thereafter I was prescribed valium medication for the next 17 years and I became painfully addicted to it to such a degree that it became detrimental to my health and subsequent personal development.

Several weeks later, visiting a pub in Greek Street called The Lamb, a shabby place frequented by prostitutes, rather late one Friday night to buy a beer, I saw a face that I recognised from when I lived in Brighton. He also recognised me at once; we shook hands and I asked him, 'Hallo Bill, nice to see you, what you doing in a place like this?' He replied as if he was genuinely pleased to see me: 'Good to see you, Barry, you look well yourself.' I ordered two pints of lager for Bill and me and we sat down at the small dirty table near the door. Bill was about twenty-three years of age, tall and slim with a long hippy hairstyle, wore jeans and a large trench coat. Not exactly the kind of chap you would like your daughter to bring home for a glass of wine with the family. He was, though, a decent sort of bloke. I had first met him some time ago in a Brighton pub, when the two of us were the worst for alcohol, no doubt exacerbated by illegal drugs. After that chance meeting we used to meet from time to time for a beer, smoke cannabis and a roasting good (Ruby Murray) curry, as Bill called it, from a little family run business near Portslade where Bill lived. We carried on chatting over at least three more pints of beer when the manager called time for us to depart, and we made arrangements to meet in three days' time in Epsom at a place where he once lived. Before we left, Bill turned round to me, rather puzzled and said frowning, 'What's the problem with your neck, Barry? It appears to be hanging to your right side or is that because you've had too much to drink, you scoundrel?' I explained to Bill about dystonia, going to meet the shrink and the pills that my GP had prescribed.

'Good to see yer my son!' Bill roared at me as soon as I had entered the old attractive Victorian pub, called the King's Head, just off Epsom High Street. 'What you having to drink colonel?' said Bill with a large smile on his face which told me he had been on cannabis. 'Cheers Bill, a pint of cider'—and so it went on for a few hours with both of us getting drunk. 'Hey Bill, shall we do some villainy tonight?' I smiled. With a wicked smile still on his face, Bill replied, 'Yes, why not, my son!' So the two of us took a cab from Epsom to my home in Runton two miles away, where I picked up my car, still drunk. We then drove to Runton village to have a look at the jewellery shops to see if it would be possible to break in at the rear of the building. We drove through the village three times to survey the area, also to reassure ourselves that this was a theft we could carry out. At the last moment we decided not to break into the jewellers at the back, but to do a smash and grab on the place. For the final time we drove back through the quiet village. At this stage I felt rather sober and parked outside the shop for Bill to get out of the car to throw a large brick through the window. There was an almighty smash which resounded through the tiny village but no alarm bells were set off ringing. He grabbed as much jewellery as he could, dropped a watch on the ground, retrieved it and the two of us drove off at high speed through the quiet roads of middle-class Runton. We eventually stopped the car three miles later on Epsom Downs to see how many items of jewellery Bill had managed to steal from the shop.

On the downs we looked at the various watches, rings and necklaces we had stolen to see approximately what they were worth. In my inexperienced estimation the bent jewellery was worth more to a Scout leader than to a crook who might possibly want to buy it from us. Of course I certainly didn't tell Bill that. Bill said to me rather eagerly, 'Let's go back to take the rest of the jewellery I left behind.'

'Okay, let's go and take the rest.' I drove back through Epsom Downs into Higher Green (we used to call it Millionaire's Row), down Reigate Road and into the village where I pulled up outside the shop for Bill to grab the remainder of the jewellery and we were away at high speed like some modern day John Dillinger and Al Capone. We drove back to the Downs but stopped at a different site where we had stopped before to do a quick calculation of how much we had stolen. As we did not have the prior intelligence of placing the stolen gear, we now had the problem of finding buyers to take it off our hands. As I looked out onto the cold dark Downs, I wondered to myself, 'What have we done?' Who will possibly benefit from our illegal activities, once the police realise this contraband is for sale to the local villains? I suggested to Bill that we now make our way home as we did not want the police stopping us with all the illegal stuff in the boot of the car. Bill looked at me and said, 'Just a moment, one more place where we can make a few more pounds.' I shook my head. 'Let's call it a night, Bill,' I said. He thought for moment. 'Look, down West Lane just beyond the football pitches is a pavilion where they keep lots of scrap metal,' he said and explained rather excitedly, 'We can put it into the boot of your car!'

I thought to myself we didn't really need the metal right now, but Bill took my silence as a sign of acquiescence. 'Okay, let's go for it,' he said, and once again I drove over the Downs through Higher Green but down a different road into the village, turning left into West Lane, passing the two schools that I had attended years ago, thinking in a flash what my former teacher and former girlfriend Christine Bungard would say right now. I parked the car at nearly the end of the Lane so we could look at the pavilion, which at this moment in time was shrouded in mist. We decided to jump over a metal fence. I felt apprehensive since I was about to commit another theft, when we arrived at the pavilion some 100 yards from my car. Bill forced the pavilion door open and we walked into a large room, but all was very dark except for a crack of light coming in through the ceiling. We were feeling our way round the room when we bumped into what felt like metal drums. Bill felt for the matches in his pockets, found them and struck a match so we could see the drums in front of us. With another light from his matches, I screwed open the top of the drum and Bill brought the match down to see what was inside. All of a sudden all mayhem was let loose in the pavilion as large flames engulfed both of us. All I remember of this terrifying experience was running out of the pavilion across the football pitch onto the road. I kept running up another road, with Bill close behind, and into the driveway of a house knocking frantically on their front door. An older couple answered the door in horror to find two young men with burnt faces, hands and clothes confronting them and they told us to come into their house. They immediately phoned for the ambulance that took us first to Epsom District Hospital and then onto the burns unit at Roehampton Hospital.

There I was in the burns unit with both my hands and face burnt, mainly superficial burns, according to the surgeon, that in time would heal but leave skin grafts noticeable on my right hand only. Bill had similar burns. There was a police guard for both of us, just in case we attempted to flee from the hospital in our pyjamas. During this time my parents had visited me in the burns unit, naturally most concerned about how I was. Two days later Epsom detectives visited me in my room to charge me with arson and two counts of theft. Bill was similarly charged. What a bloody fool I was, stealing inexpensive rubbish jewellery and then pushing my luck further, thinking there would be anything of value to steal in an old council owned pavilion. All this immature behaviour was fuelled by excessive alcohol consumption.

After ten days in the Burns Unit my parents came to collect me, as I had been discharged from the hospital, to drive me home to safety. Bill had been discharged two days earlier. Not very much was asked of my criminal behaviour by my parents but they must have been so disappointed after all they had tried to do for me over the years. But unfortunately I wasn't the first Bradbury sibling to have felt the strong arm of the law. Several times over the years, before and after my criminal convictions, my parents had the unfortunate experience of visiting the inside of a police station to support one son or another.

Ten days after being discharged from hospital, Bill and I had to appear in front of Epsom Magistrates Court which extended our bail conditions for another 14 days when we would have to appear before them once again. After the next court proceedings we were formerly charged with one count of arson and two counts of theft and we were committed to stand trial at Kent Assizes three months later. To this day I very much appreciate the anonymous person who put the money up for me to be released on bail so that I could try to recover at home. In between now and the start of our trial, I found things very difficult trying to cope with burnt healing hands, the side effects of valium, head deviation from dystonia and explaining to my family and others what had happened the night of the fire. But it is worthwhile pointing out again that my burnt hands were self-inflicted.

When Bill and I arrived outside Maidstone Assizes at around10 a.m. in the summer of 1968, we were just in time to witness the Judge dressed in a red, white and ermine coloured gown stepping down from a Bentley to open the Assizes ritual. At our trial both Bill and I pleaded guilty to all charges and were sentenced to three years each, which I thought was a rather harsh sentence. I still remember all these years later when the Judge commented to Bill and me just before sentencing us, 'I am sorry but I cannot let my heart guide me.' I have a vague recollection of this old male judge, similar to a John Bull character, sitting there with a dirty grey coloured wig precariously balanced on the top of his rather large head. At one stage in the court proceedings I noticed that he had fallen asleep in his huge brocade covered seat, probably brought about by too much alcohol at lunch time. However, it is worthwhile to reflect that no member of the public was at risk of death or injury from the pavilion fire, as it was late at night in a locked park some considerable distance from a public road.

The fact that we had both been on drugs and alcohol at the time is beside the point; we were both responsible for the pavilion fire. No doubt this major incident happening at such an early stage in my personal development, along with my other problems, would considerably hold me back even further. One important point I must clarify: It is certainly not the case, as several of my siblings have been led to believe, that I contracted dystonia due to my involvement in the fire. As this book clearly points out, the dystonia came about, for whatever reason, several months before the pavilion fire while I was driving my car home one afternoon.

Bill and I were first sent to Canterbury Prison for about two months, then transferred to Ford open prison in Sussex where the daily regime was wholly different to a closed prison. Canterbury Prison was an old decaying Victorian institution fit only to administer the harshest of sentences on those unfortunate individuals who for the most part were either mentally ill, illiterate, chronic recidivists, or all three where nothing was achieved for their betterment. My first day in Canterbury Prison I found frightening and very claustrophobic, where prison officers were shouting at cons (prisoners) while they walked from their cells to slop out their toilet waste in an alcove, one to each bleak grey looking landing. This was a practise, I thought, that goes back to the harsh inhuman Victorian days of punitive regimes but has no place in a modern prison system yet is still used to degrade life's losers. After an appalling breakfast that was not fit for a pig to eat, I had to visit the prison doctor along with all the other new inmates. The doctor was African who could speak very little coherent English, so communication was dreadful as I tried to explain to him in vain that I needed medication for dystonia; but he obviously thought that I had some sort of mental deficiency because he kept saying, 'You well, no drugs, you want no drugs.' He just about summed up the whole useless degrading institutional mentality that exists for one thing: control of the human mind.

During the day in Canterbury prison I worked sewing mail bags for eight hours a day in a stultifying atmosphere made worse by the putrid smell of outside drains and the constant farting by the older institutionalised cons, who were probably bunged up by the staple diet of too much stodge. Looking at this large room today with my mental telescope, I picture a hideous scene of mostly old age time servers bent over trying to sew mail bags that would be sent to various Banks and Post Offices who would use them to carry cash around the country. In turn, those bags carrying money would be robbed in transit and where the robber, if caught, within a few weeks might well be sewing mail bags himself. Cons receive a weekly money allowance so they can buy personal things for themselves or for someone outside, like their wife or child. Tobacco is the one currency that will enable you to buy or barter for most things inside prison. From haircuts, sexual favours, or even drugs, tobacco can afford you most unofficial luxuries that can help make prison life bearable or even liveable.

In just over two months we were informed by the Prison that Bill and I would be transferred the next day to Ford Open Prison in Sussex. Along with eight other white cons of different ages we set forth in a prison van from the confines of Canterbury Prison, taking two hours to arrive at the countrified Ford Prison which reminded me at first of some kind of holiday camp. With the sun streaming into the prison Ford Transit van, we drove into the prison grounds, laid out to accommodate single storey wooden huts with large playing fields inside and outside the prison with a single storey brick built dining hall in the centre.

The prison was originally built to house airmen in the

Second World War, which explains the uniformity of the huts and the large hard surface, probably used for parades, outside the dining room. Furthermore, airmen needed lots of space to exercise their bodies to keep them fit for the rigours of war. The prison itself was divided in two by a rather high barbed wire fence; one side where I was confined was for the younger cons and the other for the older, ageing cons. They actually lived in a three-storey newish brick building, originally built for officers, consisting of single occupancy bedrooms, large modern kitchen, day room and a well maintained garden. On the side for older cons there was a tendency, a prison officer informed me, to house the more 'sophisticated' con who could be serving five years or more for fraud or embezzlement. On my side there was mainly younger working class people like myself who could be serving shorter sentences for stealing goods from a lorry or materials from a building site. During my confinement at Ford Prison one of the red bands (trusted cons) informed us after it happened that the two spies Peter and Helen Kroger, under strict security, had met each other for a short visit.

They say that Ford prison is similar to Butlins Holiday camp but I am not so sure as there is security carried out when cons march, like a ragged army, to and from their place of work. There were hut security checks early every morning around 6 a.m. when the usual banter from the screw (prison officer) was 'hands off cocks and on with socks', and also security checks three times in an evening. Bill and I had the very good fortune to be given clean tidy work in a large hangar where we studiously placed various plastic utensils in polythene bags intended, so I was told, for the Airlines based at Gatwick. The hangar was used to house airplanes during the Second World War but had been adapted for the Prison Service to be used as a large Industrial Unit so that cons might live a productive confinement!

In the unit where I worked were men from various backgrounds including India, Israel, Africa and Europe. When I got talking so some of them, I quickly realised that they were all innocent men; in fact, most of them had been fitted up by the police. This was also the case throughout the prison where most of the cons, especially the senior cons, were either innocent or had failed to pay the police money to keep them out of prison. It appeared that Bill and I were the only real cons in Ford Open Prison, so that when the authorities found out about the mass injustice we would be left on our own surrounded by prison officers! Another charade I quickly cottoned on to was that most of the cons working in the industrial unit were millionaires with large homes in Park Lane West End, not Park Lane East Ham, had ocean going yachts moored in Barbados and were personal friends of Prince Philip. After six months the place reminded me more of Metro Goldwyn Mayer than a prison.

In reality most of the older cons were decent yet inadequate individuals whose lives had been beset by institutional confinement, prison or psychiatric institution, with very little enjoyment in between. Even today I severely question government policy that continually locks up individuals for no real reason other than short term institutional gain instead of looking at the long term development of the person.

I realised that the only way to make the best of the time in Ford prison, or do my bird the easy way, was to co-operate and participate in various activities such as football or cricket. I played for the prison team many times both inside and outside of the prison visiting places such as Bosham, Bognor Regis and Climping, all three being in the same Sussex League as Ford. On some of the away matches one or two cons would arrange to meet their girlfriends for a quick knee trembler, lucky bastards! Mind you, although it was illegal to meet anyone, as they did, without authority, those cons in question had worked hard for the football team over a period of months and, besides, it's healthier than medication or even pulling your pudding ten times a day. As a regular member of the football team I got to play against a visiting showbiz team which included Dave Webb who played for Chelsea, John Junkin, Bill Oddy, Marty Feldman, Jimmy Villiers and Kit Napier of Brighton FC. After winning a wonderfully contested hilarious match we had a bit of a party, minus the alcohol, in the visitors' room taking it in turns to have a singsong. The showbiz team also included several attractive sexy young females wearing short miniskirts, high heel boots, who typified the 1960s party scene. The visitors' room was the one place I really looked forward to every two weeks, when someone or other from my family would come to visit me for an hour or so when I could eat homemade sandwiches, cakes and scones washed down by the establishment's extremely poor coffee. I was discharged after serving fourteen months of my sentence, having been given parole for the remainder of my sentence; thereafter I would have to visit my parole officer every two weeks for the next year.

As I felt very fit and full of energy after leaving prison, I had the confidence to contact two local football teams to enquire about training with a view to playing for them. I first contacted Banstead F.C. who told me to just turn up for training. Getting off the bus surrounded by a huge Council Estate, it was clear that I would be up against some hard individuals living across the road whose only *raison d'être* for being a supporter at Banstead F.C. was to hopefully break a few legs. 'Shall I turn back?' I thought, being rather shocked at the idea of playing in front of some of those ugly morons, with tattoos on their faces, now looking at me from across the road. What was I thinking about! Fuck 'em, I've just served fourteen months of porridge, so whose afraid of those scumbags anyway? 'Hold on Barry, don't do anything irrational, for fuck sake,' I thought to myself as I looked for the bus stop that could take me back to Epsom. Anyway, I must be sensible about it as most of the young lads not thirty yards from me probably didn't even play football, never mind support a parochial team like Banstead. Besides, most of them were no more than16 years of age and probably preoccupied with sex and drugs. For the past few minutes irrational feelings had been surfacing, brought about by panic that I could feel surging through my brain—probably the side effects of valium.

During the last fourteen months I had been taking some kind of prison liquid for dystonia, and I experienced no side effects, but now back in civilian life I was once again taking prescribed valium. Already, after only several weeks, I was experiencing the side effects of valium. Once I had left the prison, why didn't I just forget about prescribed drugs and get on with my life?

I hesitantly made my way into the ground, at the same time eyeing up the place for a quick escape, to seek out my contact Pip, the trainer, who I found in the changing room. He shook my hand and said, 'Welcome, Barry, change as quick as you can and join the other players on the pitch.' At first I wasn't reassured to know that most of the players were local lads who quickly shook hands with me, which didn't make me feel at ease at all. But after a few weeks of training, things went well with my colleagues as I was eventually selected to play for the reserve team at home against Tring United in a London Metropolitan league match. I started the match well confident that I could get better, but after some 60 minutes of playing I gestured to the manager, not really understanding why my back was painful, and he called me off the pitch. After having a shower I walked out of the ground never to return again. This behaviour of flight or fight was a pattern I would keep repeating throughout most of my life and I am unable to explain why. Was it due to the long-term ingesting of valium, debilitating effects of dystonia, problems associated with being electrocuted, or the result of being unconscious which could be affecting brain function?

On another occasion, not long after Banstead, I started training with Wyteleafe F. C. located three miles from Purley Town. They played in the London Senior league, owned their football ground and were well known for their hospitality where visiting teams would receive first class facilities. After a few weeks of tough training I was overjoyed to be selected to play for the first team as a substitute at Farnham Town. Driving down in the coach with my expectations high surrounded by all the players, manager and officials, a surge of excitement came over me when I thought this time things would be different. Unfortunately, once again after playing for about an hour, I explained to the manager I was unable to keep running due to a bogus back injury. The same pattern of behaviour occurred as I walked out after the match, never to return again even though the team manager phoned me on two separate occasions to ask if I was still interested in playing for Wyteleafe F.C.

Now was the time that I had to seriously consider what to do with my life as it stood in near tatters, not having any qualifications, skills or experience to help me when applying for employment. As I was now around 23 years of age, and an individual with a voice barely heard above a whisper due to the lack of confidence and self-esteem, I think it is now appropriate to recapitulate: (1) What must be considered are the possible long-term effects of being electrocuted by 240 volts at a very young age (about 3 years) where I had received no medical treatment or psychological therapy. (2) It must be considered whether there were any long-term psychological or emotional problems after being sexually abused at a young age of 12/13 years by three mature men? (3) At the age of 17 years, I sustained a heavy traumatic bang to my head when someone hit me; I fell back tripping over a kerbstone knocking myself unconscious. Again I did not receive any medical treatment. Many years later when attending a dystonia clinic at the National Hospital in London the Consultant Neurologist asked me if in the past I had a stroke as an X-ray result had found two dark unexplained shadows in my brain. (4) At the age of 20 years I contracted torticollis (cervical dystonia) which is a debilitating illness. (5) The medication for dystonia is valium which I have been taking now for several years. The side effects are panic attacks, cognitive recall problems, sexual dis-function and lack of motivation and self-esteem. (I subsequently went on to take valium for 17 years.) (6) Although self-inflicted, I received skin grafts as I burnt my hands and was subsequently sent to prison for 3 years.

Due to the mounting psychological/emotional problems I was experiencing, I was spending more and more time on my own and isolating myself even further from the group of young people, to which I belonged at the time—young people who needed to learn various skills and support. Apparently by this stage it was not healthy to spend so much time on my own. I felt that I just couldn't cope with all the overwhelming pressures on me to conform by finding a job, be more sociable and fit in with things. At this stage of my life I had these various voices in my mind shouting out for their own identity. It was a kind of intellectual and emotional tug of war in my head for individual prominence.

By this stage I had moved back to live with my parents for the next year or so now that my life was becoming increasingly difficult. Only my two youngest brothers, George and Lawrence, remained at home and they were both working for local employers where they were learning new skills to help them make a decent living. Most of the time, unlike the years gone by, the house was quiet which gave me time to relax and think about what I needed to sort out. My parents did their best to help and support me as much as possible but I am afraid to say that I received very little support from any of my siblings, who of course had their own responsibilities. There were times when I must have descended into the realms of insanity never really knowing where to go or what to do with myself. Many times I visited, sometimes without an appointment, my GP, neurologist and psychiatrist requesting their help but all they gave were more prescriptions for valium. Never once did any of those medical professionals seek an alternative for me such as psychotherapy or a skills unit where I could train for something. My GP did make an appointment for me to attend the Henderson Hospital near Banstead which admitted people, among others, with so-called personality disorders (whatever they are meant to be). I did attend an interview conducted by the patients and it was they who voted for me to be admitted the following week, but following the same pattern of behaviour as before, I did not go back.

It was round about this time that I started experimenting wearing my young sister's clothes but I did go on to buy other women's articles in charity shops. I wore women's clothes occasionally for about three years but when living at home it was always difficult due to the number of people always around. Many years later when having psychotherapy I tried to make sense of my transvestism in terms of isolation and emotional withdrawal from things around me. I believe wearing women's clothes compensated for the lack of physical and emotional contact I failed to have with women and by masturbating on my own it became my internalised sexual love affair with myself. Regards my own shrinking emotionally bereft inner world at the time, it was J. Binswanger who came close to expressing my own painful experiences. 'The last hope of a point of breakthrough' of what he called a 'dual mode of being in the world, may be through a homosexual attachment, or the last loving bond may be with the other as child or animal.'

I also believe that M. Boss wrote about a kind of life, my life, that was fast disintegrating into chaos, devoid of human love, 'when most of his own male feelings had run out, he suddenly and for the first time in his life felt driven to open himself to a certain form of homosexual love'. This homosexual love that is referred to is different from the sexual abuse I was subjected to when I was still young, immature and at school. The reason I have cited the two pieces of text above is because they reflect my life at the time between the ages of about 23-30 years, a life devoid of any sustaining loving relationship with a woman which could be explained due to the disability of head deviation. Out of inner turmoil I was driven to seek out a same-sex relationship, not necessarily for sex, but something that could be emotionally life enhancing which would nurture my feeble emotional identity that was leading me down, descending into madness.

During this transvestism stage of my life I visited many TV clubs, pubs and shops to try and understand more about the phenomenon that affects many mature gay and straight males. In the Pink Club, in central London, I was amazed by the number of transvestites, trannies or TV's, call them what you will, men of most ethnicities, dressed in beautifully coloured female clothes beyond my comprehension and expectation. There were young oriental men who looked very feminine indeed, dressed in exotic short sexy miniskirts, long blond wigs, high thigh boots, who attracted most of the attention from the mainly white middle-aged men. By the way they were dancing it appeared that most of the oriental males were gay, some probably prostitutes, as they would cuddle up to their white gay partners on the dance floor, then retreat to an intimate part of the bar or restaurant probably to negotiate a price. Later on in the evenings, not only at the Pink Club but other TV clubs that I visited, many of the TV's would pair off together, which meant going to their hotel room for sex or going home together by car or cab.

At the Pink Club it was not difficult, the case at most TV venues, to meet a TV for a drink, conversation or something more amorous in an atmosphere of consenting promiscuity known to both parties in minutes. At the attractively decorated Pink Club, with sparkling chandeliers, pink flock wallpaper, cream carpets and well adorned lighted bars, it was like a scene out of a Dallas commercial. There were sexually erotic TVs prancing up and down the stairs to the toilets where they would repaint their faces hoping to be picked up by some millionaire sugar daddy. Many TVs that I did meet, especially white middle-aged British males, were not gay but would attend these clubs merely to enjoy dressing up in women's clothes in an environment where they would not be discriminated against. In fact, a lot of those men I met informed me they enjoyed dressing up at home with the support of their heterosexual partners who would enjoy visiting TV clubs with them.

One male I met at a TV club called the Pineapple Club—and it makes the mind boggle—used to sit in an obscure corner of the bar knitting various clothes for his straight partner back in Wales to wear. Another TV explained he and his wife would travel down to London where they would reserve a room in a posh hotel for the weekend. Visiting a TV club on his own, he would bring back another TV to his hotel where he got great delight by watching him make love to his wife. It is an understatement when they say 'it takes all kinds to make a world'!

After visiting several TV clubs, I decided that the time was right for me to experiment with various women's clothes, and for the first time to try cosmetics. I wanted to understand how and why I could fit into a transvestite environment where most of the TVs, I assume, had been dressing for some time. In most transvestite clubs, even a few pubs and one notable shop, there will usually be an experienced TV who dresses others for a fee and is usually connected, but not exclusively, in some way or other to the owner or franchise of a particular place. The same resident TV dresser at the Pink Club dressed me to my personal satisfaction on many occasions to a skilful level of female impersonation. But I didn't really know or understand what to expect from male admirers or how other seasoned TV's would react to my presence.

For the first few times I dressed, I was quite surprised how I experienced myself clad in women's clothes directly in front of other TVs. It was weird to be standing there with a painted face, red luscious lipstick, dressed in a long black wig, artificial boobs in a bra, stockings and suspenders, tight fitting skirt and high heel shoes that made me feel like some kind of Dorothy Perkins mannequin. For a while during that first occasion when I dressed as a transvestite in public, subsequently many times after, I really did feel that I had those feminine sexual qualities that other men so desired. Many men admirers, for obvious reasons, continued to give me the eye, and one particular evening a group of three Japanese men asked me if I wanted a drink, which came with added strings no doubt.

When people discuss the complexities of human sexuality and identity we are touching on something that not even the experienced gender psychiatrists really understand in any depth. The gender psychiatrist I mentioned above when I was in Earls Court many years previously is now being sued, I read, in a class action by many male to female transsexuals who claim medical negligence. Whether their case has any legal merit, I am certainly not in the position to comment, but for the record I have never contemplated, at any stage in my life, of having a sex change.

In the 1980s I met a rather ambiguously looking male in an Earls Court pub who explained to me that he used to travel every month all the way up from Penzance to be treated for his eventual male to female transsexual change. David had been married for several years to two different women without having children but insisted that he had never been gay. He went on to say that from an early age he had always felt he was a woman dressed in men's clothes; now he thought he must do something about it or otherwise he would commit suicide. His doctor first explained to David that he would have to wear women's clothes full-time in public for at least one year before he could consider giving him female oestrogen injections which would reduce the size of his genitals. As David anticipated, this would later prepare him for surgery. When I first met him he had been receiving injections for a year; later he underwent surgery to remove his male genitals, design his female genitalia and throat surgery to redesign his deep male voice. After being discharged from the hospital David did not look like a women but, more perplexing, he did not look like a man either! I subsequently read that there is a high incidence of suicide in male to female transsexuals but also a great many of them sadly oscillate into prostitution. Having thought about it, we can have all the major or cosmetic surgeries available to enhance our appearance but what it doesn't change is the mind; unless we work on that first, everything else will be a rather superficial exercise.

The psychiatrist I had consulted at Westminser Hospital, Dr Peter Dally, also managed a day hospital, St Charles, a former shabby old workhouse, not far from Kennington War Museum. I became a day patient where I received intravenous injections of valium that made me unconscious for several hours once a week for about a year. I can only assume that I received those injections to help my musco-skeletal system relax but all they were doing in actuality was adding fuel to the fire by giving me more of the medication that was causing me the problems in the first place. Doctor Dhanani, a middle-aged Indian female registrar, who was dealing with my case, asked me on several occasions if I would be prepared to answer questions about my condition in front of young medical students, which I agreed to do.

On the first occasion I walked into a small cramped stifling hot room with about forty pairs of eyes all looking at me in anticipation, I assume, hoping I would be able to explain to them what caused my dystonia problem, and why it occurred in the first place. Most of their questions I could not understand and /or did not answer in an oppressive environment with the sprightly Dr Dhanani encouraging her students to enquire about my condition although they were young psychiatrists, not neurologists. Most of them just sat there rather moronically, apparently unaware of the importance of my condition.

On one occasion a young blonde female student asked me about 'my relationship with my mother'—suggesting that my problems could relate to her influence. No doubt she was thinking of her mentor, Dr Freud, but she had raised an interesting point. On another occasion one of the students, this time a spotty looking male, asked me whether the condition I had affected my confidence and ability to develop relationships. My reply was that of course it did, and certainly affected me when walking around in public holding my head straight with my left hand while at the same time trying to act normal. Furthermore I told them that the only thing I found helpful, but was only a temporary measure, was a few beers that for some unknown reason relaxed the muscles, thereby straightening the head. It was the alcohol factor that gave me the courage and confidence to go out to pubs, cafés and other public places whereby I could at least be in the physical company of other people if not actually talking to them. The third medical questioner asked me, 'Were you a happy child and did you get on with your parents?' 'Happiness is a rather subjective term,' I responded in a firm manner, 'If I had been in your position to go to medical school, then my life might well have been different; but I had to work physically hard, delivering coal. I was one of thirteen children and my parents were quite poor. I hope that satisfies your question?'

After nearly every treatment session was completed, and I

had recovered sufficiently from the powerful valium injections that would knock me out for several hours, I would leave St Charles Hospital and make my way for a beer near Waterloo Station. I would arrive in the Cut, real name Lower Marsh, groggy, about 15 minutes later absolutely dying of thirst from the after-effects of medication that no one really knew if it was doing me any good. The Market Gardener pub became a refuge for me, not only after my outpatient appointments, but also during the years that I was wandering around London.

I got to know the friendly manager, Ted Howard, over the years quite well whose background was a rather colourful one as he explained to me one day. He was from the East End of gypsy extraction, had served six years in prison for armed robbery, and afterwards went straight so he could marry his childhood sweetheart Mary, 20 years ago. After years of self-employed building work he managed to get a job with Whitbread Beers and eventually became a manager. Since being manager at the Market Gardener he had painted the old Regency-built pub inside and outside, and had cleaned up the once derelict back garden so it could be used by customers instead of drug users. The pub was relaxing, comfortable and was used by a lot of the street market workers who I found to be a loud, funny and an energetic bunch of lads. 'So how you going Bow, just come back from the laughing house?' asked Ted smiling at me, as I walked through the stained glassed door into the bar. Ted was referring to my weekly injections at St Charles, something I had told him about when I first started using the pub. 'I am all right, Ted, a bit groggy and dying for a pint of cold lager to bring me round to sanity.' He pulled me a pint of very cold Fosters which I drank within five minutes in just three gulps. 'Another pint my son?' Ted asked, laughing all the way to the pump and back again. 'Cheers Ted,' I said breathlessly as I drank half the pint of Fosters feeling back to normality.

One of the regular customers I liked a lot was a friendly bloke by the name of Snowy Phillips, who had lived locally for many years having at one stage been a drinking partner of the late Television pundit Monty Modlin. Snowy was over eighty years old—he wouldn't tell me his exact age and I don't suppose he knew it anyway. He had worked in the docks for most of his life. When his wife died young he went travelling around the world so that he could develop his interest in photography. ''Ere 'are boy, a decent piece of meat for yer!' He used to give me pieces of meat free of charge from time to time. That was how things continued for me throughout the day nearly every time I used the Market Gardener pub.

Quickly gulping down my beer, I would usually stumble out of the Market Gardener pub to make my way to Waterloo Station to catch the last 11.44 p.m. train to Epsom. By the time the train arrived at Runton it would be well after midnight and with a further 20 minute walk ahead of me to my parents' house it was nearly always 1 a.m. before I arrived home. By this time I would think to myself that I was lost to the world with no one knowing or even caring where I had been or what I had been doing with myself. It was on one of those early morning arrivals, after another foray in London, that, on reaching home, I went to my bedroom—the one that I had been electrocuted in—and phoned the police because I felt so depressed, isolated and alienated from all mainstream life.

When the police arrived all they could do was to drive me to Horton Hospital, a large Victorian psychiatric hospital, and drop me outside the main gate suggesting I contact their emergency night staff. As I was so confused I just sat down outside the porter's lodge and cried for at least a half hour until the kindly porter came outside to offer me a hot cup of tea and a cigarette which gave me the desire to get to my feet. After thanking the porter, I decided not to contact the hospital but walk back home down the mile-long alley, parallel with St Ebbas Hospital for the mentally subnormal, that connects Epsom to Runton.

Regarding the effects of alcohol, I subsequently was to read, listen and talk to other people who had dystonia about their experiences of drinking alcohol and how it had affected their relationships, employment, friendships and so on. Many people that had dystonia found that alcohol definitely improved their quality of life by giving them the confidence to meet others in different circumstances whereas before they tended to stay at home as a relative recluse, self-conscious of their condition. Of course it is important to remember that alcohol is not a panacea for all dystonia problems, it's only a temporary measure to help the individual to come to terms about isolation and encourage those first steps to meet one or two social contacts. Anecdotally, a neurologist had informed me that excessive alcohol consumption had led to quite a few people with movement disorder becoming dependent on it, although he did find it interesting why dystonia should be alcohol sensitive.

Due to the good fortune of finding employment with Wells Enterprises I was able to save some money, the largest amount in my life so far, which would give me the opportunity to travel even to different countries. All the employment provided by Wells was contract work consisting, for example, of a few days, three/four weeks, or a contract for six months or even longer. I did have several contracts with them, the longest being for one year when I worked for a wholesale company as a fitter in Walton on Thames. Working on a contract basis was ideal for me because I did not have to go through the formal procedures of sending in an application form or attend interviews sitting in front of at least two people answering questions which I found stressful. The only downside of contract work was that some employers would give you very short notice, sometimes the same day, that you were no longer required. Nonetheless I managed to save enough money to be able to fly to Jamaica—the land of one of my former early heroes, Bob Marley—for a two weeks holiday. Ever since the early 1960s I had enjoyed listening to Scar and Reggae music on radio, records and television performed by those young Jamaican men who went on to propagate in performances their powerful message all round the world including London. It was in London that I first saw a number of young live reggae music performed in small venues in Brixton, Deptford, Victoria Park and Alexander Park full of people from various backgrounds smoking cannabis.

I remember with excited anticipation waiting for my BOAC flight that took off two hours late, full with mainly Jamaican people who were going on their annual holidays back home. I had originally been scheduled to fly from Heathrow to Montego Bay but had turned up without a valid visa so a flight was re-arranged next day for me to fly to Kingston instead. Once again I was on my own and even though I was travelling thousands of miles to another country it never crossed my mind that I should seek out other people for support or that I even felt insecure. When the plane landed at Kingston Airport we walked across the runway and into the lounge when the heat really hit me. I was sweltering as I had not experienced humid heat like that before. I remember discussing the oppressive heat with an elderly black male, who had flown on the same plane as me, and he explained how the heat combined with drugs and alcohol was the cause of so much gang violence in Jamaica.

Going through the customs I was stopped by an official looking guy who remarked to me, 'Hi brother, fancy any ganja?' 'No thanks,' was my short reply, not knowing that he could have been a police officer who was trying to apprehend drug smugglers. Besides being young and white, I stood out like a sore thumb. Outside the airport I had to negotiate the price with a young local cab driver to drive me about forty miles to my original destination, Montego Bay. Being ultra-mindful that only a few months previously a Jamaica barber had been charged with the murder of a British person, I was somewhat apprehensive when I got into Erroll's blue Ford cab. We drove through miles of beautiful countryside full of lush green vegetation, many different coloured flowering shrubs and fruit growing wild along the road ripe for people to eat. On the journey, Erroll drove me through many small villages where locals, wearing colourful clothes, sat around talking, smoking, drinking with apparently no problems to worry about. Most of the time I thought we were miles from anywhere, especially when we drove down a dirt track to stop at a bar for a bottle of Jamaican Red Stripe beer. The bar, or rather makeshift shack, was full of local chaps drinking the strong Appleton's rum chased down with cold beer. Most of them were or had been smoking cannabis which made their eyes large and bloodshot. I ordered two beers for Erroll and me, quickly followed by two more as we sat in a sauna-like temperature and I could feel liquid oozing from every pore in my body. I declined Erroll's invitation to have a smoke but accepted his offer of another cold beer at the same time thinking I could go missing here and no one would ever find me amongst the thick undergrowth of trees, water and wild animals. I was somewhat relieved when we arrived at my Hotel late afternoon in Montego Bay just in time to shake hands with a group of loud well-dressed drunken Americans who were sitting at the bar drinking scotch on the rocks. 'Hi there man, you all the way from England?' one rather fat black female asked me politely. 'Yes, that's right. I flew in today from Heathrow,' I replied, trying to get down as much beer as possible to calm my anxiety due to dystonia and to prevent dehydration. 'You'll luv it here my man,' she said, her broad attractive smile looking straight at me, 'Plenty of sex, sand and good healthy food 'cos I've been here many times and never been let down once!' It transpired that her group of about eight women were staying at the Hotel for two weeks; they all hailed from Florida which is only a two hours' flight to Jamaica.

While I was there I met two American men, Bud and Eddie, whom I was to travel with around the Island visiting many tourist attractions, eating at some very good cosmopolitan fish restaurants among the many available. Both Bud and Eddie socialised and earned a living working for a newspaper buying and selling real estate advertisements in New York. Eddie's paternal grandparents, who were poor farmers, had emigrated from Italy around 1920 to find a better way of life in the USA. Bud's family hailed from the West Coast of Ireland, his maternal grandparents having immigrated to New York, via Canada, sometime during the Irish uprising when his uncle was shot by a State Soldier. They were both good blokes with a great sense of humour and I appreciated them sending photographs to me in London taken while we were all gallivanting around Jamaica together.

Hotel Sunset was the attractive place where I stayed in Montego Bay with its private beach bar surrounded by sea, sand and sex, and was exciting, although I was unsuccessful obtaining the latter. The nearest that I came to sex was when the hotel manager George, whose parents were a mixture of English and Arab, quite wrongly assumed that as I was on my own I was there for one thing, sex! During my first night in the bar George encouraged me to stay for a late beer. Around midnight we both went to the toilet when, standing at the urinal, he turned round to me flashing an erect cock, saying in his broken Jamaican accent, 'How about that, would you like to suck it?' Wherever I went it appeared to me that the world was full of gay or bisexual men!

For the first few days he pranced round me as though I was a little boy or rather his little boy offering me swimming trunks to wear which he had to measure me for to see if they fitted. He also had drinks sent to my room on a tray which no doubt had all the hotel tongues wagging. Eventually I had to explain to the good George that as kind as he was I was not interested in having an affair with him. Bless him, out of desperation, he tried one more time to steal my heart by sending flowers to my room signed by an admirer. Given the opportunity I would have dropped the flowers plus the heavy pot onto his balding head.

Ann and Kay were another two Americans also residing at the Hotel Sunset who visited Jamaica and the surrounding Islands for their weekly holidays at least three times most years, due to the mainly cheap quick flights. I corresponded with Ann and Kay for about a year; they also invited me to stay with them in Florida but I never got round to buying a ticket. Also I got the impression that a good number of young American girls (which certainly did not include Ann or Kay), as well as European girls, went to Jamaica for the array of virile men who no doubt could provide the sex! Our hotel provided the usual tourist gimmick games such as crab and bird racing where many affluent Americans betted on the outcome, but the best attraction for me was the local reggae and steel bands that performed most days in the scorching dry sun. Our private beach was cleaned every day by a young local Jamaican who had worked for the wealthy Arab-owned hotel for at least five years. Mack, who was thirty years of age, was a tall, slim gangly person who loved all kinds of music along with his passion in life for soccer. On several occasions he would try to buy my trainers—I had brought two pairs with me on holiday—by first offering cannabis, then including two bottles of pure coconut milk, ideal, he said, 'for getting lovely suntan man for white body.' After a few days of bartering with each other, I eventually accepted his offer for an increased amount of cannabis and locally made coconut sun cream. Determined to get myself a beautifully tanned body, I sat out at the front of the hotel, then on the private beach and as my white scrawny body continued to brown, I would sit on the public beach viewing all the sun-drenched gorgeous young black women wearing their white skimpy bikinis with micro thongs. One such woman, passing me as I stood against a beach bar drinking a cold beer, looked at me and, pointing at her head, said to me, 'Hey man, straighten up your head!' I was used to that kind of abysmal attitude back in Britain, where some people would stare at me as though I originated from another planet. During those early years, when my dystonia was in constant spasm with my head leaning to one side, I must have looked to many as a forlorn person with little hope of living a normal life. I make no apologies for stating once again that dystonia is a debilitating neurological condition that affects more than 80,000 people in Britain.

Back in London one of the most reassuring places for solitude that I have ever experienced is the walk of six miles from the quiet surroundings of Wimbledon Common to Richmond Park with its large herds of fallow deer roaming free. It would restore my confidence when I found the world became too much for me, which would happen many times. Perhaps I spent too much time on my own when I should have been in the company of others. Dystonia was an unremitting, painful burden for me with muscle spasms that twisted, pulled and aggravated my neck and surrounding muscles one way and then the other 24 hours a day. The medication, valium, that I had originally been prescribed for dystonia did not alleviate the physical spasms anymore, and although it had side effects, I blindly assumed that the doctors knew best for their patients. To have places of refuge, similar to Wimbledon Common, was for me wonderful where I could sit in the wood under one of the many beech trees to read, write or just be myself away from the psychosocial conformity of talking to others.

In time walking became a very enjoyable activity and therapy where I could walk many miles into the countryside free from the intrusion of buildings, cars and pollution. Guide books informed me that I could walk 130 miles on the North Downs Way from Farnham to Dover in daily sections or walk all of it in one attempt stopping at B&B's, hotels or youth hostels overnight. Walking is both physically and mentally healthy for a person; it can also be very useful, for the individual to become more aware of their surroundings. For me personally walking offers the exciting prospect to study the flora and fauna that is abundant in various countryside habitats, where as an everyday occurrence you will be able to observe a nibbling grey rabbit or a foraging red fox.

Habitats anywhere deep in the countryside afford me the opportunity to study all alone, knowing that radios blasting out popular music, roaming gangs of youths or motorbikes will probably not disrupt my enjoyment. Above all else, long distance walks in the countryside offer us continuity with our forebears who have trod these remote ways for millennia. They would have been taking animals to be sold at market, pedlars who tried to sell their cheap wares to local people and spiritual wayfarers aiming for Canterbury Cathedral. With the never-ending encroachment of human detritus, called advancement by those in power, I know that for the rest of my life, given the opportunity, I shall retreat into those places that afford human space surrounded by peace, silence and solitude. Of course, we are social animals but as existential beings it is irresponsible to depend on others for joy, for what is in essence a conditioned superficial joy, but once seen through it becomes joyless.

Roehampton Hospital wrote to me stating that there was a place available for me in one of their beds under the care of Doctor Dally of Westminster Hospital fame! When I arrived at the hospital one rainy Monday morning I made my way to the ward, called P1. I was not surprised to find that the ward was really called Psychiatric 1. In the ward each patient had their own bed space sectioned off with curtains, carpets to give it the feel of a homely, some would say institutional, space, where the individual could be on their own at times of uncertainty or for more personal reasons such as masturbation or suicide. Due to institutional dogma every patient had to keep their pyjamas on for seven days, then allowing for good behaviour, their civilian clothes would be returned. It is hard to believe that in the enlightened 1970s medical or nursing staff still demonstrated their punitive mentality by confining mature intelligent people to a ward for seven days by stripping them of all dignity. The Wards called P1and P2 were the only psychiatric beds in an otherwise large General Hospital. According to the charge nurse, these wards admitted those patients who had mild to moderate neurotic problems, not dangerous or serious illnesses like those found at the Maudsley or Ashworth Hospitals. But in reality most of the patients that I exchanged personal information with about their admittance to the ward had social problems and not some psychopathology. There has been a concern for years of the growing number of people who are being medicalised for social and not medical reasons

On one occasion two mature patients, man and woman, had been 'caught' having sex on the floor of the ward kitchen which they had locked for the purpose. When the staff eventually opened the door, they were both told to change back into their pyjamas as a punishment and were confined to the ward for seven days instead of encouraging them to openly enjoy each other's company in a more discreet environment. Surely by being honest with people it can then become an integral part of their therapy. Both of those two people had most of the time experienced a somewhat hard upbringing on a large London Council Estate which was devoid of physical and emotional human enjoyment.

On another occasion a new young attractive female patient and I had made love standing up, crudely known as knee trembling, in a small cleaning room halfway down the long corridor some distance from our ward. When we returned to the ward she was coerced by the nursing staff into explaining where she had previously been with me. Later on that day the Nursing Sister came up to me and brazenly asked, 'Had any new conquests recently?' Once again a punitive comment from a senior nurse.

When I met the psychiatric registrar, an Indian male, he explained to me that the treatment I would receive was called bio-feedback therapy using lactic acid—at first I thought he said lysergic acid (LSD)—after which my neck should feel better. The next day the nurse took me to a small room, closed the curtains explaining that the doctor would place an intravenous drip into my right arm which would take about two hours to empty. This treatment went on for five days when the delighted doctor said to me, 'We have now completed the treatment and you will be taken back to the ward. Do you have anything to say?' 'No,' was my instant reply. I thought like asking him if I was going to see Doctor Dally, being afraid that he might ask me about the grunting again! I walked back to the ward where I was handed back my clothes to wear for the duration of my stay at the hospital.

Three days later after finishing my ward evening meal, I was free to walk down to Roehampton Village fifteen minutes away to have a drink in one of the local pubs. After buying a beer I sat down in the corner of the pub out of the way of others when I observed a few seats away the young Portuguese psychiatrist who was one of the staff at wards P1 and P2. Inevitably we got into conversation about psychiatry and I asked him about the bio-feedback treatment I had received which had not made the slightest difference to my neck spasms. His reply must be the classic of all time when he said, 'It did not work because you did not want it to work.' Dangerous people, those shrinks!

Later I got talking to another patient on the female side of the ward, called Georgina Still who lived nearby. Apparently she had been admitted with one of those mild neurotic conditions she had found disabling while at the same time teaching, living with her husband and young son.

As she had been in the ward for more than three weeks she was allowed to have a day out to spend time with her family which she told me went very well although she got a bit drunk. Georgina, or Gina, as she preferred to be called, had long red flame-coloured hair, was tall, of medium build with blue eyes and was a very sexy powerful woman who had the confidence to engage intellectually or otherwise with any person she so wished. As she was being discharged from hospital we arranged for me to visit her in her Victorian terraced house in Barnes, not far from the Thames. For good behaviour, how pathetic, I was allowed to have a day out, when I of course duly visited Gina for what I hoped would be an exciting time. As I left the hospital to walk to her house about a mile away, I became rather anxious as I looked at the large detached professionally decorated houses around her area, thinking that I might be out of my league when it came to intellectual conversation. At least Gina knew all about dystonia. There was also another male about my age also on the ward with a similar medical problem as mine. Incidentally, in time Gina also ended up shagging him as well. Gina immediately reassured me that 'you can relax in my house where everything is informal, just enjoy yourself darling'.

The downstairs front and back rooms where full of books by authors that I had never heard of before such as Newton, Cohen, Marx, Davies, Miliband and T.S. Eliot. As I was reading the vast amount of names of the authors stacked on the shelves in her attractive yet cosy front room, Gina called to me to go upstairs to join her in the bedroom. There was a feeling of anticipatory excitement welling up inside me as I reached the top of the winding timber stairs where she was waiting for me with nothing on except her beautiful red hair that was flowing down over her feminine milky coloured skin. At once I pulled her close to my body and put my arms round the back of her waist, kissing her red thick lips; she took my hand and led us into her bedroom smelling of a divine perfume. We made love for what appeared to be ages but was probably no more than ten minutes in an atmosphere of intense emotional and physical sex that I had certainly not experienced before. Love-making with Gina in the last few minutes made me feel so wanted and needed that it has stayed with me for the rest of my life. She has since constantly reminded me of one of Rossetti's beautifully painted women that I would love to meet on a warm evening on the Serpentine for discreet sex. When we went downstairs for a drink, I asked Gina to explain to me some of the various themes and theories behind some of the books on the shelves by authors such as R.D. Laing, David Cooper, Joseph Berke, Herbert Marcuse, Erving Goffman and many, many more.

Due to Gina introducing to me the work of R.D. Laing in particular, I came to understand some of the work about one of Britain's famous psychoanalysts and psychiatrists whose unorthodox practises were sneered at by the establishment. Because Laing found conventional psychiatric practise in the large mental hospitals unacceptable, he opened Kingsley Hall in the East End of London for people to live out their experiences of madness in a positive and supportive environment. There were a number of psychiatrists and therapists who worked with Laing and/or supported the ethos of human transformation that could only have happened, so they thought, outside of institutions. For all his human frailties, Laing had a major impact on those around him, determined to do all he could to ameliorate human suffering. Because of the work of R.D. Laing, and others, I was able to understand, and to a certain degree address, problems that had caused some of my own suffering for so many years of my life, especially the way he articulated the schizoid personality experience in his much read book, *The Divided Self*.

Something that still interested me was horse racing which had become over the years more than a hobby. Due mainly to dystonia, I no longer drove a car but depended on good public transport services to get me around the country, which meant I could drink as much alcohol as I chose without being stopped by the police. My favourite racetracks in those days were Epsom (my local track), Kempton Park and Sandown Park for flat racing, while the steeplechase courses I visited were Fontwell Park, Plumpton and Exeter. At the time there was nothing quite like taking the early morning train from Paddington to Exeter where you could see a large number of punters on board the train reading their sporting life or racing post all trying no doubt to pick the winning horses. Many of those middle-aged blokes I spoke to briefly on trains, at the race tracks or in various bars, appeared to be loners who for one reason or other never really wanted to engage in conversation.

Other than travelling to Exeter races, it also gave me the opportunity to visit Exeter Cathedral, for at the time I had a passion for visiting Cathedrals. This fine Christian Cathedral gave me the time, before racing began, to seek out spiritual sustenance among the many scholars, knights, clergy and many other historical figures who did much to defend Christianity against hostile adversaries. Although I am not a Christian, I am nonetheless attracted to its many fine church buildings around Britain. Especially as a walker I have found sanctuary in many small countryside churches where the doors, despite the increasing theft of valuable artefacts, remain open.

Places like Exeter were ideal for me because no one knew who I was or where I came from, so what was important for me was virtual anonymity where no one could interfere with my fragile identity. If someone were to look at me even quite innocently in a bar, I would become anxious to the extent that I would walk out until the danger had gone, or if that was not possible order a couple of large scotches. My life at the time was preoccupied with being seen and not being seen based on my inner life of observation and fantasy. How very odd that a young man, as I then was, should be in the world craving to meet someone and at the same time doing nearly everything to avoid human contact. Was it caused by madness, an anxious self-consciousness due to the debilitating condition of dystonia, or the side effects of taking valium for several years, or one human being just trying to make sense of his world?

When I wasn't working for Wells Enterprises, or other employment agencies, I would go travelling for two or three weeks at a time mostly on the Isle of Wight or down to the West Country where I knew that both places would have many good enjoyable solitary walks. On the Isle of Wight, walking involved taking a short bus ride from where I was staying to the coast path and along flat paths that can be enjoyed by virtually anyone. One evening after finishing a 15-mile walk on the coastal path, I managed to find a small family run B&B down a track not far from the coast road in Freshwater. I knocked on the door about 8 p.m., and after a few minutes a lady answered and I asked if they had any vacancies; to my delight they had. After being shown to my small single room for the night, the landlady explained the time of the breakfast to me. I then said goodnight and closed my door. The room had a pale green ceiling and walls with modern furniture, which didn't look very appealing to the senses but was practicable. After completing my daily diary of activities, I fell asleep, having had a strenuous day walking on Tennyson Down and the attractive Alum Bay with its coloured sands, which is not far from the former government weapons establishment next to the Needles.

I woke up round about 6 a.m. with a strange notion running through my mind about the landlady wanting to get me out of her house very quickly but being unable to so would phone the police who would come to eject me. I felt so uncertain about my security in this house that I did not go back to sleep, but dressed and waited in my room for breakfast to be served at 8.30 a.m. when I thought all would be well again. Breakfast time came but I refused to leave the security of my locked bedroom, now thinking that the landlady was conspiring with others to get me out of her charming detached house. It was now 10 a.m. and I had not been down for my breakfast when there was a knock on my bedroom door from the landlady, as she wanted to inform me that if I did not come down I would miss breakfast. I remained silent, not knowing what to say or what do in the awful predicament I thought I was in. I was so determined to get out of the house that I slung my rucksack over my back, walked down the stairs, left the

£25 B&B charge on the counter and rushed out into the road and away.

During those past hours in Freshwater I had undergone an odd experience in the B & B, of not being able to distinguish fact from fiction. I was engrossed entirely in my own thoughts and emotions to the point that at some stage, I believed I was the only person alive on the Island capable of sorting out the world's problems. Like most of these experiences it is inexplicable to account for what had caused my strange, odd behaviour. One can imagine, if I had presented myself with those symptoms to a psychiatrist he would no doubt have diagnosed me with 'schizophrenia'.

Not long after my trip to the Isle of Wight I had this impulse to make my first visit to the famous Old Bailey criminal courts, not this time as a defendant on trial but as an interested tourist trying to find out more about the judicial system. Unlike visiting today where security is very tight, many years ago one could just walk to any court to listen to proceedings where barristers ply their trade in a world of adversarial language. On this occasion I was directed, along with others, to the famous or infamous No1 court where most of the high profile cases are heard. On his feet in the well of the court was a senior barrister or QC who was defending an Irish male charged with manslaughter for killing another male outside a public house in North London. The British judicial system is interesting and at the same time archaic with the presiding judge dressed in his red, white and ermine robe looking down at everyone with a solemn piercing look. Directly below him are the QC's, behind them the junior barristers and others behind them going down the hierarchy with the clerks way down the pecking order sitting in some obscure seats near the exit. While I sat in the public gallery listening to the QC's arguing the case for Crown and Defendant, I thought to myself that the whole scene came across like actors expressing themselves on the West End stage.

Just before lunch a middle-age male, who had been sitting not far from me listening to the proceedings, spoke to me in a broad Irish accent saying that the defendant, who was his brother, should not be on trial due to mistaken identity. That statement of mistaken identity immediately conjured up in my mind a vision of Ford Prison where most of the cons had been incarcerated for exactly the same injustice! During the lunch break we both went into a public house opposite the Old Bailey for a beer and sandwich followed by members of the public, young barristers and court security staff. The Irishman I had met in the court introduced himself as Patrick Duffy living in a North Kensington rented flat where he lived with his brother, Danny Duffy, on trial today, and a younger brother. He explained how one night, three months ago, the three brothers were drinking in a public house when another Irishman had started arguing with the youngest brother Aidan Duffy, accusing him of deliberately spilling beer over his shoe. A fight broke out between those males when someone from behind hit the deceased on the back of his head with a bottle, killing him. Patrick Duffy went on to say a member of the public had told police that his brother Danny Duffy was the guilty party. But he said 'it is a fecking frame up by the police so we are hoping that our witnesses will be able to get Danny a not guilty plea'. With that I said goodbye to the Irishman wishing him the best of luck as I left the public house to make my way to Kensington Gardens, though I read subsequently that the defendant had been found not guilty.

After another night on the drink, this time in a road near to Waterloo Station, not for the first time I felt quite desperate but I was unable to pinpoint exactly why. Out of impulse or panic I went to the nearest telephone box, dialled the emergency 999 to ask for an ambulance by giving the operator some sort of confused message. The ambulance arrived with flashing blue lights ten minutes later, where I was sitting on the pavement outside an all-night café in Lower Marsh, known as The Cut, the place I used to visit for a few beers after completing my several hours of so-called treatment at St Charles Hospital. I was taken to Westminster Hospital A&E department where I gave the young doctor a half-truth story about not feeling well and hearing voices brought on, I said incoherently, 'by drinking excessive amounts of alcohol with my medication valium'. The concerned doctor said, 'You will have to be admitted for the night for observations until a doctor can assess your position, probably tomorrow.' I was taken to a men's medical ward, fell asleep until about 7 a.m. when a nurse woke me up with a hot cup of tea.

I felt very embarrassed when some of the patients started asking me questions about why I was in the ward, what was wrong with me and I didn't look unwell, to which I replied that I 'just didn't feel well when out with friends'. At last the doctor came to assess my medical condition knowing, I suspect, that I gave his colleague a spurious story in the A&E department the night before. I tried to explain to him that I had been drinking alcohol combined with valium, that at the end of the night, not for the first time, I had for some reason began to panic which consequently led me to phone for the ambulance. He wrote down a few notes, said he would write to the fictitious doctor that I gave him and handed me a prescription for valium. The danger of mixing valium, and other similar tranquillisers called Benzodiazepines, with alcohol, is well documented and should be avoided. Furthermore if I had known that such concoctions could have led to panic attacks, abnormal behaviour, cognitive impairment and even mental illness, I would not have gone on to repeat further frustrating visits to A&E departments.

On another occasion I had been drinking late one night when again I had this overwhelming impulse to phone 999 requesting an ambulance when I said something confused like, 'I don't feel well and I need help and support right fucking now!' This time I was taken to St George's Hospital A&E department in Tooting where on arrival first a nurse, then a young doctor, started to assess my medical condition asking me what I thought the problem was with me. All I could mumble was something about the detrimental effects of mixing alcohol with valium scenario again. 'Please, please help me,' I remember pleading with the doctor.

The young Indian doctor, who examined me, asked me several questions about my background: 'Are you lonely, depressed, and are you being treated for a mental illness?' On this occasion I was honest with the doctor, unlike at Westminster Hospital, explaining to him that I had been diagnosed with dystonia more than six years ago and had been prescribed valium 30 mg three times a day which I had been taking ever since. Also, for the first time, I gave him my correct name, address and name of my GP. He admitted me into a hospital observation ward until the next day when I would then see a doctor who would look at my problem. The morning came and after I was given breakfast, I washed myself and went along to see a consultant psychiatrist who was sitting in an office the other side of the hospital. He didn't say very much other than it was a 'rather immature thing to drink a lot of alcohol on top of 30 mg of valium and then expect the hospital to sort out your problem'. I must say that I did not disagree with the doctor's statement. 'I am not going to prescribe any medication,' he said, and added, 'Instead I shall write to your GP to request further information from him about your medical condition.'

During this time the hospital had phoned my mother to explain that I had been brought to the hospital the night before in an ambulance, was admitted, had seen a doctor and I was being discharged. About two hours later my mother came into my ward looking rather anxious, expressing her concern for me even though I was in my clothes and chomping at the bit to get out of the hospital. Some of the first words my mother said to me were, 'Don't worry, I won't tell anyone you have been here.' I remember not long after thinking to myself that I am crying out for help, badly in need of the support of others, and that was the only thing she could say to me on the subject. This incident with my mother demonstrated to me how emotionally cold we were as a family; when anything of this nature happened it was never discussed. When strong feelings or emotions came about in the family, they would be denied or suppressed, aggression being the only answer.

That was tragic because I could recognise problems that some of my siblings had when I last saw them many years ago, realising these could relate to unresolved conflicts from their childhood.

By now all my siblings had left school and were trying to make their way in the world. By this stage Martin had been married for over ten years, producing four boys who were all doing well. For most of Martin's working life I think he did mainly semi-skilled jobs such as building work, driving a lorry and for a number of years was a London Transport red bus driver. I did not see very much of either Jennifer or James throughout the years; suffice to say they were both married with children, and both had full-time occupations, which meant, unlike me, had everyday responsibilities to their families. Jennifer worked in the West End for a European Merchant Bank as a full-time secretary where she was put in charge of ten other typists in a busy environment. That doesn't surprise me as she trained hard at college as a shorthand typist so that she could pass the relevant qualifications to work for a West End bank. It is thought within the family, I don't know for sure, that James did well in the construction industry, going from strength to strength particularly during the Thatcher and Major administrations, which probably explains why he has a middle class lifestyle in a small Kent Village.

Regarding David, Bob, Margaret, Sid, Susan, Wayne and Gordon, they had all moved away from the family home, getting married at various times, working and had young children to socialise with. Only George and Lawrence remained at home who both worked for local employers learning a trade with skills that would help both of them later on to earn a good living. I never did spend very much time with any of my siblings with the exception of Martin, who I used to visit for a beer during the few years when he lived in Croydon.

My parents were also both well, active and engaged in the lives of some of their children and grandchildren. My father was still working for the family-owned building company in Esher that I originally got for him in 1967 and he would remain there until he retired at the age of 73 years. He kept on working he told me because he needed the money; he was healthy and would receive a bigger pension when he retired. All my family were doing relatively well considering none of them left school with any qualifications, but some of them did excel in their chosen way of life. It is incredible to think that my parents had their 13 children in twenty-three years from 1936 to 1959. My parents were not Catholics or Protestants, nor were they affiliated to any other ideology that expressed a certain way of family life. One explanation why my parents had so many children could be that as an only child my father was very lonely, which could be the reason why he had so many children himself, or more likely they probably never thought of the consequences of unprotected sex.

But from a very early age, I do have some fond memories of my father being active with his children in the long back garden that backed on to common land next to a small wood. My father built a small pond for us to play in where at times among the thick mud we found huge frogs to play with. We would also hide them in my mother's jacket when she wasn't looking. We had some wonderful times climbing trees, fishing with a net and jar trying to catch pop bellies, red throats and sticklebacks in the local Hogsmill River.

On one occasion I was on my own climbing trees in the woods, when I was about 8 years old; an older man came up to me saying he had found a bird's nest with eggs, and would I be interested to have a look at them? Naturally being inquisitive at that young age I went with him; it was an age of innocence, and as I went to look inside the nest he grabbed my genitals from behind. As I was terrified the only thing I could do was to run off in the direction of my home. To this very day I don't know why I did not go straight home to tell my parents that a male sexual abuser had grabbed my genitals in the woods. Similar to later incidents that happened to me, and my siblings, nothing was ever discussed, so memories of such incidents were repressed. Due to the early training of young children who now have the confidence to explain to their parents or teachers certain behaviour that they feel uncomfortable with, they are taken seriously which builds their confidence and trust in people.

The reality for me now was that I very rarely socialised locally with friends whom I had known for some considerable time such as Peter Upton and Melvin Cross who, I heard through the grapevine, were doing well. My life consisted of socialising with people whom I had not known for very long or not at all, in the kind of places that were frequented by a transient crowd that were here one moment and gone the next. The kind of crowd that you would get drunk with for several hours, lend them your money, then they went from your life as if they had never existed. Two young South African lads in particular I found interesting who came to London, so they told me, as the police were after them in their own country for writing an anti-government anarchist newspaper. They were staying in a run-down seedy B&B in Paddington where the owners at the time didn't give a damn who you were as long as you paid your rent in cash and on time. This meant that the two South Africans could bring back to their room all number of disreputable people, including me. At one visit to their large dirty room I met three other radicals who had fled from South Africa for subversive activity and who were now trying to organise student demonstrations in Britain. I didn't hang around for too long, not because I did not support their radical political views, I certainly did, but after serving a prison sentence I didn't want the police feeling my collar. Besides, I had to find myself a job so that I could pay my rent. In London, Paris and other Western European cities at the time there was an outpouring of intense radical demonstrations against Western policy that was detrimental to people with different ideologies.

Although on my own a great deal, I still kept visiting Steeplechase and Flat horse race meetings at mainly Epsom, Sandown Park and Kempton Park. At one Sandown race meeting that I attended I saw my old friend Peter Upton dressed in a flashy blue pinstriped suit with a snazzy hat and a large pair of binoculars strapped over his shoulders. With a large smile all over his face Peter came up to me. 'Hello Barry,' he said, 'so good to see you once again. What you been doing with yourself?' I replied, 'I am well, Pete, how the hell are you? Blimey, you look very prosperous—have you robbed a bank?' With that Peter laughed and responded with a smile all over his face. 'I'm doing well now working for a bloke who sells precious jewels in Hatton Garden,' he said, adding, 'Got the job by luck when I answered an advert in the *Evening News* some three months ago. The geezer has a right few bob and if I play my cards right, who knows what might happen.' Peter went on to say that he was here at the races with his boss mixing work with pleasure, which meant wining, dining and hopefully extracting money from some of the potential wealthy customers living it up in the private boxes. After a quick beer we parted, exchanging telephone numbers, hoping we could meet up once again at one of the local racecourses. It was good to see Peter as he looked so mature, professional and self-assured, and so different from that young lad of a few years ago who looked, similar to me, so vulnerable.

It was at the same time that I became interested in the Theatre, especially musicals such as *Evita*, *Hair* and *Jesus Christ Superstar*. Andrew Lloyd-Webber the musician and Tim Rice the lyricist were behind many successful musicals that would over the years become internationally renowned for their most brilliant stage work. When I wasn't working I used to sometimes wait in long queues for lunch-time stand-by tickets that sold at knock down prices to see many international actors perform in West End theatres.

When I was working on another Data Employment short term temporary job, this time portering in the West End, I was in the fortunate position to be able to buy two tickets that had become available from a colleague to see the new musical *Evita*. *Evita* was the musical about Eva Peron who rose from a very humble background to become the President of Argentina. I contacted my brother Martin to offer him the opportunity of coming to watch the musical, and he duly jumped at the chance. I had not seen him for some time, due to his being married with young children, living in Sussex and busy working in Worthing as a self-employed builder. It was a memorable evening sitting beside Martin enjoying the opening performance of *Evita* which starred David Essex, Elaine Page and Joss Ackland in front of a sell-out audience.

These were the times when another kind of angry young men were around, called Punks and symbolised by rock bands such as the Sex Pistols led by the singer Sid Vicious. At a Sex Pistols concert you were at least guaranteed noise, drugs, sex and for the lucky few a weekend of sleep in a psychiatric hospital. I too was becoming angrier at myself, my family, at anyone who just happened to be around at the time. Some of that anger, most of that anger, I felt, were the reactions to the side effects of my prescribed medication valium, or as it was called on the packet, diazepam. When I didn't want to take the medication or forgot to take it, I would get the shakes quite badly or experienced involuntary movements and that would exacerbate a dystonic reaction. Other times when I missed taking valium, I would panic especially when other people were in close proximity to me which would cause me to sweat and head for the nearest exit. Things would settle down when I topped the valium up with copious amounts of alcohol to the extent that after 30 minutes or so I would be totally relaxed, or even at times in another world.

It was at this time that I started using pubs mostly in Kingston which also attracted lots of middle-class youngsters from the affluent areas of Richmond and Twickenham. A lot of these Hooray Henry's would get blind drunk on alcohol and take various types of drugs from 'uppers' to 'downers'. Most did not know what they had ingested, and they made their way to Eel Pie Island in Twickenham for more hedonism or the new Kaleidoscope Project for social support. Eel Pie Island had become a most notorious club for the drug taking counter culture since it was first used in the days of the Rolling Stones and Yardbirds. Invariably I spent quite a lot of time there during the 1970's drinking too much alcohol, taking illegal drugs such as cannabis and amphetamines, shagging lots of girls and living a useless life with no direction except oblivion.

I did meet some decent young people around my age who were trying to get away from their parents who had, so they said, unrealistic or unreasonable expectations of them. These young men and women were angry because they didn't want to attend university, get a good job and get married just like their parents had done thirty years earlier. Even at the time, I thought coming from my background, these young people were so fortunate to have so many opportunities at such a young age. On one occasion I left a club in Richmond with one young guy I had met only the night before, Tony, who invited me back to his home in Richmond. His peaceful home was a huge Edwardian detached house occupying several acres of land resembling the love nest of a movie star or business tycoon. Sitting Inside the beautiful house was a most thrilling experience for me to behold, taking into account the quality of my life so far. There were large rooms with several sofas in each, televisions, pictures on every wall, gadgets galore and a full length bar stacked with drinks of every possible description. 'Get the fucking booze out Tone,' I said in a most obnoxious manner, not deserved by a decent chap, as he was.

Tony explained to me candidly how 'I am very privileged and spoilt to live in such opulence that my parents have provided for me'. He went on to say, 'I am an only child but my parents expect so much of me, which I find suffocating.' In an uncomfortably voice he went on, 'I have rebelled by going to dives like Eel Pie Island to escape from the conformity of my background, but I expect I will eventually do what is expected of me.' Along with others, Tony and I continued to meet occasionally in Richmond, Kingston and other places until he finally went to Cambridge University to study medicine. The young white middle-class people that I had met at this time, in the numerous pubs, clubs and cafés had informed me about a way of life that hitherto I had only dreamed about while drinking in some down and out place a million light years from their reality.

Horse racing still had some sort of interest, not to say vague status, for me in a world which gave me the motivation to get out of the house to seek a purpose or challenge elsewhere. On one of my visits to Sandown Park races, while at the bar buying a beer, I got talking to a fellow drinker who, like me, was seeking that obscure fortune as a successful gambler which never materialises. Bill was 36 years of age, short with a balding head, lived in Lewisham, and had been made redundant from his job as a printer after twenty years working for the same employer. We sat down to our beer to try and pick the next winner as Bill had been told by a stable lad friend of a horse he thought would win that day. Bill convinced me that the horse Tapestry at 10-1 would win so I gave him £20 as he walked to put the bet on for both of us with his favourite bookmaker whose name, he said, was Dave King. As I watched the race unfold it became clear that Tapestry was about as fast as a rocking horse, finishing last of the ten runners. As for Bill, he was not seen again that day or any other day, doing a runner with my money; he was, of course, a fraudster who had told me a pack of lies. So much for seeking purpose elsewhere! As they say, there's one born every minute.

On another of my forays into the seedy world of drinking in West End pubs, I met a black chap called Sammy who was about 30 years of age standing in the corner of a rough Edwardian pub called Tiffany just off Regent Street. This pub was well known for prostitutes who would come in for a drink—a latch opener they called it—after they had done the business with a punter, as they so eloquently called the men that kept them in money. Sammy had come to London during the 1960s to find work so that he could send money back to feed his wife and six children in Barbados. Regarding his children, he said to me laughing, 'Too many kids mon, must tie a knot in me prick!'

I bought us two pints of lager, for he was broke, probably on the ponce, but he didn't tap me for a few quid, so that we could keep chatting in the corner of the bar away from prying ears for an hour. 'What do you do for a living, Sammy?' I asked, and ever smiling he replied, 'Me do fuck all mon, I am looking to do some crime.' He looked at me with his black piercing bloodshot eyes, no doubt caused by smoking too much cannabis. When he invited me for a smoke of cannabis outside the pub, Sammy put it to me that he had a shop sussed out in Soho that we could break into during the night to steal thousands of cigarettes.

'Well,' he said, 'are you up for it man?' I shook my head. 'No, sorry, not me Sammy, I've done one dose of prison and that is enough for me,' I replied. We were about to part when he turned round, smiling of course, and said, 'Nice to have met you brudder, here is my phone number just in case you change your mind.'

That same evening at around 11.30, I had just come out of another pub (the name of which I forgot due to intoxication) after being accosted by a prostitute, when out of impulse or panic, I phoned 999 for an ambulance. The ambulance arrived about 12 minutes later with its flashing blue lights lighting up the whole narrow street. A tall Indian male came up to me, as I was sitting on the ground, to ask if I had called them out. 'Come with me Sir to the ambulance, and let's see if we can help with the problem,' he politely suggested. The other worker was also an Indian or Pakistani male who told me to 'kindly come into the ambulance, Barry, and let's see what the problem is right now, so we can help you'. He went on, 'What have you been doing this evening that made you phone for the ambulance?' He smiled reassuringly at me. 'I have been drinking too much and I don't feel well; also, having smoked cannabis earlier on...' After they had a brief discussion they told me I was being taken to St Phillips Hospital in nearby Euston.

At the A&E Department a young female doctor came to question me about the reason why I had phoned the ambulance and what the problem was. I told her the usual misleading information about hearing voices or that I had not taken my medication for it and that I was also taking valium, for dystonia (that part was true) which was causing me various side effects. I went on to say, 'Please let me stay in the hospital overnight as I feel frightened at the prospect of walking the streets of London on my own.' With this the doctor made arrangements for me to be taken up to the male medical ward where I was met by a rather frosty looking weighty matron who insisted that I remove my clothes forthwith and get into bed. After a weak cup of tea I fell asleep in the observation ward until being woken some time later with the words, 'Are you all right Mr Morris?'— a name I apparently gave the doctor last night, by a young nurse holding a steaming cup of much needed tea.

'After breakfast, Mr Morris, you will be seen by the registrar who will assess your medical position,' the nurse said rather kindly. Around 11 a.m. the registrar arrived, a young white male with reddish hair, to escort me to his very colourful looking office two minutes from the ward where he asked what I thought the problem was and could he help. I managed to give him my usual bullshit citing mental health issues, which turned out to be correct many years later, and various problems in my life that I was unable or unwilling to cope with. He discharged me with a prescription for a month's supply of valium made out to one Mr Morris which of course I duly had dispensed. I am eternally grateful and at the same time most apologetic for the way I have in the past misused the ambulance service for my own personal gratification. Furthermore, the ambulances could have been used by people who genuinely needed them and at the same time I was adding more financial expense onto the hospital. In hindsight I have realised that I was crying out for help and support, yet the way I went about it was rather bizarre; but what else could I have done when you consider that even my GP or neurologist had little knowledge or understanding about the causation of valium addiction and origins of dystonia.

Margaret Thatcher, the shopkeeper's daughter, had been voted into office with a new sweeping manifesto to change Britain forever. She would go to war with the miners and beat them, get rid of most of the heavy manufacturing industry and bring the militant unions into line, thereby introducing the new British service industry financed by private investment. Along with all these radical changes, Britain, once the workshop of the world, lost many of its industries which now went abroad. Thatcher's government made it more difficult for unions to go on strike, with a repeal of many trade union laws, which saw the development of a more modern union culture in Britain. Central to her manifesto for the first time in Britain was the right of council tenants, later to include other tenants, to buy their homes, many at knock-down prices whereby they emerged as the new lower middle classes. For the first time many working-class people moved away en masse from their traditional neighbourhoods. I was pleased that several of my siblings benefited from the Thatcher policy of 'right to buy'.

Another emerging cultural/social change that was coming out of the concrete jungle in Britain at the time was the fusion of white and black music. It was also considered that the television soap *Brookside*, among others, epitomised the mixed classes under the Thatcher ideology; however, after all this huge social change accent still defined who you were. Coming from my background, accent was something I had always been self-conscious about, mindful that others spoke well, had good jobs and sexier girlfriends.

As I was by now the only sibling still living at home with my parents, both my two youngest siblings having got married and moved to live with their wives, I encouraged them to have a party for a family reunion. We made arrangements to buy in the alcohol from a local sale and return shop and the catering was carried out by a friend of the family who used to live locally but had since moved to a new restaurant in Kent. Unfortunately we only sent out invitations to those family members we had addresses or phone numbers for but about 15 people arrived for what turned out to be an enjoyable night. I had not seen some of my siblings for some considerable time, including David who informed me that we had not met for at least ten years. Not surprising, as the evening progressed people consumed more alcohol, dancing along with the many records that various members of the family had brought. My mother and father were in good form, dancing about the floor having consumed quite a few drinks between them. Martin, Sid and Gordon were also at the party with their respective wives, but none of them brought along their children, who no doubt would not have been happy among the older family members.

When I later met my mother in the kitchen she said, in her usual intense voice, 'Things are going well son, are you enjoying yourself?' 'Yes,' I said to my mother, 'It makes a change to have a laugh once in a while, doesn't it?' 'It would be good,' she said in a sharp manner, 'if you could straighten out that neck of yours!' I was rather flabbergasted by that comment but realised that she did not understand the nature of dystonia notwithstanding the volumes of information that I had given her, and my siblings, throughout the years. Over the years none of my family members ever asked me why I had severe neck deviation even though it was obvious for all to see. Around 10 p.m. people started to leave the house due to the long distances that some of them had to drive. At 11 p.m. my parents and I were the only three left remaining in the house. 'It was good to see so many of you lot together again,' my mother said with a broad smile on her face.

I could see the sadness in my parents' eyes, realising it must have been an enjoyable evening seeing some of their family again, but now all was quiet. As I looked around me nothing had appeared to have changed in the house since all those years ago when I was young. One small change, however, was instead of having open fires they now had installed gas fires in the two downstairs rooms. My siblings used to take daily turns cleaning out the grate full of ash and replacing it with fresh paper and wood ready for the evening fire, when we all congregated into one small room to keep warm.

My mind went back to when we were children running up and down the stairs shouting and screaming at each other and my mother trying to keep control of the situation. I remember the fights between siblings, which frequently ended with my mother slapping all concerned around the head. Sadly I could also recall how my mother used to hit us frequently, sometimes for no obvious reason. I recalled the mayhem she caused when on regular occasions she used to shout, swear and bang the front room door at the neighbour, Mrs Hillbrook. During those most desperate times, it was surprising that my father never tried to stop my mother from the insane behaviour that sometimes preoccupied her. Although little was known about the subject at the time, it is probable that my mother suffered from post-natal depression which could have explained her unpredictable and aggressive behaviour.

Many evenings I would try to find a spare corner place in the front room, to sit down to read my cherished soccer programmes and Ian Allan train locomotive books. Years later my younger siblings, when I was at school or work, would tear them up or throw them out of the bedroom window. Also, as I sat there, I wondered if my parents had fulfilled some of those dreams and aspirations they first had when arriving in Runton as young people all those years ago. Trying to feed and clothe 13 children throughout the years must have frustrated and overwhelmed my mother most of the time for what must have been for her an unhappy life. It is remarkable that one woman gave life and put air into the lungs of all those children. I do remember her saying on more than one occasion, 'I did my best to feed and clothe you all.'

Although my father was still working full-time for the building company he started with in 1967, he suggested that we could also advertise for landscape gardening work, which if successful, I could use his tools and he would drive me to the various jobs. My father and I agreed to make a go of it, so we got many trade cards printed locally and placed them in many different shops, cafés and gardening centres. After a month or two, work such as weekly lawn cutting or garden maintenance started to provide me with an income for the first time in at least two years. Things were also working out well in my working relationship with my father, who was a good, decent man, as he would help me in the mornings to load the tools required for the day then drop me off at the required location, collecting me later on after he had finished his own work. I was always open and fair in the financial dealings with my father, and I always gave him half of what I had earned at each gardening job. Although my father did make an effort to co-operate with those he had dealings with, he wasn't a particularly assertive, confident or demonstrative person, which is one of the possible reasons why my mother became a more dominant personality within the household.

One potential customer who lived in the affluent area of Claygate, Surrey, phoned to request a price for various gardening work they needed done in their garden. When we arrived I was amazed at the size of the house and the garden, flabbergasted that people could afford to live in such luxurious surroundings. After negotiating a price with the male owner I proceeded the next day to start work on reducing the height of the long100-feet hedge, laying bricks round the trees and digging the borders and beds. On the second day the attractive middle-aged wife of the owner came out to give me a cold beer accompanied by two succulent sandwiches filled with salmon. As I sat on her patio eating she came back out to ask if I required another beer. When she returned with it she asked me rather provocatively if I would be interested in being her model. She went on to explain that she was an artist, a figure painter, with a private studio in Esher besides running classes twice weekly for art students in Kingston. As she had been watching me laying bricks round numerous trees in her garden she said to me openly, 'I can tell by the way you are using the bricks that you are a creative person and would do well as a live model in front of art students.' I thought about it for a minute, then somewhat confused, said, 'I am interested, but how would I get to these places and how much would I be paid?' She said to me in a rather reassuring sort of way, 'Don't worry about the details, I shall sort them all out for you.' With that in mind I explained to her that I first wanted to finish landscaping her garden; then we agreed that I would phone her to arrange further details.

Suffice to say that I did not phone her, but as usual, with the garden contract completed, I convinced myself that I did not want to see her again. This particular proposition could have been the ideal opportunity I had been waiting for so long and yet I let it slip from my grasp without even giving it a chance. Here was the potential to develop new skills, get to know new people, earn a living and move on with my life, but I did the same as before which meant being stuck in the same predicament. Once again I was overwhelmed by frustration, not knowing how to change my life for the better, thinking suicide the only way out.

Realising that I was now 36 years of age with very little prospects of sorting out my life to any satisfying degree, I decided to take up the offer my older brother Bob gave me to play football in his team. It wouldn't immediately bear fruit such as getting a job from one of the players or their friends, but at least it would place me in a position where I could get to know some people. Bob introduced me to the players three nights before my first match, although I already knew some of them socially from the years gone by. Just before the end of the first match I signalled to my brother that I had hurt my hamstring and could not continue playing. My brother was fine about me coming off, having played a good game considering that I had not played in a competitive football match for several years. The next time Bob phoned me to play in another match I told him I did not want to play anymore, making an excuse that I had found a job in Putney. Bob phoned me several days later to ask, 'What is the problem, Barry, you played well last time, considering you were not fit?' For the first time I explained to him 'that for some reason, Bob, I lack the motivation to do things'. With that my brother told me there was always a game available if I was around.

Being directly around other people at my brother's football club, did at least give me the impetus to buy a ticket to see Neil Sedaka in concert at Wembley Arena. Since the age of 15 years, I had been a great lover of Sedaka's songs such as 'Oh Carol', 'Breaking Up Is Hard To Do' and 'Calendar Girl'. He was born in Brooklyn to a father of Turkish origin who had made a living as a taxi driver and encouraged his son to train to be a classical pianist at the world famous Julliard School in New York. He had turned to pop singing/writing along with his school friend, Howard Greenfield, to earn a living. Most of his earlier songs were dedicated to his former girlfriend Carol King who herself went on to develop a successful singing/composing career. I went on to see Neil Sedaka in concert four more times in London, the last two in the 1990s when he was accompanied by his talented daughter Dara. The one big thing that attracted me to Sedaka, and I realised this at a young age, was the sincere way he sang live on stage determined to reach his appreciative audience.

Another singer, altogether different to Sedaka, who I

enjoyed seeing live was the American protest/blues/soul singer Bob Dylan. A disciple of the late blues singer Woody Guthrie, Dylan came to prominence singing about the abuse of various peoples by governmental power around the world. He reminded them of their responsibility to humanity via some of his songs, such as 'Times They are a Changing', 'Hey Mr Tamborine Man', 'Love Minus Zero, No Limit', and 'Maggie's Farm'. Although I went to at least five concerts of his the best was without doubt when he performed in an open-air concert at the disused Blackbush Airport with Eric Clapton and Joan Armatrading in the early 1980s. Dylan was the kind of singer that aroused the deepest feelings in you, to stand up and do something about the predicament you find yourself in, something very pertinent to my own experience.

Whether it was the powerful message in Dylan's singing I don't know, but I decided to spend some time in the Mediterranean country of the Holder of the George Cross, Malta. I flew Air Malta from Gatwick to Malta Airport, then went by bus to Bugiba, the small town where I would stay for ten days. The hotel I was booked into was designed by the former Prime Minister of Malta, Don Mintoff, who years ago when in charge had expelled many British people from his country for abusing the tax and residency laws. Some commentators had said that it was like giving Malta back to the Maltese. I enjoyed travelling around the Island on the former London Bedford single decker petrol buses that had been bought by local people to earn a living.

The waters around the coastline were a beautiful translucent blue and ideal for swimming, skiing and sunbathing. I also took ferries to Gozo and Comino, two small Islands off the mainland, which are havens for sun-loving tourists. While I was there I met three English lads from Yorkshire on holiday for two weeks, who were having a whale of a time, sampling all the local wines, which were very cheap indeed and guaranteed to give one a severe headache. No doubt they sampled the young women also. Due to the water shortage most hotels, including mine, turned the water off for several hours during the day causing an almighty smell that drifted from place to place almost gassing me unconscious. However, I must say my all-white decorated room was very clean with matching curtains, and had a multi-coloured terrazzo floor. The food although not cordon bleu was also very well cooked. Most of the hotels appeared to be used by British people taking a holiday away from the cold chilly weather of the homeland. On the second to last day of my holiday, along with twenty other tourists, I went on an organised motor tour of Malta when I got chatting to the rather attractive blonde woman sitting next to me. She was on holiday with her mother, a rather sad looking woman, to escape the intensity of her dental work back in Poole, but she did explain how she enjoyed living in rural Dorset notwithstanding the encroachment of a housing development. After a glass of wine together in one of the local tavernas, we exchanged phone numbers and went our separate ways. Back in England I dutifully phoned this lady, whose name was Gwen, and made arrangements to visit her home by train the following Saturday arriving early afternoon to be greeted by her and her silver-haired scowling mother who was no more than five feet tall. It was not surprising that her mother, who owned the three-bedroomed thatched detached house, with attractive front and rear garden, kept eyeing me up every five minutes to see whether I was making sexual advances to her daughter—no doubt, in her mind, with a view to marrying her whereby I could then rob the old woman of her house. That was what it felt like at the time. Suffice to say that after eating a snack with Gwen I left the house around 5 p.m., saying my goodbyes to both of them, vowing never to return to that depressing family environment. Once again it demonstrates for me the fundamental difference between meeting a person (especially a woman) socially, to meeting them in her home, where you can understand how some of them have been detrimentally conditioned by their families.

After my foray into Dorset I came to the conclusion, rightly or wrongly, that I needed the fetid air of the West End once again. On this occasion I hunted down some of the pubs that I had not used for some considerable time, including those in one of my favourite haunts, Soho. There you could be anyone you chose to impersonate in a world of near make believe, which fitted in well alongside all the different peoples from around the world, briefly passing through its narrow dirty streets. As I passed a sex shop there were two middle-aged prostitutes standing in the door touting for work, who shouted in their Cockney accents, 'Want some fun darling?' One woman had long blonde bleached hair with eyes painted like a panda while the other resembled a former Dickensian boxing booth character with a face ready for instant action. I eventually recognised that the place where the women were was the actual shop that my friend Howard and I had entered some twenty odd years previously to watch rather ageing women taking their clothes off to simulate sex with a cigarette to a tune by Elvis Presley that I have now forgotten. What heady days!

Around the corner from this dive was a rather attractive Georgian pub called The Three Grapes, another haunt of mainly prostitutes, pimps, ponces and pretenders, a place where nearly all of life within those few square feet was represented. As I entered my attention was drawn to a young attractive black woman who was singing soul music at one end of the pub next to the exit, which was covered in flyers of all descriptions, but mainly selling sex. With a beer in my hand, I sat down next to a black guy of about 40 years dressed in a black velvet jacket, white trousers and black shoes. 'Good evening brother, how are you?' the well-dressed handsome looking man asked me in a deep Jamaican accent. I returned the courtesy: 'I'm all right friend, and how is yourself?' 'Good, good, brother,' was his reply. It transpired that the young black woman singing was his sister who apparently sang around different pubs and clubs in London. Jack, that was his name, and his sister Marcia both came to London together about ten years previously from Jamaica to try their luck in the big city, having lived on little money in a rather small poverty stricken village in their own country. Having previously shared a rather small cramped flat with five other people, Jack and his sister now lived together in a two-bedroomed council flat in Brixton. Neither of them could find any regular work, both of them having done unskilled temporary work in the catering trade, so they decided that they would concentrate on developing Marcia's musical career instead. Marcia set up a limited company with a solicitor, her brother became her agent and she set about registering with a music school in Westminster where she took advanced tuition with one Peter Fenwick who specialised in soul/blues vocals. After two years of tuition she had done very well, according to Jack, having performed at numerous pubs, clubs and cafés around London at the same time earning a living for herself. During the next stage of her work she was hoping to record several songs with a small recording company in Soho where her music would have the potential of reaching a much bigger audience. I am constantly reminded of the way people struggle to survive in the human jungle. After a beer with both of them we exchanged phone numbers, one of many that I had collected over the long years of accidentally meeting people, wished each other well and I decided to move on to another pub around the corner in Greek Street.

Around 9 p.m. I walked into the Golden Arms pub that was packed with a mix of art students with long hair, local prostitutes, theatre goers and a small group of men from the local football team. The pub was owned by the former British boxing heavyweight champion, Danny Osborne, who had been the governor for about 15 years, with a well-known reputation as a bruiser around Soho for throwing out drunks from his pub. After buying a beer I sat down next to the bar when, in time, I was accosted by an attractive Indian female with long black hair who explained to me that she was on the game. No surprise there, I thought. She asked me whether I would be interested in going back to her place around the corner. 'No thank you sweetheart,' I told her most emphatically, but she persisted in trying to get me to be her next punter. 'Darling,' she said, smiling at me with thick red painted lips, reminiscent of Coco the Clown, 'I don't charge very much and I do a blow job for just a tenner.' She went on and on about her mother being sick with cancer and that she needed money to send her to a private doctor in Harley Street. 'I will only charge you a tenner darling for full sex, and I will wear my sexy black undies just for you.'

After this exchange, I finished my beer, went to the toilet and walked out of the pub into another, the Smiling Monk, 50 yards down the same road. The Monk was a popular pub for local Soho residents, having live international jazz bands perform there at least four times a week in front of appreciative well-informed customers. Since his arrival some five years ago, George Selby, the owner of the Smiling Monk, had skilfully and sympathetically decorated the Georgian pub with an extensive international menu cooked by Roland, a well-known, so I was informed, Danish chef. The evening I was there it was full of locals congregating into small groups, discussing the proposed plans to sell Ronnie Scott's jazz club (of all places) and turn it into a large Chinese restaurant seating 400 people. The last I heard of the proposals was that the local people had sent a petition to the council opposing such a development.

Dave was a local betting shop manager at Corals in Dean Place where he had worked for at least 20 years, first joining as a board man. He was born in Stepney of mixed black and white parentage, his father originating from Trinidad. I liked Dave, as did most of the locals and customers, from the first time I had first met him in this pub which must have been at least ten years ago. At that time I remember that I had been drinking far too much alcohol and I was sitting on my own, although that was not unusual, when Dave came up to me and asked if I was all right. He bought me a coffee, reassuring me that he would be there for me if I needed any support. From that stage forward, whenever I was in the Monk pub, I would seek Dave out for a beer, chat and have the occasional Chinese meal together in nearby Hong's restaurant.

I left the Monk pub to walk round the corner into Greek Place and into another pub I had used for some years called The Wayfarer which was owned by Tommy Webb, an East Ender from Bethnal Green. This being another Georgian Pub, Tommy had decorated the outside with lots of flower baskets which looked very attractive and on the inside he had decorated the walls with a horse racing theme depicting photographs of various Derby winners. As it was now getting towards closing time I ordered two pints of bitter, sat down on a chair next to an old chap who was reading the *Sporting Life* and thought about what I could do later on in the impersonal city called London.

By the time I had finished drinking my last pint, I realised that I was going to phone 999 and ask for an ambulance to take me to an A&E somewhere in Central London. I left the Wayfarer pub nearly drunk, but feeling determined more than ever to reach the phone box, which was outside a charity shop across the road. In the phone box I dropped the receiver twice but on the third occasion I managed to phone emergency to ask for an ambulance which duly arrived ten minutes later to drive me to the familiar site of an A&E department. Inside the department I gave the usual fictitious story about why I had phoned 999 to a young white male doctor who seemed most concerned about my medical condition. After about 20 minutes he decided to admit me into the hospital for the night, and in the morning I would be able to see a doctor who would help me. I was taken up in the lift to a medical ward for older men where I was greeted by a young white nurse with a kind smile. By this time I had sobered up sufficiently to be aware of my surroundings to respond to the nurse's questions about my name, age and address, giving fictitious information once again. In the morning after having my breakfast an older looking doctor came to the ward to ask me some questions about why I had phoned for the ambulance, and other familiar questions such as: did I have any current illnesses and/or was I taking any prescribed medicines? After 15 minutes he said he would write to my GP about the incident and discharged me onto the wet depressing streets of London with a prescription for valium which I had dispensed in two hours. Later on in a pub near Trafalgar Square, I sold the medication to a young man for £2 so that I could buy some more beer.

After another absurd experience of being discharged from a London Hospital, where nothing was resolved, I decided to go walking in the West Country. The next day I took the train from Runton, where I had been staying with my parents since I last returned two years previously, to Waterloo from where I took a fast train down to Poole. I stayed in a local B&B that night, got up early in the morning to have my breakfast and made my way by bus to the start of the southern section of the 630-mile National Trail of the South West Coast Path (SWCP). Feeling free with the wind blowing in my face, I walked out of Poole around 10 a.m. with my mind set on enjoying myself, determined to walk the eight miles to reach Swanage by the end of the first day.

In Swanage, a sizeable town with lots of accommodation, I found myself a B&B nearby to the SWCP which allowed me time to have a few pints in the local Fisherman's Inn. Inside the pub there were the usual crab pots, fishing nets and sea shells fixed on the white-washed walls. I was among the many tourists who were sitting down eating, drinking or conversing while others milled around the pub reading old newspaper articles of Weymouth's former trading days fixed on the walls. After many similar trips to the West Country, I came to realise that most of the people that own these local businesses have made money elsewhere and originally came from cities. Also, a lot of affluent townies have bought second homes in the West Country, thereby increasing the prices of homes and adding more pressure on local youngsters who have to move into larger towns to find affordable accommodation.

One of the good things about some of the local home produce is the strong local ale that is brewed for local consumption. In the past years there has been a steady increase in the number of small breweries that have opened in the West Country. Ever since I can remember I have been a great fan of strong ale brewed around the country by local people. After several pints of ale I felt relaxed and confident enough to interact with other customers in the Fisherman's Inn. And of course it helps when I've drunk a few pints of alcohol, as it relaxes my sternomastoid neck muscles whereby I become less self-conscious of my head deviation.

Moving on from Swanage, I continued to walk along the SWCP, passing Kimmeridge Bay, Lulworth Cove, Osmington Mills and on to Weymouth sea front, the end of my walk on this occasion. I had walked 40 miles in four days which I thought was a good achievement considering the situation I was in at the time. As I have mentioned before, walking or just sitting gives me a great sense of freedom; whether it is sitting down pondering on the fundamental complexities of this magnificent world, listening to a singing blackbird or observing a shimmering primrose next to a long distance path, it is all so breathtakingly beautiful. I decided to stay in Weymouth for three days more to take in the various surroundings, especially for a walk round the Isle of Portland to view two Tudor Castles, Portland and Sandsfoot.

That evening I found a decent little old pub called Hopes Reach, not far from the statue of George the Third, where I got into conversation with two local men about long distance walking, remembering that the SWCP goes via Weymouth Town and the Isle of Portland. Harry, one of the chaps I engaged conversation with, said, 'It is only right and proper that an Englishman should have the right to walk over the land that he and his forebears have fought and died for.' Harry had been born 80 years ago only a few miles down the road from Weymouth in a small village called Chickerell. After five years of local education he left school to work on the land, first as a labourer for 25 years and thereafter as a cowman until the age of 70 when he retired, having worked for the Grant family who had owned the local farm, Treetops, for several generations.

Wally, who was approaching 78 years, had been born locally in Bincombe some six miles west of Weymouth. After working for ten years as a farming labourer he went to sea in the Merchant Navy where he travelled the world returning for a short while to stay with his parents. But he soon got itchy feet and returned to the life he loved so much until retiring at the age of 60 years. 'Tell you what, Wally,' Harry ruefully remarked to his lifelong friend, 'our generation should have spoken up more against the power of the Grants and Steels, who not only exploited us but also refused to let us walk over their goddamned land to collect the likes of mushrooms and blackberries.' 'Well, you are quite right there, Harry boy, that old bastard Steel did not even allow the local women's guild to walk over his land for the autumn festival,' remarked Wally, drinking his 4th pint in just over two hours. 'Anyway, son,' admitted Wally, 'I am pleased you have a legal right to walk the SWCP, and not only that, in some places you can wander off the path to walk over other land too.' I explained to both of them that I had to go and find myself a B&B for the night as the time was now nearly 10 p.m. After I bought them a pint each, and shaking their hands goodbye, Wally explained that I could find a decent local B&B at Holly Bush House, the home of former farmers Jeremy and Diana Worth.

On the morning of my final day in Weymouth, while I sat in the Worths' warm and comfortable guest house, I decided to walk the five miles north-east to Osmington Mills where Jeremy Worth had recommended a good pint of locally brewed cider that could be bought. Booking out from Holly Bush with my sturdy rucksack on my back, I had a strenuous and enjoyable walk uphill past Overcombe into Osmington Village, arriving about two hours later to find the pub nearly packed. I soon fell into conversation with two young local males who both worked in the travel industry in Lyme Regis for a small local family business called Start Travel. The two men, Peter and Wayne, when they were not working would spend most of their time drinking in this village pub called The Nelson. As they were single with little responsibility except for themselves, they usually had long cider sessions with other men from the area whose sole intention was to drink as much of the strong locally brewed cider as they could. Peter explained the strength of the cider was 7.9 ABV (alcohol by volume, which is very potent indeed) but both of them would not touch a drop, so they informed me, when they were working. After I had consumed four pints, I realised that was enough for me so I decided to say goodbye to my co-drinkers to walk the five miles back to Weymouth where I took the train to London.

We must applaud the wonders of British rail engineering that transformed Britain in the late 19th century and early 20th century from sleepy backwaters to thriving economies. That transformation continued around the world especially in countries such as the Indian sub-continent where today their thriving world economy is largely dependent on its British designed railways.

CHAPTER FIVE

MY FIRST CONTACT WITH BUDDHISM, SEXUAL RELATIONSHIPS AND MY FIRST STEPS TO RECOVERY

Not long after walking on the SWCP, looking a little fitter and tanned, I read there was an art exhibition by a local artist, Brian Connelly, being held in Croydon library. Connelly painted live countryside scenes from around the areas where he lived in the small village of Downe, once the home of Charles Darwin. I enjoyed viewing Connelly's impressive paintings as they were full of a mix of exciting natural environments that spoke of a way of life that is largely forgotten since mechanisation. Now 60 years of age, he had himself worked in the countryside, first as a dairy man, then thatching for several years, later managing a smallholding for twenty years before deciding to take up painting full time. As I made my way to exit the library, I saw a small colourful advert on the main notice board advertising meditation classes every Wednesday evening at the Croydon Buddhist Centre only 100 yards from where I stood.

Having read about meditation before, but not really knowing or understanding what it really meant, here was the opportunity to find out. Having had two pints of beer to help me relax somewhat, I made my way rather anxiously to the Buddhist Centre where a white young male of about 25 years was sitting behind a small table with various flyers in front of him. 'Good evening,' he said smiling at me in a friendly manner. 'Welcome. Have you come for the meditation class?' I felt a little uneasy at this stage. 'Yes I have,' I said nervously. 'My name is Sanghadeva,' he told me with a larger reassuring smile on his youthful looking face. 'What does that name mean?' I asked, somewhat puzzled. The young man himself came across as an intelligent articulate person. Blimey, I thought to myself, bet he comes from university. He explained the meaning behind his Buddhist name which was given to him when he was ordained. He went on to say that as the meditation classes started in ten minutes, would I make my way up the stairs to the shrine room? He gave me two flyers advertising future Centre activities as I departed.

At the first meditation class the teacher talked us through the various stages of a meditation practise called the Mindfulness of Breathing which lasted for about a half hour; then we meditated ourselves for another half hour. The teacher appeared to be so calm and focused, explaining to us that if we wanted to benefit from meditation then it is best practised every day for at least 15 minutes. Later I came to know the mediation teacher as Satyraja who was a kind, friendly and reassuring human being. Not surprising at first, I found it difficult to take in, understand and perform some of the Buddhist practises especially in the shrine room, where for some reason or other I would become rather anxious if it was occupied by a lot of people.

So began, in 1985, my contact with the Friends of the Western Buddhist Order (now the Triratna Buddhist Community) which continues to this day although I must confess that for most of that time, especially from 1992 onwards, my presence had been at best irregular and most of the time non-existent although I have been on retreat a few times in the Norfolk countryside. However, the first day that I met that young order member called Sanghadeva, was the first day of a friendship that continues to develop, I hope, to this very day. After several weeks of regularly attending meditation classes, which I found helped me relax although I found interacting with others there difficult, I booked to attend my first two weeks Buddhist retreat in Battle, Sussex. Led by Nagabodhi, who had been an order member for many years, I found the mixed retreat of men and women interacting with each other strange at first yet it became quickly uncomplicated and interesting. This was especially the case at evening meals which were held in peaceful silence, not something I, or others, had practised before. The private school where the retreat was held was ideal for the purpose, having small comfortable well-decorated dormitories where groups of men and women could sleep in comfort and privacy. Group workshops in the warm orchards I found most enjoyable for the whole two weeks, and each group was conducted in an atmosphere of kindness and friendship. The respect that men and women had for each other was something I had not experienced before, which demonstrated that we can, with effort, overcome our conditioning. The one consensus that was overwhelming was the vegetarian meals that were well cooked, yet nearly everyone was bunged up.

During one of the retreat workshop tea breaks I got talking to an individual, who was by profession a practising psychotherapist in London, about tranquillisers (EG: valium, librium and temazepam, etc.). Over a period of two evenings we discussed how prescribed valium was having an impact on me, considering that at this stage I had been taking it for at least 15 years. I explained to Brian that when I had forgotten to take the medication, I experienced side effects such as increased anxiety, panic attacks, tinnitus, cognitive recall problems and social phobia. Long-term valium use could also be exacerbating dystonia whereby the muscle spasms and contractions are increased in severity. Furthermore, another point that we overwhelmingly agreed on was the detrimental effects that valium can have when mixed with alcohol. The therapist explained that he currently had four people in therapy who were all trying to address their tranquilliser side effects or withdrawal addiction problems. He gave me his contact details so that at some stage, if I so desired, I could make arrangements to visit him which I never did.

After what I considered to be a successful retreat, although a subjective analysis, I continued to attend weekly meditation classes at the Croydon Buddhist Centre where things were going quite well considering my somewhat precarious position of trying to manage head deviation, side effects of valium and at the same time have meaningful interaction with others. I was back living at home with my parents; all my siblings had moved out for one reason or another. I felt increasingly at the age of 37 years that I was a failure, considering that nearly all of my siblings were doing well. My parents did their best to support me with everyday practicalities such as cooked meals, clean clothes and a comfortable bed, but they had a limited understanding of the wider world. As the medical profession had caused most of my medical problems, which had developed into social isolation, yet were unable to offer any long-term beneficial treatment or support, it was totally unrealistic to expect my parents to resolve things for me. Unfortunately, similar to other people, including my siblings, my parents placed the emphasis for all my problems on being burnt at an early age which was not the case, although even to a trained mind, including doctors, my position had become very complex indeed.

In a free local newspaper that was delivered to the house one afternoon I was attracted by an advert whereby males could meet the opposite sex who were single yet had children. After paying my £30 registration fee with an agency in Sutton, I was sent the names and contact numbers of three women who lived in the local area. One of those women was Judith who was then aged 40, had three children and lived nearby in Worcester Park. We made arrangements to meet in a local pub where things went well; we both enjoyed walking and theatre, so we decided that I would visit her home to meet her three children. Feeling anxious, mindful of my own family experiences, I knocked on the front door which was opened by a smiling young boy around 11 years old who asked me into the house explaining that his mum was in the garden. There I was greeted by Judith looking attractive, dressed in a pink summer frock with matching flat shoes. She was tallish, well-built though not big or heavy, had short fair hair interspersed with highlights. Along with the older boy who had opened the front door, Judith introduced me to her attractive three children, two boys and a daughter, who were all understandably rather shy in meeting this strange man in their house for the first time.

After going out together several times with Judith and her three children, enjoying visiting various places, we thought the time was right for me to move into her household. We discussed this significant change to their household with her children, especially the older two, as best as they could understand taking into account their personal feelings of having a father they visited fortnightly. This was the first time I had lived with another family by choice, but from the outset, not surprisingly, adapting was difficult for all of us. With hindsight I felt guilty about not explaining in depth my own medical problems to Judith who no doubt would have seen things differently about us living together. But with failure hanging over me from all sides, like the sword of Damocles, I thought that by living with Judith I had the opportunity to be in a warm family setting with young children that in time I could help grow up into strong productive people. At the same time, I reckoned, I could also sort out my valium problem, find a regular job and contribute to a happy household.

I did manage to find work most of the time, mainly through employment agencies, so that I could contribute some money to the household which did please Judith, and for a time things went well, especially my relationship with the children. There were times when I would go out on my own. Judith saw no problem with that, but on one occasion I stayed out all night drinking, arriving back home at 8 a.m. next morning. Judith was not angry as she was so concerned about what might have happened to me; in fact, she had phoned my parents expressing her alarm. As I had been on my own for so long it didn't dawn on me to phone to reassure her that I was all right.

After several similar incidents the time was right, now that I had been living with her for some nine months, to be open in great detail about past events. At first she was angry but after a while all she wanted to do was to support me to wean myself off years of valium addiction. As I did not have any confidence in the medical profession I started my own withdrawal programme, but it was very difficult to achieve due to the fact that I had been taking 30mg per day of valium for over 17 years. But slowly over the next few weeks I reduced my intake of valium. At first I started sweating profusely, especially if I was in the company of others; the tinnitus in my ears became a lot quieter; and I had a rebound effect with anxiety which happens to a lot of people coming off tranquillisers. I still used to panic when in enclosed spaces and my libido increased after years of sexual inactivity. Later on in many different enclosed settings, including social work training, panic would at times bring me close to the edge of a complete breakdown. Many times, for example, I left the training or lecture room determined never to return, yet I kept going, realising that failure meant the end of me.

For the first time in 17 years, I felt a lot more motivated and emotional; whereas before I left things unchallenged, now I was becoming more assertive. New things started to appear in my consciousness for the first time. It has been found by various researchers over the years that long-term ingestion of tranquillisers represses the emotions by putting them into a kind of cold storage. I had come to realise that my own emotional responses to other people, including praise or anger, were cold, blunt or inappropriate. Over the years I must have come across as a rather immature person which of course I was and this was brought about by years of addiction. One of the major legacies of long-term ingestion of tranquillisers is a poor short-term memory recall, something I still experience today.

By coincidence, at the same time as I was trying to withdraw from years of medical abuse, Esther Rantzen was hosting a Sunday programme in which she was encouraging those people who had been taking prescribed tranquillisers to write to her about their experiences. With the strong support of Judith, I wrote to Esther Rantzen regarding my own experiences of valium, detailing the many years of medical abuse during which time not one doctor, considering the various GP's I had registered with, had even looked at my case to see if medication was still appropriate, or perhaps I would benefit more from a talking therapy. Ms Rantzen (or the programme makers) did not contact me regarding the letter I sent them but for the first time in many years it was clear what had been detrimental to my health, and vague as things were at this stage, change was in the air at last.

Suffice to say that I lived with Judith and her friendly children for two years which for me was some sort of a minor miracle, taking into account my abysmal record of not committing myself to anything. That lack of commitment can now be understood as the powerful side effects of taking valium unabated for years. Judith was a very good person and I appreciate the opportunity she gave me, with sincere open arms, to live with her and her family in a warm home where I experienced kindness. To be honest, I was not mature enough to be able to look after three young vulnerable children who required to be loved simply for themselves. Although it was just the beginning, there would be many difficulties ahead. Living with Judith allowed me to take some first tentative steps forward towards developing new social, cognitive and psychological skills that I would desperately need for the future.

After my short-lived positive experiences of living within a supportive family unit, of which I am eternally grateful, my new GP made an appointment for me to see a psychiatrist at the Maudsley Hospital due to the side effects of withdrawing from valium, and which I thought had brought about an obsessive/compulsive disorder (OCD) problem: With regards to this possible problem, later on in 1992, I obtained legal access to all my medical history case notes. Within that bundle of notes was a letter written by a Professor Ellis in 1984, who worked at the Maudsley Hospital at the time, explaining that when I last saw him12 years previously in 1972 the schizoid personality disorder (SPD) which I suffered from was more disabling than it was in 1984. SPD was certainly not a diagnosis that I had heard of before—and why had someone not told me about this problem all those years ago way back in 1972 when it might have been possible to have done something about it sooner rather than later? Without doubt Professor Ellis or my GP should have brought it to my attention; indeed, they had a legal or moral duty to do so. If I had been made aware of the so-called SPD all those years ago it would have been possible to have made a much earlier focused withdrawal programme from BZ along with other opportunities that could have helped me such as education or skills based work. I felt so let down once again by the medical profession for not explaining to me what personality disorder was, how it came about and what could be done to throw its shackles off my back. Never thinking I was a victim, however, many times I wondered what I had done to have received all this incompetence heaped on me.

It is now Hospital policy to copy all consultant letters to the patient for their own information when they have attended for diagnosis/treatment. Professor Ellis' letter went on to state: 'I am in fact struck by the remarkable improvement since I last saw him 12 years ago. The torticollis has virtually disappeared. In the early 1980's he seems to have managed to wean himself off Benzodiazepines. As to the specific complaint, I do not think that he is in fact suffering from OCD at all but is complaining of a certain amount of distractibility which is quite normal.'

Professor Ellis' letter had added one more 'medical problem' to my list of six problems recapped above by diagnosing SPD in 1975 when nothing was done to help me cope productively with my ever-growing burden; yet my GP went on prescribing valium for another ten years, aware that I had been diagnosed with SPD! According to the British National Formulary: '...cautions against issuing Benzodiazepines where there is marked personality disorder.' If I did have a pre-existing personality disorder, why did the prescribing doctor not pick that up at the time? On the other hand, if I did not have a pre-morbid personality disorder, then the only explanation is that 17 years of valium ingestion and underdevelopment has caused the problem. Once again quoting from the British National Formulary: 'Tolerance develops relatively easily to the anxiety-relieving and sleep-inducing properties of benzodiazepines within 3 to 14 days.'

Regarding personality disorder, I would like to quote the full statement written by Dr Marjan Jahanshahi on my behalf for the Legal Aid Board in 1992: **'It could be argued that the possible concurrent personality disorder referred to in the medical records could have been a more fundamental cause of the abuse of alcohol and medication, and underdevelopment of social life and career. Although this cannot be ruled out completely, it should be noted that individuals who suffer from chronic neurological disorders such as spasmodic torticollis, that are not that well understood even by doctors, have been in the past regarded as demanding and as having odd personalities by the medical profession, because they tend to be persistent in seeking relief for their illness although no single treatment has been universally effective and thus end up being perceived as demanding and illogical.'**

The reason I have highlighted this full statement will become clear later on in this work when the above statement was used in a civil medical negligence case.

Around about 1986 there was a significant development when several people who had contracted dystonia got together and started an organisation called the Dystonia

Society. With few resources yet with much commitment those early heroes took the Dystonia Society forward, trying along the way to contact those individuals, often isolated, and with no support to reassure them that they were not alone. In those early days dystonia was considered to be a psychiatric abnormality. Trying to get a correct diagnosis often took ten years and limited treatment was available.

In the early 1990s, I worked as a volunteer for the Dystonia Society at their offices at the time in North London. During my time there I met so many decent hard working volunteers who freely gave many hours of their week in helping to take the Dystonia Society forward into the effective neurological charity it is today. The Dystonia Society today 'exists to support people who have any form of the neurological movement disorder known as dystonia, and their families, through the promotion of awareness, research and welfare'.

Over the years the Dystonia Society has always been there for me when I have needed various support, including written neurological evidence to help me win my incapacity benefit appeal to supplying well informed dystonia leaflets for my local GP centre. Being a quintessential loner, I have not attended many dystonia activities, both nationally or locally, over the years, but I am eternally grateful for the work the Society has done, and continues to do, for all those people whose lives in one way or another has been affected by a movement disorder. We certainly now have a great deal to celebrate!

Due to living with Judith for over two years meant that I

attended the Croydon Buddhist Centre during that time only occasionally. Now that I was back living with my parents, it gave me the time I needed to attend meditation classes, hoping it would give me the impetus to think more deeply about how I could develop my life from now on. As soon as you walked into the Croydon Buddhist Centre there was so much for a new pair of eyes to take in. First there was the library that sold many different books by various Buddhist authors from around the world, including inspiring books and taped lectures by Sangharakshita, the founder of the Friends of the Western Buddhist Order. Also, you could purchase most other related paraphernalia from incense, candles, jewels to brightly coloured serene looking Buddha figures. At the weekly meditation classes we would congregate outside the shrine room chatting to anyone who was around; people were there from all walks of life including care workers, therapists and building workers. It was interesting and reassuring to know that so many different people who were from a wide background were interested in understanding more about Buddhism. Once in the shrine room the teacher would take us through the various meditation steps for that particular night. Usually two different meditation and complementing practises were taught: (1) the mindfulness of breathing and (2) the development of positive emotions. Including instruction, both practices would last for about an hour.

Back outside the shrine room the procedure was to have tea in usually small informal groups standing around discussing personal experiences or other matters. This was an ideal occasion to deepen your friendships with those people you had previously met at meditation classes or other centre activities. After attending weekly meditation classes for about four months where I spent productive time with men who had been practising Buddhists for some time, especially order members such as Sanghadeva, I was encouraged and supported to become a Mitra, a good friend.

Over the months and years, Sanghadeva and I did a lot of enjoyable things together, mainly walking, visiting public gardens and inhabiting cafés. He moved from the Croydon Spiritual Community to live, work and practise in the FWBO College in Birmingham. I have enjoyed visiting him several times at the college where I have been impressed by how mature, focused and happier he now appears to be. It is not surprising that for a time he became disappointed and unfocused when the Croydon Buddhist Centre restaurant, Hockneys, went out of business. He had been an integral part of its success. Sanghadeva is a kind, friendly supportive man who is full of energy where, in Birmingham he is the college gardener, cook and teaches meditation and Dharma study to local people. All the time I have known Sanghadeva, I have never seen him angry or resentful; instead, he puts his negative energy into practising Dharma.

In the summer of 1988, I decided at the time I wanted to make a definite link to the order and with Sangharakshita who is head of the order. Sangharakshita, who was born in London, had played a key part in the revival of Buddhism in India, particularly through his work among the ex-untouchables. In 1967 he created a new Buddhist movement in Britain called Friends of the Western Buddhist Order (FWBO) and the following year The

Western Buddhist Order (WBO) when he ordained the first order members. In a public Mitra ceremony you offer flowers, a candle and a stick of incense in front of the image of the Buddha in a devotional ceremony called the sevenfold puja which was in front of Order Members, Mitras and members of the public. After the thought-provoking Mitra ceremony, where others also went through the same ceremony, I made a definite decision at the time to become more involved in things around the centre but with my past experience of non-commitment at the forefront of my mind.

My visits to the Buddhist centre now included attending regular Mitra classes and supporting various inspiring Dharma talks that were given by order members from around Britain. Although my life was more stable, mild to moderate anxiety was still an issue for me and has remained so throughout my life. About three months later I joined the successful Hockneys vegetarian team where in the mornings downstairs in the large kitchen I prepared vegetables along with my mostly young idealistic colleagues. At Hockneys most lunch times, and some evenings, we were very busy as people from far and near would turn up to eat Sanghadeva's deliciously cooked food. It is not surprising that due to Hockneys' success, mainly because of good management and professional acumen, over a period of several years the Croydon Buddhist Centre was able to finance a thriving creative arts centre attracting well known poets, musicians and writers.

The intense financial culture and rich social life of the time reflected Margaret Thatcher's policy to give working people of Britain a bigger choice of what to do with their hard earned money. Sadly her financial policy did not last as recession hit people badly throughout the country where unemployment rose and many homes were repossessed. Hockneys was not immune from the recession and in the end due to mounting overheads and lack of income it had to close.

However, the health food shop at the centre, run by women, did not close but continues to be successful even as I write these words. For some unexplained reason, other than in the shrine room, during the years I was around the centre men and women had very little contact with each other. At the time it was mooted that there was a clique of feminists in the health food shop who wanted only minimal contact with men. The only time that I spoke to one of the female shop workers I'm afraid to say she gave me short shrift; indeed, subsequently I thought that maybe I should have tried working in their shop wearing my TV attire! On a serious note, there was around this time at the centre a sexual demarcation line that one did not dare venture over. It is understandable in an intense spiritual environment where young people, for the first time, were doing their utmost to change their lives that a considerable amount of projected negativity is used to justify certain behaviour. On the whole, allowing for discussion and personal reflection, such behaviour can afford individuals, as was the case at the Croydon Buddhist Centre, the opportunity to move on with their lives.

After numerous occasions throughout the years living temporarily in my parents' home—and I appreciated how they had always welcomed me—I had now left for good. But after two years of living in two different bedsits, I had further accommodation problems of my own to resolve when Neil Goddard kindly invited me to live with him and Paul Prince in his three-bedroomed terraced house just off the A23 in Purley. Unless one is disabled or has children, single people like me have to rely on the private housing sector to provide, sometimes inferior, short term accommodation. By this time both Neil and Paul had been having regular contact with the Croydon Buddhist Centre attending various Dharma courses; subsequently they both became ordained and moved away to live and work for the movement in another part of the country.

I no longer worked at Hockneys, although I got a lot out of being with others, so the first phone call I made to Wells Agency successfully found me a temporary job for one year as a supervisor/driver for Leatherhead Council Social Services. The job entailed supervising 12 males of varying ages between 28 and 62; all of them had some kind of learning disability, with various rubbish cleaning tasks in the community. Apparently this working scheme came about through government policy where Local Authorities would have a duty to employ people with varying disabilities being discharged from the large institutions into the community. Most of the group I worked with had received institutional care but they all, except two who lived at home, were now in a supportive housing environment closely supervised by a carer.

I really enjoyed working with those men who made me laugh nearly all the time I was there, especially John who would often say to me, 'Bowie, have you seen porky pig around?' John had severe learning disabilities but had the strength of three men when it came to digging or shovelling rubbish onto a lorry. In the mornings I usually picked the men up in a designated area and drove them in a 12-seater van to various places that needed to be cleaned of rubbish, overgrown vegetation and abandoned bicycles, etc. Typical places they cleaned were the long alleys that ran parallel with railway lines which are ideal places for throwing away various unwanted items. I would space them out along the alley every 20 yards or so, depending on the length of the alley, but when I used to return to see how they were progressing one hour later they had all congregated back as a group. I highlight this point because it demonstrates the power of conditioning in the large Institutions where most of them lived for varying lengths of time.

I lived with Neil and Paul for about two years. At the time we did not see a great deal of each other as we all worked in different places. Neil worked for Legal and General in Kingswood, Paul was still working at Hockneys, and I for Wells employment. We all got along with each other quite well but I did not experience any real depth within the household which is understandable considering the differences in age, background and socialisation. We did, however, on rare occasions visit one restaurant and had walks together on the local Downs.

While I was living at the 'semi-community house' I was active attending various things around the FWBO. There were regular Mitra study groups held at the local men's spiritual community, called Aryatara, in Purley, which was only half a mile down the road from where I was living. The men's community which is a large detached house has been around for some considerable time, housing men who used to work mainly at the Croydon Centre. In study groups you will find other Mitras who can offer support, guidance and friendship which is important during a time of possible transition and change that can come about from intense spiritual practise. Outside of Mitra study there had been times when my visits to Aryatara were met by unfriendly remarks from some of the community members who expected me to phone them before turning up unannounced. But most were sympathetic towards those guys whose only *raison d'être* for being there was to seek out a friendly chat with someone.

This all sounds so re-assuring—for practising Buddhism—but during these times things must have been difficult for me because I started visiting prostitutes in London, decadent behaviour that would last for a few years. After finishing work one day I took the train to Marble Arch where occasionally I would use a quaint old Regency pub off Oxford Street which was owned by a former actor whose name I never found out. This particular evening I remember having a meal there—the pub was well known for its English food—when inexplicably Marylebone station came to my mind as I thought of the times I had worked in the area when I used to observe street prostitutes diligently plying their trade.

Some thirty minutes later, battered by the insane experience of travelling on an underground train full of commuters, I found myself outside Marylebone main line station in the pouring rain looking at the many different coloured cards in the four public telephone boxes advertising various sexual services. With no real preference or understanding, my eye was directed to a red coloured card advertising 'Strict Correction given by the local senior black magistrate'. When I phoned the number a female voice said rather seductively, 'Senior Correction Magistrate, what can I do for you, darling?' I was rather flummoxed by her straightforward approach and immediately put the phone back down. Five minutes later, bracing myself, I phoned her again and when I received the same question I answered nervously, 'Are you available now?' 'Yes I am, darling, where are you at the moment?' I explained where I was and it turned out her house was only five minutes down the road from the station. Her front door was downstairs in the basement and she came to the door wearing just a black gown and high heeled red shoes. 'Hello darling, come in,' she said to me in a pronounced Jamaican accent, 'follow me into the room, and we shall see what I can do for you.'

Rose—that was her name—was at least six feet tall with long black straightened hair; her large luscious lips were painted with ultra-red lipstick and she had a feminine sexy body which by this stage I was craving to touch. She explained the various services she could provide, starting with a body massage, which meant masturbation, which would cost £40 up to the most expensive, £100, for which she would place you into basement stocks and administer her Senior Magistrate speciality of a severe beating. I was certainly not attracted by the proposition of having my bottom being beaten black and blue, so I chose most weeks, with the confidence obtained by drinking a bottle of white wine, to have my little member rubbed and squeezed by her shovel-sized hard black hands with pink nails, ably assisted by her muscular Mike Tyson lookalike arms.

Regarding the social effects of the growing prostitution or seediness around London Terminal stations, I'm afraid Alan A. Jackson (*London's Termini*, Pan Books, 1969) got it wrong when he thought that there was hardly any degeneration around the Marylebone area. Not only are there several telephone booths outside the station full of prostitutes' calling cards, but there are also telephone boxes around the neighbourhood displaying naked ladies on colourful cards, sometimes with lurid messages, explaining the pleasures that await you.

Infrequently thereafter for several years and under the influence of alcohol, I visited up to about ten more prostitutes in and around Central London who all had their quirky ways of attracting punters like me. One such lady of the night was called 'Pussy'—a terribly indecent name, I know—a young West Indian whose speciality was tying the hands of a male behind his back while she would urinate all over him for the sum of £70. 'Pure hedonism, darling, for the initiated,' she said smiling at me with the most sexy African lips which almost lured me into performing another version of water sports. 'No I'm not really into that sort of sex,' I said, explaining that my own degrading choice was simple masturbation with the practitioner wearing plastic yellow gloves of the heavy industrial duty kind.

The one thing I do regret doing when I used to visit prostitutes, nearly always under the strong influence of alcohol, was to smoke marijuana and sniff poppers. Both substances then can be dangerous if used regularly. On a serious note, visiting prostitutes on a regular basis cannot only be expensive to one's pocket but also dangerous to one's physical well-being due to their precarious lifestyles. Many prostitutes have drug addiction problems, so they need to work to buy drugs to fuel their habits, and some are controlled by pimps who claim to protect them, yet at the same time abuse them. It is not unknown for punters, the name given to customers, to have been beaten up by prostitutes' minders. All I will say on the subject is: stay well away from that dangerous environment.

From hedonism to spiritual aspirations: by going on retreat with other men to Padmaloka Retreat Centre in the Norfolk countryside was a positive experience which gave me the opportunity to deepen my commitment of Going for Refuge to the three Jewels: The Buddha, the Dharma, and the Sangha. It also gave me the opportunity to meet the residential Community and other men from around the movement. I have been on retreats at Padmaloka when there have been more than 80 men in the shrine room intently performing the sevenfold puja in an atmosphere charged with much positive energy and goodwill dedicated in a ceremony to the Buddha. Puja, which means devotional worship, is a ritual practice performed along with others focusing on the beauty of the shrine. After most sevenfold pujas that I have actively participated in, I have nearly always experienced a feeling of deep insecurity. Why that should have happened is not particularly clear but one explanation could be that due to the powerful nature of Dharma our emotions are exposed to refinement. After 1992, I attended several retreats at Padmaloka but I found them uninspiring possibly due to inexperienced teachers who did not live in the community there.

Some of the most enjoyable times I have had with other

men in the FWBO have been on gardening retreats held at both Aryatara and at another community called Rivendell, a beautiful rambling detached house with large attractive gardens in Sussex. On one of the Aryatara gardening maintenance days, organised by the young community members, a Swedish order member came up to me late in the afternoon to inform me that my dystonia was the result of negative Karma from another lifetime. At first I just accepted what he had said about dystonia, as this was something I blindly and ignorantly believed in those days from Dharma study groups without having the confidence to challenging its merit. Later I discussed with another order member what I had been informed about of my personal connection between Dystonia and Karma but his response was that 'the Swedish order member had been misguided. Only Enlightened beings would have that insight'. Two days later I realised the probable explanation behind the misguided statement the order member had made to me. Three months earlier at the Croydon Buddhist Centre I rather insensitively and incorrectly suggested to the Swedish Order Member that he was a homosexual notwithstanding that within days he was seen in the company of a rather attractive young blonde woman. I did admire his swift action in finding a woman that at the same time refuted my absurd suggestion that he was gay—one positive example of action speaking louder than words.

There is one final comment I would like to make about some of the former members of the Aryatara community going back to the years of 1987/1991. For whatever reason, I am not speculating why, but at the time Aryatara attracted very young men. Since it was the first time that most of them had left home, it was not surprising they were greatly inspired by the experience of practising the Dharma with older men. On many occasions it personally irritated me when one or other of these young men, some no more than 18 years at the time, would insist during study that I was not living my life very well, saying I should follow the Dharma if I wanted to find the answer. Well, if only life were that straightforward! None of them, understandably, had ever worked or fed themselves by their own hands, none of them had ever had to work hard to pay rent or mortgage or experience being homeless with nowhere to go except to bed down for the night under the nearest bush. None of them had been chronically ill with an incurable condition or had to battle against a drug-induced addiction. Being given access to Dharma can act as a powerful antidote indeed.

As gardening retreats were informal it gave you the opportunity to meet men you had not seen before or those you were already friends with in a relaxed and convivial atmosphere. The gardens at Rivendell were large and magnificent, full of shrubs, plants and flowers from around the world including many different coloured rhododendrons. Many men who at the time were living there spent a significant amount of their small income on buying plants to enrich their surroundings. Also at Rivendell, an ideal place for spiritual practise, there was a facility for individuals to carry out a single retreat in a ready-made well-insulated shed at the back of the garden, furthest away from the house activities. Individuals have informed me that after two weeks of solitary practise you had to be careful when re-engaging with the mundane world due to 'spiritual alienation'.

Of all the various FWBO places that I have had the pleasure of visiting over the years, Rivendell is the one I have most enjoyed being around. Apart from its imposing beauty, it was the surrounding countryside that I found most enjoyable, fresh in contrast to the vagaries of the modern world full of stressed people inhabiting polluting noisy cities. Having walked past Rivendell, a former vicarage, many years later, the area still conjures up fragments of a peaceful way of life that was lived there more than a century ago.

Wesak (Buddha Day) was a particularly special festival that is held every year at the Croydon Centre, and all over the Buddhist world, that attracts large numbers of people to celebrate the life of the Enlightened one. This particular day consisted of meditation, study groups, communal lunch and in the evening a sevenfold puja. For the day itself the whole of the inside of the centre used to be decorated with beautiful colourful images of various Buddhas and Bodhisattvas who gave you strange piercing looks determined to move your blocked emotions or even move you enough to run back out of the centre.

It was on one of these enjoyable Wesak days that I met a rather shy tense young man, not unlike me a few years before, who was attending for the first time on his own. Graham was 25 years old with long curly hair, wearing old worn out clothes that were given to him by a local charity about six months earlier. When I got into conversation with Graham he explained how he had left home at the age of 17 years, having had numerous rows with both his parents because, he said rather sternly, 'I just didn't fit in with what my parents want me to do with my life.' After thinking for a couple of minutes he went on to say in a rather sad, dejected manner, 'They wanted me to attend university and be successful but that is all vague and bullshit. It doesn't fit in with the plans that I have for myself.'

Trying to be sensitive about what I said to him, I explained to Graham about my background and how very difficult life can be. 'I suppose your parents love you and want the best for you in a world that is increasingly difficult for young people to find suitable employment.' With that we both left the centre that Wesak evening to walk onto the pavements of a hostile and insecure world that has the capacity to bring down its full force of suffering upon you. Briefly discussing Graham's life with him reminded me of those young idealistic middle-class men that I had met in Richmond all those years ago who were so desperate to break away from their family to find their own way in life. Of course it is healthy at various stages in our individual lives to make decisions for ourselves, but it is also important to remember the security our families can give us so that we can take risks in an uncertain world, mindful that we have a home to return to.

There are many people I have met during my years of travel where they, including myself, would certainly have loved to have had a family background where one does not have to continually worry about earning money to survive. It is nearly always about balancing wants with needs. As the existentialist might say, don't waste your precious time making money or buying houses or clothes—you are free to choose any path you wish to walk, but the reality is something else.

As the Buddha said, all conditioned things are impermanent. Those conditions applied to me at the house where I had been living for the past two years. Neil wanted me to move out of his house—we were never particularly close—as that would allow his friendship with an order member to flourish. So once again I had to find new accommodation, if I could, in the nearby locality. There was some tentative discussion that I had at the time with several order members about renting a house together but nothing became of it. After many phone calls to advertised accommodation, I managed to rent a small self-contained bedroom where I would be sharing the rest of the small terraced house with the owner, a friendly chap called Simon. It transpired that he had had his own problems with prescribed tranquillisers and alcohol years previously, having been subsequently hospitalised to treat the withdrawal effects of both.

The year was 1991, and at the age of 44 years, I wasn't making a great deal of progress towards developing a better quality of life for myself although it was great to be free of valium. In a quiet household where we respected each other's space and understood the problems we both had with tranquillisers meant Simon and I got on well together, going for occasional walks and trying to knock into shape his overgrown garden. My bedroom was clean, tidy and well-decorated with a light blue ceiling, ornate coving and lemon soft walls. Within those small cosy bedroom walls I slept soundly at night remembering the arduous path most of humanity has to walk before some kind of peace descends upon them.

Nearly always on my own, I still continued to visit the West

End for drinking sessions in various pubs, preferably where I was not known by anyone, not that I knew that many people anyway due to being a quintessential loner by nature. After drinking in at least five different pubs around Soho, I took an underground train to Earls Court where you will find a mass of cheap hotels, cafés and gay pubs. Walking aimlessly can be important, sometimes, to observe your environment, as I did around Earls Court, passing many of the attractive red brick Victorian flats that overlook their own spacious well maintained gardens, locked so that the local drunks, drug addicts and drifters can't urinate over the prized roses. Back onto the Earls Court Road, I looked into one of the many Estate Agents in the area advertising local flats for sale starting at a million pounds in the most densely populated four square miles in the world, so I was informed by some knowledgeable drunken middle-aged male. After moving on from the Estate Agent, realising that I didn't have the money to buy a cheap coal bunker, I started walking down the dirty windswept road for about two hundred yards when I came across a small bar called Naughty Boys. Not an auspicious sign, you might think.

Being a gay bar, it was not surprising it was packed with men, a few women, in an atmosphere of thick cigarette smoke, noise and music with the Petshop boys blasting out from a gadget in the high white ceiling above. I had to fight my way to the bar, bought a drink and sat down outside the pub on a cold bench where the table was full of empty glasses with soggy cigarette ends snubbed out inside them. After ten minutes a rather camp looking male with long black hair and green jumper spoke asking if he could join me at the same table. He lived in Battersea where he worked as a waiter in a small wine bar just off the High Road. 'Do you enjoy coming to this area for a drink?' I reluctantly asked the chap. 'Oh yes, of course my dear, I can visit any number of gay pubs and clubs where I will be safe in the arms of another man.' Be careful, I said to myself. He came across as a younger version of Quentin Crisp minus the colourful clothes, but certainly used flamboyant gestures with his very small effeminate hands. He did not hang back when he said to me, 'Would you like to come back to my place in Battersea for a drink, my dear?' At the same time he was measuring me up and down with his piercing black eyes. 'No thank you, I have to meet someone else later on,' I replied rather hesitatingly. 'Well, at least take my phone number, won't you my dear?' He passed me his white card containing his name, Benjamin Carne, and contact details. I thanked him and made my way back to the dirty grimy Victorian Earls Court underground station to take the train back to the West End once again, the gravitational pull being too powerful for me to overcome.

By this stage the heady mix of at least six pints of beer was making me rather confused, so much so that I started to panic and I rang 999 requesting an ambulance to be sent as I did not feel well. As I could not explain to the operator my location with any clarity it took the ambulance a while longer to find me sitting on a pavement propped up by a telephone booth. The two workers who were very friendly asked me various questions about why I had phoned them—had I been taking drugs, and how could they help me? Explaining that I did not feel well, they drove me to a small NHS hospital somewhere near Marble Arch, arriving ten minutes later at the A&E which was full of noisy people. As I was lying down on a trolley waiting to be seen by a doctor, those noisy people were being rather rude to each other—some even started swearing aloud. At one stage a security officer had to be called into the A&E to inform several people to behave.

About twenty minutes later a rather young looking small Oriental female doctor came into my now curtained space to ask why I had phoned the ambulance for help. Giving her the usual bullshit, in line with my usual spiel at these places, she was taken in by my pleadings and told me that I would have to wait until tomorrow when I would be seen by a senior doctor. The same procedure followed when I was taken up into a dark lift to a male medical ward, where I was told to undress and change into hospital pyjamas. I was put into a small observation side ward after the young attractive nurse had first taken my pulse and blood pressure. Sometime in the small hours, I'm not sure when, the same nurse, who noticed that I was still awake, came up to me to ask me rather apologetically, 'I won't say anything but are you working as an undercover (forgive the pun) reporter for a World in Action television programme?' 'No, of course I'm not, nurse, I don't feel well—that's the reason I am here.' Nurse David—that was her name—said, 'I do apologise for asking questions, but you are young, intelligent, healthy, so I wondered what you are doing in here.' She accepted what I had to say and went away to make me a cup of tea which tasted delicious after nearly a gallon of beer. But it was very interesting what the nurse had to say about my admission to her ward as she probably realised that all was not as it seemed to be.

Around 11a.m. next morning a different nurse took me to

another floor to meet the senior white doctor who would assess my position. He asked me in a kind manner why I had phoned the ambulance for assistance last night. He asked me a number of other questions about the medication I was taking—was it for mental health problems and did I reside in a psychiatric hospital? After piercing and probing questions, the most thorough so far, I was discharged back onto the streets of London but also without a prescription for valium medication.

Like most other uneventful Hospital discharges that I have experienced, after only twenty minutes I was back in The Black Lion pub just off Oxford Street. But mercifully, that would be the last time, after having drunk so much alcohol, that I would ever phone for an ambulance again and spend the night in a hospital ward hidden away from those who could potentially support me. I am truly sorry for wasting the time and resources of hospital staff but at the time I must have been crying out for help, as it is quite obvious that my behaviour was not normal. It is interesting to consider that at this stage I had not been taking valium for some years, yet my rather irrational behaviour continued. Had it been the years of emotional instability or insecurity, caused by the detrimental effects of taking valium and alcohol together for 17 years, which might account for my continuing abnormal learned behaviour? Or is it important to consider the impact that dystonia has had on my life since the age of 20 years? Dystonia is a rather debilitating neurological condition, and in my case, a chronic problem. Or did SPD already exist before I contracted dystonia?

Perhaps the reason for bringing my occasional bogus

hospital presence to an end could be explained by the fact that during that year I had been meeting infrequently a black nurse whom I had first met in a café in central Croydon. Linda, who was about ten years younger than me, had trained and worked as a nursery nurse for several years in Mayday Hospital, Croydon. She lived on her own with her 5-year-old son who attended the local school. After some discussion we both decided that if we wanted to take our relationship forward then it was best if we started living together in her small attractive terraced house in East Croydon. After collecting my belongings and saying goodbye to Simon, who was a decent person whose company I had enjoyed during the six months living in his house as a lodger, I moved in with Linda and her son Paul.

As I was now in my 45th year, I really convinced myself that now was the right time to settle down into family life with Linda and I had high expectations that, at last, I would be in a successful relationship. I found myself a decent full-time job working for a local builder repairing customers' gutters and drainpipes. Things in the house with Linda were going well. We put our money together to buy food and pay the bills for the running costs of the house. We spent some money on painting some of the internal walls and doors of the house; we also laid new turf and planted various flowers in the back garden. Linda drove us to various interesting places in the countryside where we would have picnics, play games and generally enjoy being together. I used to look forward to those times out with Linda and Paul very much indeed. Linda had a secure, well paid job which she enjoyed very much, and I had a full-time job, not temporary like before, for the first time in years and I was bringing home a regular wage to help pay my way and, to cap all things, Paul appeared to be happy. By this time, it was 1992, and I had not seen any of my family for some considerable time. For one thing, I did not know where most of them lived and, not being a close family, I was not that concerned although I did occasionally phone my parents so see how they were. As I was living in Croydon, I assumed the nearest of my siblings lived somewhere near Epsom which is some distance away, and besides, with 12 siblings in my family they could have lived all over the country for all I knew. In fact, there were at least four siblings that I had not seen for about 20 years, which meant I would probably not even recognise them. Also, I could understand that they had moved on with their own respective lives with a commitment to working hard for their own families.

It was Derby day in Epsom, the premier horse race in Britain where the fastest and strongest 3-year-old male horses do battle for the richest prize money and the privilege to procreate at all the prestigious stud farms. Being born close to the racetrack, I had been attending Derby day from an early age when my parents first took me there, but for some reason they did not take my other siblings. I have a vague recollection that my eldest brother was also there wearing a dark blue trilby with black silk braid on the side of it resembling a George Raft lookalike. During the last 15 years I have only been to the Derby infrequently due to living too far from the racetrack or else I have been working and been unable to attend.

When I was working in Croydon as a builder, three colleagues and I decided to take the day off and head for the open blustery Epsom Downs where every day of the year local racehorses can be seen working out on the nearby undulating gallops. I was also pleased that after discussing the prospect of attending Derby Day with Linda, she thought it would be good for me to spend time with my colleagues, especially as Epsom was my place of birth. All four of us arrived at Tattenham Corner station around midday amid the mêlée of people pushing each other out of the packed dirty smoked-filled trains along the platform and onto the nearby road just a few yards from the five furlong starting gates. From this road you could see the throng of people scattered all over the windswept Downs, walking like ants into the many side shows and beer tents that are assembled every year for the world famous Derby race.

The train itself was full of various people from different backgrounds such as middle-aged Cockneys who were no doubt full-time punters, mothers and fathers with young children and young people with their bags full of cans of beer, all determined to enjoy themselves. 'Yus Bert, we will 'ave a monkee on that O'Brien two-year-old today alright,' said one of the smiling Cockneys. 'Make no mistake today Teddy my son, we will 'ave a good touch on the 'orses,' was the emphatic reply from Bert, who looked about 55 years of age and had short black hair, dressed in a smart blue suit. Once we were out on the road my three colleagues and I made a beeline for the large pub called Tattenham Arms which was only a stone's throw from the station. Once inside, the place resembled something like a psychiatric ward with people shouting, singing and swearing at each other in a near drunken environment. As Bob, who was one of my three colleagues, was over six feet tall and built like a brick shithouse, he volunteered to buy the beer from the crowded bar. The bar itself was large, well decorated with a delightful blue chandelier in the middle of the room where amid the uproar a young drunken male was jumping up trying to pull it down. Several drinkers nearby were shouting, egging him on to 'bring the fucking thing down my son, there is a large scotch if you succeed'. Another colleague, Sidney, who was a hod carrier with tattoos all over his chest, bought the next round of beer from the frazzled female barmaid. Three or four drinks later we joined in with most of the pub who by now were singing various London songs which would have been a familiar scene to my late maternal grandfather who was himself once an avid crooner.

Out of the mayhem I managed to get to the toilet when in front of me in the queue I saw two old former school buddies who I had not seen for some time, Pete Upton and John Wilshaw. Both of them looked well even though Pete, now working for a property dealer, had lost a considerable amount of money recently on horse race gambling. 'What you doing with yourself Pete?' I asked my former smoking partner at school. 'Started working a year ago for a property company in the West End, not bad money but I spend a lot on the horses, drinking and women,' he said with a glint in his eye. He went on to say that he had left his wife, whom he had met in Spain, and his son two years ago to move in with his current partner, Susan, who was an accountant in the same company he worked for. I was impressed how in every way he had grown since those heady days at the junior and senior schools in Runton where academic achievement was unheard of by us thickheads.

Although I had also known Johnny Wilshaw since our

schooldays, I had not been so close to him as I was to Pete Upton. As I had not seen John for many years, when I first saw him in the toilet, I was not sure it was him standing six feet tall with long blond hair wearing a dandy light brown mohair suit. At school he was short, not very imposing, but with the passing of the years he had filled out into a handsome well groomed individual. 'Nice to see you, Barry, after so many years,' John said. 'I often wondered what happened to you.' He looked at me with his kind brown eyes. After explaining the position I was in, John told me of the various countries that he had visited on behalf of his employer, a legal firm for which he now worked as a senior clerk. He explained with great enthusiasm how hard he had worked having spent three years at college to pass the relevant qualification needed for the senior job. Like Pete and I, John had left school without any qualifications to seek his fortune in the world but it had proved difficult to move on to something more enterprising. Throughout the years he had struggled to find nothing more than semi-skilled work which he found soul destroying and ultimately utterly useless for him. It was at this stage that he started to do something about his lot in life, realising that only he could change the predicament he was in. 'That started the educational climb,' as John put it, 'from the bottom of the educational heap starting with an Access course, designed for mature students without qualifications, moving on to a read for a Law degree at South Bank University.' He passed with flying colours achieving top marks.

Having moved outside the Tattenham Arms pub due to the noise, John continued explaining to me how he had found the advertised Law position in London then gradually worked his way up to the senior clerk job. 'The senior clerk job entails, amongst other things, briefing barristers about forthcoming court cases so you have got to be aware of communicating factually correct information,' John was at great pains to explain. This gave him the confidence several years ago to buy a small mortgage so he could then ask his girlfriend to live with him and for the first time in his life he felt really confident about the future. I was so pleased to hear about John's successful development from college to full-time employment.

While I had been talking together with Peter Upton and John Wilshaw about our younger lives, my three colleagues had joined me outside away from the deafening noise of the pub. They both, Pete and John, gave me their contact numbers and departed to head for the racetrack Grandstand 100 yards away to have a bet on the first race which was in ten minutes. Bob, Sid, Billy and I also headed for the Grandstand taking up our seats for the first race where only Billy, my third workmate, had had a £10 bet on the local trained horse Melton Flyer which finished unplaced similar to all our bets before the Derby race itself. The Grandstand was packed with thousands of expectant male punters all trying to win their fortune, which is to be expected on another exciting Derby Day, but very few would return home with more money than they set out with only hours earlier. As I made my way down through the masses to the smell of male urine in the toilets I unexpectedly bumped into my older sibling Bob accompanied by his eldest son called Tony. 'Hallo, Brains, how is it going?' Bob asked, half shocked to see me there. Brains was another nickname I had acquired over many years, from whom I don't remember, but is a reference to the Television series *Thunderbirds'* male character who wore thick horn-rimmed glasses similar to the glasses I used to wear. Throughout the years in the Bradbury family most siblings have had a nickname of some description. Here they are: Belly, Wiggy, Fatty, Skinny, Skimbleshanks, Dillinger, Bungard and Annie, to name but a few of them.

Bob was in good spirits, having backed the first winner at odds of 8 to1 and asked me whether I fancied a beer, but I explained I couldn't as I was with friends. He told me things were going well in his business—all his family were well and his second son Joe was getting married in three months to his childhood sweetheart. We shook hands, said our goodbyes, and went our separate ways back among the bustle of hundreds of people standing around the numerous bars eating and drinking, no doubt a few celebrating with their winnings.

One thing that was guaranteed at Derby week was the amazing number of characters who would be drawn like a magnet to the Grandstand and Paddock areas. Without doubt my favourite was Prince Honolulu who hailed from Hackney but told the world he lived in a Royal Palace with his wife, twenty children and servants in Southern Africa. You would see him every year standing on the grass in front of the Grandstand looking a real spectacle wearing African tribal clothes and shouting, 'I gotta horse, I gotta horse!' After a few minutes he had amassed a large colourful crowd around him who were anticipating buying one of his horse tips sealed in a small envelope originally for half a crown (about 12p in today's money). 'Here you are Sir, I gotta horse, I gotta horse,' he would keep repeating like some old gramophone record until all his tips had been sold, at which point he would make himself scarce, not to be seen until the next day or the next Derby meeting. It was thought that all his envelopes contained the names of different horses and most knew it was all a bit of a joke played out in front of people looking for a bit of theatre.

I remember meeting a character just by chance from Hackney in one of the Grandstand bars about four years prior to this Derby Week. He told me that Prince Honolulu was in reality one Moses Best, who was born in Hackney about fifty years ago to African parents who immigrated to this country to find a better life. Moses, who was one of ten children, worked in a local public house cooking the lunches six days a week, but on his days off would travel to all the race tracks in and around London practising his art of tipping horses. Incidentally a drinker in the Grandstand bar told me with a twinkle in his eye, 'The furthest Moses has travelled to is Bognor Regis for a holiday twenty years ago!'

We were about ten minutes' away from the start of the Internationally renowned Derby, where the heavily backed short priced favourite Noble Saint looked in peak condition to win the big prize for Ireland. With the favourite being at such ridiculous short odds, we decided that between us we would have £10 to win on four different horses, all of them at good prices. Taking our beer back to the Grandstand to watch the last three furlongs of the Derby, we were amazed to find that one of our backed horses, Great Fell, was at least six lengths in front of the rest and remained there up to the winning post. We were all dumbstruck! We could not believe our luck as we stood there shouting, as did many others, for we had won £100 between us. After we had collected our winnings from the irate bookmaker, who at first was reluctant to pay out, we made our way along with hundreds of other people back to Tattenhan Corner station. The paper-strewn platform was packed full of disgruntled punters waiting for the train that eventually took us to East Croydon and into a local bar we all knew well. I arrived home that night quite merry while trying to explain to Linda that I had a wonderful time winning £25 racing with colleagues.

Early in the morning before the two of us left for work, Linda and I had to start the process to find out what the problem was behind her son's belligerent attitude towards me. As the months went by Paul would increasingly go out of his way to make my life difficult. On more than one occasion, when I had asked him to do something reasonable, he would retort by saying I wasn't his dad. Paul's irritating behaviour had been going on now for some time and was particularly obnoxious when he had returned home after spending time with his grandmother who used to collect him from school in the afternoons, due to Linda working at the hospital. Naturally both Linda and I were very appreciative of her mother collecting Paul from school, taking him home to her house for his tea and allowing him to watch television or listen to music. Several times after I had returned home from working, Paul said in a loud manner to me that he referred to himself as Jamaican and wanted to live there when he was older. The fact of the matter is that after his father married his mother, he had lived with them for only a few weeks, and not wanting the responsibility of looking after his son, had walked out of the front door never to be seen again. The one pleasing period for me, hopefully for Linda too, was when, after much encouragement from me, she enrolled for a nursing course which she passed, as a result of which she was eventually promoted to a RGN with the prospects of senior positions with enhanced pay.

The atmosphere in the household was not improving. In hindsight I realised that someone was sabotaging my relationship. The untenable position I was now in, sadly, was the beginning of the end of my relationship with Linda. There was, however, some good news for me around this time as I had been accepted on a local Access course, notwithstanding that I had enquired at several different Job Centres over the years about such courses only to be told that they were no longer available. For the record I had requested information about Access courses in Kingston, Croydon, Sutton, Epsom and Westminster but all to no avail. Those public servants all demonstrated an indifference, which was my experience, to the needs of the people they should have been serving. Some of their attitudes were downright abysmal, not fit for someone supposedly trained to provide a public service. But I'm afraid to say that public servant mentality has been my experience nearly all my life. There I was at the time, lost in the world, a young immature person with no roots or ties to hold me secure. Not knowing what to do or where I could go for support, I would retreat to the one place I knew well, the pub.

After living for over two years together, Linda and I realised that our relationship was irreparable so we decided to go our separate ways. I was very fortunate in that

Simon, the person who I had lived with prior to living with Linda, had sold his house and he was in the position to give me the contact details of the housing association where he was now a tenant. In the space of two days I had contacted Mace Housing, completed an application form, been offered, and I accepted, a self-contained studio flat in Crystal Palace. With the hot morning sun blazing above me, I moved into the studio flat carrying my few worldly goods accrued over the past years mindful that once again I was on my own.

It appeared that I had failed to develop a long-term relationship with Linda but I was aware that having done my best at the time there were other factors beyond my control that were determined to make our relationship come to an end. I also realised that Linda was heavily influenced by her mother's strong-willed attitude towards certain things. Anyway, I had to move on hoping that I could use my past experiences to make me stronger, more committed toward something that could help me develop a productive life. I painted and decorated my studio flat, as that was a part of the contract, bought some second-hand furniture, and generally made an attractive home for myself.

It was at this time that I left the building job that I had had for some time, and started to do more long distance walking, mainly on the North Downs Way (NDW), a 130-mile picturesque walk from Farnham in Surrey to Dover in Kent. The NDW can be walked in one go over a period of 10/12 days or walked in daily sections the way I did it. I have now walked the NDW from start to finish on four separate occasions and still find the walk wonderfully inspiring, when I take into account the diverse flora and fauna one can experience along the way. For example, I would sit down on a fallen log or on the open chalk downland grass to eat my sandwiches and listen to a blackbird singing to me or ponder the complexities of this truly marvellous planet we live on.

Occasionally I would meet a fellow traveller walking in the opposite direction who would nod approval or give a reassuring smile, suggesting that we were both on the right highway of life. Other times I would come across those truly hardy souls on the downs or woods bedding down for the night in tents, or have seen them getting up in the morning to make breakfast outside their tents, using a little gas bottle to make tea or eating bread and sharing it with the birds. Most of the souls I meet walking along various tracks or byways of Britain have to a certain extent given up or never had a family life; they prefer their own company. I find it reassuring that increasing numbers of people are taking to walking in the environment in which our species evolved and in which we are adapted to live.

CHAPTER SIX

SOME SUCCESS AT LAST: UNIVERSITY LIFE. THE BENZODIAZEPINE LITIGATION, VOLUNTARY WORK WITH VICTIMS OF TRANQUILLISERS AND MEETING ANNA

Fitter and healthier from my long distance walking, in September 1992 I started my Access course in Croydon with renewed vigour, determined to be successful at something. The Access courses are nationally accredited by LOCF (London Open College Federation) with similar status to A-levels and can act as a springboard for those mature students who wish to go on to University, similar to the route my former school friend John Wilshaw took. LOCF provided-courses afford a comprehensive framework for the accreditation of adult learning. My Access Programme was based on obtaining credits; one credit represents notional learning of 30 hours, which is the total of average self-study time needed to achieve specified outcomes. I was awarded 29 credits at the highest level 4, and one credit at level 3. From the very outset I was motivated to read, write, listen and learn as much as possible having at the forefront of mind those bleak days when all seemed lost especially the overwhelming disappointment of being denied the earlier opportunity to educate myself. I was determined that the Access course I had embarked upon would be the start of my ascent to a higher way of being and understanding about myself and my existence.

The one-year Modular Access Programme was built around three main subjects of Psychology, Sociology and Social and Community Studies with other supporting subjects: Self-Management, Communication and Information Technology. What was interesting for me was that most of the various books that I had read on my own over the years in isolation became valuable tools when formally researching the main authors or ideas of a particular subject. For example, when researching for the Psychology element of the course I found, among others, that I had read and analysed some of the work of R.D. Laing. Others in the same or similar field of research that I had read or found useful for my essays were Freud, Jung, Ericson, Skinner and Rogers.

At Selhurst College where I read for my Access Programme, there was a large and modern up-to-date library system the likes of which I had not seen since my days at Hurst Road school. It was absolutely wonderful to be let loose as a student to be able to walk round at one's leisure looking at the huge number of books, papers, articles and DVDs available. When I was at school all those years ago I did not appreciate or understand the great value in book learning.

Another Access Programme subject that I was interested in was Sociology which included scientific materialism, the work of the German philosopher Karl Marx who wrote so powerfully about the human predicament in relation to alienation and capitalism. Alienation is something that I have experienced for most of my life whether in employment or not. But Marx highlighted the powerful demand that capitalism has over our waking lives for the incessant desire to keep making money for our masters, to the detriment of our individual freedom. That is why from a personal point of view I also became interested in existentialism with its inquiry into human beings, their freedom, responsibility, isolation and despair. Regarding my own wanderings throughout the years it could well be that I was fighting for my own freedom to choose, but at the same time was suffering from the punitive treatment prescribed by doctors who see patients as some sort of problem and not as a combination of a physical, mental and spiritual entity.

On a practical level I have thought more about those Victorian working-class heroes who refused to work in those dens of hell called factories. Instead they took to the roads, the byways of Britain, walking mainly around the countryside trying to scratch a living wherever they could, or even begging when things became tough. Indeed, I myself still observe this similar type of behaviour in individuals today when I have been long-distance walking around various places in Britain. By far most of them are males who for some reason, which I am unable to discern, stand out as being not just walkers but quintessential wanderers, loners or free spirits searching for their inner freedom. They appear to be all types of ages, classes, dressed clean and tidy notwithstanding that most of them have been camping or sheltering out on their own in solitude. But I am sure that there are many others who would label such people as shirkers, benefit cheats or workshy. All I say is, may those free spirits enjoy their wanderings off the beaten tracks, among nature, away from noise, pollution and the concrete jungles.

At this time my own personal life was back on an even keel. I enjoyed being on my own and my Access course was developing well, when one particularly sunny morning I received a phone call from one Dr Reg Peart who lived in Bournemouth. He went on to explain to me that he had trained as a nuclear scientist and had enjoyed a successful professional career both in the USA and Britain where several of his articles and papers had been published. Due to feeling unwell with a relatively minor problem, he consulted his GP who prescribed him tranquillisers (valium) which he took as he was told for one month. At the end of the month he went back to his GP as he did not feel well and explained that he thought his medication was now causing him a problem. His GP gave him another prescription for tranquillisers explaining to Dr Peart that it was his problem, and not the medication, that was causing him to be unwell. Visiting his GP for monthly consultations went on for a considerable time until he felt so ill that he had to take time off from his professional work.

Taking more time off from his job due to sickness was now causing him problems with his employer who after several months asked him to leave due to his ongoing medical condition. He continued to take tranquillisers until his medical problems became so disabling that he had to be admitted to a psychiatric hospital where he was given various treatments including electro convulsive therapy, without his legal consent. Electro convulsive therapy, not surprisingly, detrimentally affected Dr Peart's memory recall for the rest of his life. After his initial contact with the psychiatric services he never worked again; at one stage during his scientific career he was head-hunted, being admitted to various hospitals and clinics until he realised that all along it was tranquillisers that had caused him so much suffering. After that horrendous experience he refused all treatment and withdrew from tranquilliser addiction on his own which he found very difficult and without any support from his GP or NHS services. After my own experiences of withdrawing on my own from valium addiction, I can only applaud Dr Peart's courage for what can only be described as a brave act of self-reliance. Along with tranquilliser addiction he had also developed an alcohol problem so he started attending the weekly ten-steps to recovery programme run by Alcoholics Anonymous as a result of which he received great relief, being able to think for himself after several years of cognitive impairment. That initial powerful telephone conversation I had with Dr Peart had set in place for me the history of the Benzodiazepine prescribing culture that had been prevalent during the previous 20 years in Britain.

Due to the withdrawal of Legal Aid, Dr Peart, along with another person, had in 1993 started a self-help group called Victims of Tranquillisers (VOT) for those users who had been prescribed tranquillisers (which belong to the group of drugs known as Benzodiazepines (BZ), for example: valium, librium and ativan) and were now causing them various problems, including addiction. VOT was a self-supporting organisation without membership fees, its members being self-financing through their own efforts. Dr Peart had been given my contact details by a solicitor who was acting on behalf of many claimants who had been awarded legal aid to bring a class action for medical negligence against two of the pharmaceutical companies who had manufactured tranquillisers. After a lengthy telephone conversation with Dr Peart during which we discussed many things about tranquillisers, he offered me the voluntary position of London representative for VOT, and we made arrangements to meet several weeks later at his home in Bournemouth.

The Access Programme was progressing well and I was still focused on what I have called the main subjects of study: one of them including sociology, also the work of Marx whose formidable presence still continues to influence some of the world's political ideas today. Social mobility encouraged me to seek out education as a means to changing myself. There were other sociologists, such as Weber, Durkheim, Parsons, Miliband and Barrett, whose work had a forceful impact on my thinking at the time, and the latter would later become one of my sociology lecturers at City University. All of these people, and others, wrote about power stratification within competing groups relevant to class, gender and race and their arguments came to influence the way I understood the effects on the working classes and their life chances.

One's primary socialisation, influence of parent(s), money, material acquisition, education, all have their impact on the growing person and can dictate one way or another what a person can achieve in his life. At the age of 46 and after an intense year's study at further education, I had finally achieved some success by passing the Access

Programme which had come my way by hard work. It was a very moving moment for me when on the 18 July 1993 in the packed Fairfield Halls in Croydon, I walked up onto the stage, (the last time I did that was years ago at Hurst Road School), to receive my Access Modular Programme Credit Certificate from the principal of Croydon College. When the principal handed me my certificate, I thought, for a split second, that I was looking into the eyes of my smiling former Hurst Road headteacher—bless him. During the evening of celebration I sat down on a seat to cast my mind back to those dark days when I fought so hard to hang on to my sanity, and dare I say, there were occasions when I ventured into the realms of madness. However, along with some small success, which passing the Access Course gave me, there also began to emerge a muffled voice that I had not heard before but one that intermittently started to speak for me, unlike before, with a friendlier intention.

With a little success behind me, I was inspired to take the train down to Bournemouth station where Dr Peart was waiting to drive me to his small flat just off the main Boscombe Road. During the ten-minute drive I got the impression, subsequently confirmed by other visits, that it was a mainly middle-class area with well-maintained detached and semi-detached houses. There were also some family run hotels and B&B's, many with colourful large front gardens. Mind you, I nearly always visited Dr Peart when it was sunny so I may have got a false impression of the place but of course there were pockets of relative poverty.

When I entered Dr Peart's flat the whole living room space

was full of ring binders, books, bound articles, DVD's, videos and other paraphernalia, to the extent that there was just about enough room for two small armchairs which we occupied. There were books and ring binders even in his small hallway and bedroom. It is true to say that his whole *raison d'être* for living was to find the truth that lay behind so many innocent people being damaged by tranquillisers. Reg, as he preferred to be called, explained to me that other than a few books of his own, all the other information was connected one way or another to BZ litigation which he had collected from many sources during his VOT travels. When I first met Reg he was in his sixties, under six feet tall, a full head of hair, friendly, intelligent and a chain smoker. He had chain-smoked all his life, he explained to me, and years later he managed to stop smoking which, not surprising, caused him various problems. But I do not know if those related medical complications eventually killed him in October 2009.

During that first meeting, Reg and I discussed the many varied issues outstanding regarding the BZ class action. After the struggle to free himself from BZ, he had set up VOT because he believed that 'thousands of victims of tranquillizer damage are suffering alone in their homes all over the country, getting little or no support from the medical profession, but too frightened to venture out to seek help for themselves'. Due to his own painful experiences of BZ, Reg was acutely aware of the lack of support for people with tranquilliser problems and the ever growing social problems it presented, so that by setting up VOT there would be a phone number or postal address to contact where users would receive a friendly and supportive response. That was the reason why VOT had put in place representatives, who themselves had first-hand experience of tranquilliser damage, around Britain.

My role as the London contact for VOT would be to act as a supportive and sympathetic friend. Also as a representative one could, among many other things, help promote the understanding of the long-term physical, mental and sociological damage caused by BZ to the thousands of innocent people in Britain. At the end of the day, after many hours of discussion, I was emotionally and physically drained but had a much clearer understanding of my own 17 years of experience of taking BZ and how they had damaged me to such an extent that at times I was unable to function. Also I was now able to relate to the bigger BZ picture that was happening to many other people who had taken BZ in good faith and now had a drug-induced addiction.

On several occasions when I visited Reg, we would walk down to nearby Boscombe to have dinner together, sometimes in a local public house or in a cosy little family run café that he had been using since he first moved to Bournemouth. When I asked him about his life, he would reply in his usual calm manner, 'Well, at this stage in the game, what can I do about it? I took their medication in good faith and look what happened to me.' As a youngster Reg had been involved with most things, he played football, rugby, cycled a great deal, had many friends and enjoyed his life. He was also a studious person passing his A-levels which gained him a place in University where he excelled in the sciences passing out with a first class degree. He went on to research for several years eventually being awarded a Doctorate in the Atomic Sciences which would be his professional life's work, writing many science papers along the way. I asked Reg, when we were in a local café one day, what had happened to him, and he responded, smiling, 'We must go forward as there is much work we must do in bringing this BZ prescribing culture to the attention of politicians, the media and the medical profession, of how innocent everyday people's lives have been destroyed by Benzodiazepines.' That response was typical of him; he always wanted to use his limited time on this earth helping others. I shall always remember what he used to say or write to me: 'Don't let the buggers get you down.'

Back in London I had received a letter bringing good news informing me that as a consequence of my interview I had been accepted on a three-year philosophy course at City University in London to start in September 1993. I was so pleased all the hard work I did on the Access Programme had led to the beginning of a degree course which I would commence in September. During the last few months I had beavered away making several university applications for various courses around philosophy/sociology/psychology through the university admissions system but had only received two interviews with one acceptance which was fantastic for me because I would be going on to higher education—though I was also anxious about what lay ahead; anxious because most of the students would be young, energetic and motivated to be successful. Another factor I had to consider seriously was the financial consequences of studying for three years and how I would maintain myself on a meagre maintenance grant and student loans which would mean, I later realised, that I would also have to work at least part-time to supplement my income.

Over the past years I had continued to attend various concerts on my own in and around London. As my interest in the exciting era of rock/blues era grew I was still intrigued by those performers who were, by now, beginning to age somewhat. With that in mind, I bought a ticket to see Elton John at Wembley, not for the first time, to experience live the great showman that he is; moreover, I was intrigued to see him playing his diamond studded piano and singing a medley of his most successful songs that date way back to the days when he wore flamboyant clothes, glasses the size of a modern television and real hair. A true pinball wizard!

Another favourite singer/songwriter favourite of mine is still Bob Dylan (born Robert Zimmerman) who led the way in the 1960s with protest songs, something missing today, against American power that was constantly bombing those countries that did not fall in line with their values. His hero was the late Woody Guthrie who espoused the life of the Hobo travelling the railroad of the USA seeking a simple yet human way of life while at the same time singing songs that gave a voice to the downtrodden many. I first saw Bob Dylan perform live in the late1960s on the Isle of Wight during those heady days of beatniks, flower power and anti-establishment ways of living. Due to many bent tickets that were sold illegally, no one really knew how many people attended that Dylan concert but it was way beyond the official figure given by the police and local authority that tried to play down their security responsibilities.

I was there on one of those packed trains setting out early from Waterloo Station, full of young people with long hair carrying rucksacks and smoking cannabis unaware that the unsuspecting people of the Isle of Wight would be in for a torrid time from revellers. On the whole things went well with little criminality involved except bouts of drunkenness, cannabis smoking and minor damage to private property. Not surprising, the whole area of Freshwater was near packed with thousands of young people attending the concert who with flowers sewn in their long hair, danced and sang into the small hours. One of the problems I had, similar to many others, was going to the toilet in the early hours when it was still dark, and trying to find your way back among the thousands of small tents occupied by young vocal lovers expressing their passion for each other. Several times returning from the toilets I tripped over the guy ropes of tents when you usually heard 'fuck off' or 'steady on man' or 'are you blind you cunt' from the irate lovers inside.

During those very hot sunny days varied performers would occupy the stage for most of the day, strutting their stuff which varied from rock, blues, soul or protest within an atmosphere of friendship and goodwill. On the final two days of the concert I struck up a good camaraderie with a group of people from Scotland who were tenting not far from where I was pitched. They were all vocal Celtic football club supporters; when they were not listening to the live music they would sing football songs motivated by alcohol and their hate for Rangers supporters. But they were decent working people trying to make sense of the complex world they inhabited. After the concert had finished we exchanged personal details with one another but as usually happens on these occasions I did not hear from any of them again.

What did please me very much though was how relaxed and confident I felt now that I had been free of BZ for ten years. Cervical dystonia I would have for the rest of my life, there is no cure for it, but it was still a physical problem that I have to manage the best I could from day to day. The one major problem I had to contend with was the occasional jerking movements of the neck or body. Now that I did not have to contend with the debilitating side effects of BZ, I used relaxation exercises or meditation to help reduce the abnormal size of the left sternomastoid muscle which can send out painful muscle spasms or contractions. As I have highlighted above, alcohol is the one tried and tested method that always works when I am anxious, especially in stressful social situations. But of course one must be very cautious about not drinking too much alcohol to the point where it starts to become a difficult problem, although I must say I continue to drink on a regular basis aware of its positive and negative qualities for me.

Among the many other rock concerts that I have attended over the years, that stand out for all round professionalism, are Pink Floyd, Rolling Stones (and I have to state it once again) that melodious voice of Neil Sedaka. For the final time in 1994, I watched the latter, accompanied by his maturing daughter Dara, perform at the London Palladium in front of an appreciative maturing audience hearing him sing those golden oldies from the 1960s. It is not surprising that a few years ago Elton John, who so loved his singing, signed Sedaka up on his record label to perform at a number of venues and record songs with him. To conclude my experiences of a great performer, I was fortunate to see him many times and he epitomised those innocent teenage times by writing painful love songs. His appeal to many people, rightly or wrongly, was his clean cut straightforward image that portrayed a kind of honest decency.

The Rolling Stones is another band that I have watched quite a few times over the years, including in one of my old haunts in Twickenham, Eel Pie Island. In those early days the Island was full of young children seeking an alternative lifestyle to the one proffered at the time by parents and politicians, but it may well have changed or even closed since I went there. I went to many of those types of dives because you could be anonymous; in fact, that was part of the cult or game, so you score or buy illicit drugs from gangster-like figures who abounded in those places. The usual spiel in those days were 'Want some dope man?' or, 'Want some shit man?' or, 'Wanna buy blues, brother?'—things I was constantly asked by mostly young black men who had started frequenting those clubs.

Wherever they performed, the Rolling Stones were electrifying, especially in the 1960s when most of their music was free flowing, spontaneous and enjoyable. I was fortunate to have seen the late Brian Jones perform on the drums without constraint or inhibition, for several hours where without taking drugs it would not have been possible. The Rolling Stones, I remember, wrote the lyrics called 'Mother's little helper', referring to valium, and included in one of their songs, which at some stage in the 1970s was the most prescribed drug in the world.

Of all the rock groups that I have seen live, the most effective for me was Pink Floyd. When they performed at 'The Wall' concert at Earls Court, it remains the most powerful and memorable music that still resonates today. The packed arena that night experienced music integrated with physical symbolism most had not seen before. Along with a very high artificial wall, with its powerful, oppressive reality, various flying mechanical objects rained over the populace below. I suppose one of their most memorable songs was called 'Wish you were here', dedicated to one of the original band members, the late Sid Barrett. He only made the first record with Pink Floyd after contracting mental illness brought about by taking acid after which he slowly declined into oblivion. Among other considerations, the Pink Floyd with all their wealth and security were trying, I was led to believe, through their music, to understand the predicament of life. But it does help if you are in a predicament that you at least have enough money to fall back on until times change. The further lyrics, 'Two lost souls swimming in a fish bowl' from the above song somehow reminds me of the terrible predicament I was once in chasing my shadow or perhaps still am.

After studying for several months at the City University, where I found academic life at first to be quite an alien environment, things gradually began to fall into place with the support mostly from fellow students in my tutor group. Having at least half of your tutor group being mature students most certainly helped at first, like when it came to just finding your way around a large university, especially the next lecture room. But also other important places such as the restaurant, academic offices and of course the bar, where most social life went on, or if you preferred, you could use the small garden as a retreat for a short while detached from the onslaught of student life. There were two mature students in particular that I started hanging around with and in time a sincere friendship developed between the three of us. That friendship was confined not just to the University though that itself was enjoyable, but later on we met in various places around London such as the inevitable pubs, restaurants or parties. Due to the depth of my friendships with both Maria and Martin at the time, I would like to write en extended piece about both of them, bearing in mind as I do the extent of their influence upon me:

Maria had grown up in Manchester where her parents had developed a successful furniture business but had moved down to live in Virginia Water—a wealthy area in Surrey. In Manchester, after attending three different private girls' schools, her parents once again found her another fee paying mixed school for her down in Surrey which she said she did not like at all as most of the children there were snobs. In vain she asked her parents to move her to a state school without success, when suddenly one day when she was 14 years of age they relented, agreeing to her request to join the local state school. That did not last as Maria was not doing well academically so she was given a private tutor who helped her pass two A-levels. When she had finished with her private tutor she went to work for a friend of the family as a personal assistant to a solicitor for ten years. When I met her at the City University she was nearly thirty years of age and needed a degree to move on with her life. It was not surprising that Maria did well at University as she was intelligent, articulate and friendly. She was popular with most people, no doubt due to her genuine smiling face, positive attitude, and she became an integral part of social life, even performing in more than one of the plays there. During the short time I was at City

University, I think Maria and I fancied each other for a while but nothing came of it.

The other mature student that I got on well with was Martin:

He had been brought up somewhere not far from Rochdale where, during his early years, he had attended three local state schools, passed three A-levels and had worked for a local building company as a trainee engineer. He was thirty-five years of age when I first met him. Tall, well-built and handsome, Martin had been a successful rower, winning a bronze medal for the Great Britain team in the Commonwealth Games a few years ago. Unable to find or keep a decent job going, he had even tried unsuccessfully to work for his father who owned a large manufacturing business, but decided to move to London to read philosophy at City University.

The anticipated financial concerns that I had before the degree course started were well founded as four months later my cashflow was becoming stretched. I had at this stage thought about taking out a loan from my bank but was discouraged due to the high rates of interest. After seeking some employment guidance suggestions from Martin, I decided to follow up the temporary jobs adverts in the *Evening Standard* by faxing my C/V to them in Oxford Street. Fortunately I was interviewed at their plush West End premises by a rather high flying chap called Tarquin, (yes I know), who promised me the world; he explained he had placed me as a table clearer in an Italian restaurant in Soho for two weeks, back on my old stomping ground again, after which he would get me a temporary job as a night porter.

What an education it was being a table clearer in Soho, much more insightful than cramming for three years on a degree course! The owner was not Italian, but French; his wife was Danish and three of the other staff were Indians who could not speak very much English and looked like the Asian version of 'Last of the Summer Wine'. The last employee, Sammy, was a third generation Italian who could not speak the language, was born in Cornwall but sounded like a cross between Barbara Windsor and Frank Bruno. There was laughter every five minutes especially when the oldest Indian chap, nicknamed Rooney, used to regularly put the wrong food on customers' plates. Rooney prepared the food at the back of the restaurant, usually wearing an 'I love Imran Khan' T-shirt, constantly playing 'Jerusalem' so loud that you could hear it coming from his earpiece as he happily chopped the tomatoes or garlic.

The French owner, nicknamed President DeGaulle, and another one of the Indian workers, nicknamed Alex Ferguson, used to have regular shouting rows with each other. De Gaulle would shout something at Alex Ferguson in French, raising his clenched fists as he did so; then the latter would shout back in Urdu holding a rather large spatula, intimating that he would smash it over the boss' head. The French owner's wife, nicknamed Lulu, at the end of the day would try to wash the kitchen floor free of the accumulated day's fat and vegetable peelings when on cue Sammy would walk straight through it wearing his Wellington boots, to the anger of Lulu who would invariably tell him to 'piss off, you moron'. And so it continued as the third Indian male, nicknamed Winston, would ask his colleagues who wanted an afternoon drink. Winston would ask me, 'Mr Bazzy you like drink today?'

'Yes!' I would say with devilment in mind, 'I would like lavatory varnish topped up with Brylcreem please Winston.' He would go off happily to make drinks for all of us. When he returned on this particular occasion he said, long faced to me, 'Today no drink you want Mr Bazkan please. De Gaulle say no wood varnish left.' Incidentally, according to De Gaulle, Winston had been trained in Bombay as a heating engineer, but when he came to London some ten years ago he was unable to work due to his inability to communicate effectively in English. Winston's hobby was collecting cigarette packets which he picked up anywhere in public.

The restaurant itself had been professionally decorated only three years before when the present incumbent bought the place before running a small popular wine bar in Rupert Street. The present restaurant in Greek Street had been painted gold, blue and silver in mixed parallel lines with new air vents, decorated with masses of Italian plants intermixed with soft warm blue lights. I must say that the French owner had spent a lot of money on the place, even though I thought he did not use the space to its full potential, insisting that his late mother's old gold-plated vase be the centre of attraction on the counter, though certain employees used it as a spittoon or tried to push it over onto the floor.

Notwithstanding all the foibles going on, it was certainly attractive and popular enough for the many customers who would travel far and near to eat some of their favourite Italian dishes at reasonable prices. For two hours at lunchtime and three hours in the evening the restaurant was very busy serving meals and where I would work non-stop clearing the sixty covers that would be occupied during peak time. Many times while clearing tables I would accidentally drop crockery and cutlery, mostly on the floor inside but occasionally on the ground outside the restaurant. Fortunately for me I only ever dropped one piece of crockery, a plate with left-over vegetables on it, over one of our regular customer's clean trousers, who was most kind over the incident and brushed aside any concerns.

Another time a rather attractive well-dressed middle-aged Frenchwomen called one afternoon to order cake and coffee. She removed her rather elegant tortoiseshell coloured hat and coat, and placed them over the chair next to her so she could start to eat her cake; when I walked past I somehow caught my foot on the rather large strap of her white leather bag, thereby dragging the bag, jacket and hat with me for a couple of feet. I was so embarrassed by the incident, even more so when I realised that I had inadvertently dragged her attire through tomato sauce on the pavement. After apologising profusely for my behaviour to the relaxed smiling woman, I volunteered to take her clothes to be cleaned at the back of the restaurant. I even agreed to take the clothes for the lady right away to a nearby shop to have them cleaned and I would pay the bill. Both the owner of the restaurant and the lady concerned refused to let me take her clothes for cleaning as the incident was an accident and no lasting damage had been caused.

That job in Soho, which was originally only for a few weeks, eventually came to an end four months later when they took on a full-time employee. Although the money had been very useful, if I wanted to be successful now was the time to start making more of an effort with my BSc course. I found the sociology lectures given by Michael Barnett very interesting; he talked articulately about the position of women within industrialised societies from a Marxist point of view. My weekly tutorial groups were also very interesting. The diversity of the students, who came from various backgrounds, certainly made for fiery debates. I also found study groups useful, bearing in mind I had returned to education after some thirty years' absence; indeed, I found the approach to research sometimes difficult to sort out. It was helpful to work through small projects at home as this gave me more confidence, I thought, when exams came round. I managed to present my essays on time, covering several different subjects, and overall I received a pass mark for my academic work which I found reassuring. Three weeks prior to the exams I read for about twelve hours a day at various times so that I could cover most of the subjects we had researched during the year. I can remember it was a very stressful time indeed for me where eating meals at proper times, sleeping and even washing had to fit round my near obsession of focusing on passing my exams. On the first day of my first exam, sociology, I felt terrible and in no way did I feel prepared for sitting a three-hour exam. After the first exam I joined my fellow students in the bar for a well-earned pint of beer, not forgetting that within the next four days I would have to pass three more exams if I wanted to progress into the second year of the BSc course.

I was mortified when three weeks later my exam results were posted through my letterbox stating that apart from sociology, I had failed all my exams. At this stage I had to give clear thought to where I was now going and what I wanted to do. For example, did I want to re-sit the failed exams, or move onto another degree course at a different university, or finish with education altogether and find a job having at least passed the Access Course? I decided to discuss my options with Martin, Maria, my Tutor and Anna who was my neighbour.

Anna is an attractive blonde, a Danish woman who I had first seen sweeping the leaves from her front garden path. I decided to ask her out for a drink and ever since we have had on the whole a most enjoyable and rewarding seventeen years' relationship that continues to this day. She had herself trained as a fine artist at Goldsmiths College in South London and subsequently went on to follow a teacher training course at Surrey University. As she was now teaching, Anna was very well placed to give me professional advice about my next educational move or tips about re-joining the world of work.

In January 1993 many thousands of claimants in the BZ medical negligence case were informed, by the large number of solicitors involved, of a significant court appearance in the Strand, London. The court appearance was the beginning of the discharge of Legal Aid Certificates that would see a huge number of claimants reduced to a small group. Victims of Tranquillisers from now on would represent, along with a solicitor who worked for free, former claimants at various court proceedings where we would henceforth be known as Litigants in Person. Over time a lot of those former claimants would express their understandable bitterness at being damaged by BZ, unable to work for many years due to addiction and now they were being denied their day in court.

Furthermore, due to individual BZ problems, many of them had only managed to buy no more than a small house, and along with the support of spouses or families, were not prepared to finance their own court case by jeopardizing their only security. In the wake of BZ Legal Aid being withdrawn from a number of solicitors, users and many other interested bodies involved in a whole range of activities, there was a tumult of activity. This included television and radio interviews, conferences with different health professionals to discuss a way forward, court appearances to discuss the financial viability for the BZ class action, meetings with case experts and finally at the House of Lords an Appeal which led to all BZ cases being struck out.

Undeterred, we continued on with what we considered a justified action even though we had been badly let down by the Legal Aid Board. From originally acting as a pressure group, VOT now saw itself as a pro-active medico-legal group as well as having to support claimants with their many problems, who had nowhere else to go, as their former professionals had dumped them. As mentioned above, that was when Dr Peart's great practical idea of having VOT representatives at the end of a phone in various places in the UK very helpful for those people who were still suffering from the intrinsic addictive properties of BZ. As the London VOT representative for several years, I was shocked, saddened and angered by a lot of the painful stories I had listened to by people of different class, race, sex and age. Many times in the small hours, when my phone was ringing, I had been wakened by a frightened, sobbing person who was confused by the various BZ withdrawal symptoms they were experiencing and yet had no-one to turn to. In was at these times that I thought about my own pernicious experiences of BZ side effects and withdrawal that no doubt induced me to wander aimlessly all over London crying out for help yet lost to the world. One woman phoned me on a regular basis for at least two years since she was experiencing particularly nasty withdrawal symptoms, whether in actuality or otherwise, of insects crawling over her body.

Another woman who had been taking BZ for many years had been diagnosed with various mental health conditions such as schizophrenia, depression and personality disorder. She had also been sectioned on two occasions, been thrown out of her social housing and ostracised by most of her family. There was one man who used to phone me, usually at night, when he had powerful impulses to visit various places where he thought people might help him even though he had no connection to these places. Other times he was desperate to visit as many doctors as possible to explain to them the massive BZ problems they had caused innocent people around Britain. He articulated that by travelling to obscure places where he was not known, only then could he be himself and act spontaneously. All the above are by no means isolated or unusual as I have spoken to many people who hitherto had normal behaviour but had changed abnormally when they started ingesting BZ. The three people cited above all recovered from their awful way of life. Also what must be remembered today in the 21st century is that even short-term ingestion of BZ can develop into a hidden addiction where most people do not present themselves at GP surgeries or hospital waiting rooms for treatment.

It is heart-breaking to think that there are still many users out there who are addicted to their prescribed medication and yet the medical profession is doing nothing about it. Similar to my own experiences, very few people are offered any alternative non-medical treatments such as psychotherapy or counselling. Benzodiazepine prescribing is on the increase and has been for a number of years, but the new British Government (2011) have said that they recognise there is a problem with BZ and are going to put in place effective treatment programmes to support those people who are experiencing side effects and/or withdrawal problems. We are not overly optimistic that these 'new' treatment regimes will ever be implemented. Hitherto most BZ users had nowhere to go for help; instead, like Reg Peart and I, and no doubt countless hundreds of others, had to experience the shivers of 'cold turkey' or replace their current BZ with another abuse of more alcohol. I certainly wish all those years ago I had been informed of the inherent dangers of mixing BZ with alcohol whereby my quality of my life could have been very different. Over the years many GP's had neither the time nor the inclination to educate their patients about the pitfalls of taking BZ medication, and instead had complete faith in what they had prescribed.

Over the years many former BZ users who had been withdrawing from BZ were offered anti-psychotic drugs which is very short sighted treatment indeed, as many people regard their use over the last 40 years as scandalous, since they have multitudinous side effects. Largactil is one of the notorious anti-psychotic drugs that was the drug much abused in the days gone by in the large psychiatric hospitals. Indeed, my former friends who worked as nurses in a psychiatric hospital in Epsom during the 1960s saw how detrimental Largactil, and other anti-psychotics, were to the well-being of patients. The only time I presented myself when drunk or experiencing BZ side effects at my local Epsom Hospital was sometime in the 1970s. After waiting for three hours, a psychiatrist arrived from one of the local former large hospitals to talk to me. Straightaway I recognised his face, although I had never been one of his patients, through photographs in the local newspaper as being one of those old time servers, institutionalised, similar to his unfortunate patients. He didn't want to hear about my problems, and within three minutes he had prescribed me a month's supply of Largactil which I thought grossly incompetent; but in those days, who would have been prepared to listen to a uneducated immature young working-class person? Suffice to say after I took two Largactil, which knocked me senseless, I threw the remainder of them into the Thames. Finally on the subject of anti-psychotics, I was researching the subject on a BBC 4 programme in 2010 when the late former consultant psychiatrist at one of the Epsom psychiatric hospitals stated that anti-psychotics were all but useless treatment for patients. Suffice to say there is a huge list of BZ symptoms that can detrimentally affect people for many years, but the painful effort to withdraw from these drugs is worthwhile because eventually a different person will emerge to re-engage with the world once again.

There was one last BZ action we could embark on and that was an appeal to the European Court on Human Rights. Liberty took up the VOT case, introduced under article 25 of the Convention against the United Kingdom, and argued unsuccessfully that we were entitled to have our case argued in open court. There are many good decent people that I have met during the whole BZ saga who I cannot name due to legal reasons or the restrictions of this book. Suffice to say without their professionalism, commitment and humanity we would not have got this far with our justified case. There were a few claimants, including myself, who were fortunate enough to have their individual cases assessed by two case experts who did support most of the claimants. I would now like to give a brief synopsis of the two medical assessments carried out on my behalf by two case experts for the Legal Aid Board:

(1) 'The chief symptoms complained of retrospectively are characteristic of those listed in the Roche data sheets. The severity of the symptoms and their duration individually cannot be supplied at this late date, and the client should not be discredited for his difficulty in accurately remembering or for the lack of documentation to support his contention. His account given in the above interview, together with the summaries of the notes and records obtained, give a sufficient general picture to support the issuing of proceedings. The very substantial recovery following withdrawal tends to further support his claim.' P. Graham Woolf, Consultant Psychiatrist. 1992.

(2) 'A conservative estimate would be that at least 80% of the mild cognitive problems revealed by the neurological assessment, that is, poor short term retention on material and some discrepancy between pre-morbid and current intellectual ability can be attributed to chronic Benzodiazepine use with some confidence. The doctor makes a conservative estimate that about 50% of your

underdevelopment in the social/career spheres of life can be attributed to chronic use of Benzodiazepines which obviously in this case is Valium. Therefore the report does support in parts that you have suffered from cognitive problems being the result of chronic Benzodiazepine use.' Dr Marjan Jahanshahi. 1992.

Finally the one person I would like to thank publicly is the late Dr Reg Peart whose unstinting hard work and commitment in trying to obtain justice for those individuals damaged by prescribed BZ would have been more of a tragedy without his skilful intervention. It is commendable that this stoical man beavered away month after month in his little flat trying to bring attention to the many different professionals and Institutions the insidious BZ prescribing culture that had silently but powerfully overtaken the inner lives of millions of innocent people. I am most grateful for what Reg achieved for me and many other people who at least had the opportunity to understand through his hard work, and others, that it was BZ medication and not our personality deficiencies or character weaknesses that damaged us.

During this most intense time of VOT legal activities, I had applied and been successful in securing a place at Kingston University on their two-year Diploma in Social Work course starting in early1995. Finally I came to the conclusion that at the age of 48 it was clear that I needed to earn a living from any subsequent education or training in which I had participated, and importantly, I knew I had to take out loans to support myself through two years of study. The Social Work course was a practical based course where in time I could make a living through my own efforts and also I could bring a wealth of personal experience to the course to guide me through a sustained two years of study and two demanding work placements. Having been personally addicted to prescribed BZ with all the problems that had caused me, perhaps it still does, it could give insights whereby I could hopefully support those people self-harming and suffering from drug misuse to gain some control of their lives.

The student group at Kingston University was very much larger but racially similar to the one I had seen on my course at City University. Of the approximate 50 students on the social work course, about 50% were non-white people, which I thought at the time more than represented the diverse society we all lived in. When I first arrived at Kingston University, I was based at the Kingston Hill Campus which was going through an extensive building programme to bring it up to a University level standard from its previous status as a Polytechnic. Among other changes they made, the University greatly enlarged the library, lecture rooms, access roads and parking facilities in particular, which was reassuring for those mature students who had to drive cars to collect their children after lectures. Some also went on to work in the evenings.

In common with most institutions that I have been to, it took me time to settle down at Kingston University by regularly attending lectures, visiting the library to take books out for study and research which I mainly did at home. It was very interesting listening to the stories that some of my colleagues had to tell about their experiences of care work in various Local Authority, Independent, and Private residential homes. Most of what these students had to say was relevant because of the nature of the social work course where we would soon all be on our first year placements working with different client groups. There were a few students in my cohort who had no practical experience of care work but were on the course due to having brought up their own children. Many of the lectures we had were interesting and yet hotly debated by some of the more vocal students in the group who had the confidence, unlike me, to challenge the status quo espoused by various researchers.

Being acutely aware that dystonia can at times be severely exacerbated by anxiety, I came to realise, pretty quickly, that I would have to try to make adaptations at Kingston University. Most of the time I used to sit at the back of the lecture room or tutor group hoping that I would not be recognised too much which was unnecessary as I was undermining myself. On one occasion, when I had to deliver a piece of work myself in front of students, I completely froze, unable to get the words out. I was so humiliated and devastated by the experience that I did not return to the afternoon session with my fellow students. Instead I took the bus to Kingston Town to get drunk.

Many times when I had been drinking I would become aware of how a random innocent look from someone in the same pub could sometimes be frightening to the point that occasionally it seemed to penetrate my inner life. It was only around about this time that I became preoccupied with how much energy and time I was wasting on unproductive observation and fantasy. I had even thought about throwing it all away, even though I had done well so far at college, because I could not take any more of being constantly undermined by my past life. However, probably due to the nature of the social work course, I did at this time begin to think that I must have had difficulties developing close emotional relationships due to the fact that I nearly always chose solitary activities. That meant over many years I had not received the warm support that friends and family can offer, but what about those individuals who are loners, like me, who appear to function quite productively on their own? The realisation was that I had not functioned as a mature person very well at all, and it began to dawn on me once again how underdeveloped I really was.

After several months of diligent study both at my home and down at the local library, where I managed to present all my essays on time, I was so thrilled at the end of the year to have been informed that I had passed all my work which was for me a minor miracle. Socially I did not spend much time with any of my cohort except with a chap called Gordon who lived not far from London Bridge. Gordon had throughout the years worked in many different social care jobs but was unable to apply for the more senior positions due to being unqualified, hence his presence on the course. He was about 40 years of age, short, with longish brown hair that reminded me of the hippy days in the 1960s. Born in Cornwall, his parents were divorced, his mother moved to London, where she found a job at Harrods as a dress designer where she worked for the rest of her working life. Gordon went to local schools but as he did not get any qualifications he left school aged 16 and found a semi-skilled job working as a technician with the BBC based at Shepherds Bush. 'Do you know, Barry, that people used to call the BBC the "bum boys club" but it has changed a lot in the last twenty years or so?' Gordon told me, smiling, sinking his second pint in thirty minutes. We used to enjoy going for a few beers together in Kingston Town after lectures or occasionally when we had a free day off from University.

When it came to money Gordon was a shrewd character, as he knew lots of people where he could earn cash in hand working on building sites, or driving or even putting flyers through letterboxes. There was something I really liked about the initiative and common sense that Gordon had in his everyday dealings with most people. I thought he would make an ideal social worker who would be aware of the practicalities of people needs, and how to empower them to speak up for themselves.

There were two important issues that I would have to deal with if I was to make progress with my social work course. Fast approaching was my first placement that I would have to prepare myself for as it would be in a very demanding methadone treatment centre in Kingston called Kaleidoscope. The other issue was similar to my short time stint at City University. I had to find a job to earn some money to pay my way as the student maintenance grant topped up with loans would not be enough to see me through the course. With some luck one of the students on my course had been working for an old established social care charity called Safecare based in Sutton and he informed me they were opening up a new residential home for users with mental health needs in Kingswood, Surrey. After a successful interview for the job of carer the charity placed me at their new mental health home in Kingswood working three evenings a week from 7 p.m. to 10 p.m. I found the work demanding which is not surprising considering that during the day I had now started my first placement which I had to attend five days a week. All this travelling would not have been possible if Anna had not been so kind to drive me to the evening job and drive me back home. At Safecare the evening work was mainly assisting the five residents to cook their supper, clean up after they had finished and give them their medication. Sometimes I would work the occasional weekends to cover staff sickness or holidays; this was when I was assigned to take out one of the residents who had a mental health abnormality called obsessive compulsive disorder (OCD). As Safecare was my first paid care job, I had not seen this type of unusual abnormal behaviour before although I had seen this cruel condition explained by psychiatrists on the television, radio and I had read about it in various books. I used to walk with the young man in question for about two or three hours around the local woods occasionally stopping for him to collect various leaves he would later draw in his room.

On one particular occasion while I was out walking with Richard, he got hold of a wastepaper bin and threw it into the air emptying all the rubbish on to the ground. Only some 50 yards away was an elderly lady who was taking her dog for a walk on the attractive downs and saw what had happened, then made her way towards us. At first, understandably, she pointed at Richard, asking in an irritated manner, 'Why did that young man throw all that awful rubbish onto the ground?' 'I am so sorry madam,' I said apologising for his behaviour and I explained to her that he had a mental health problem called OCD to which she was very sympathetic. I continued working for

Safecare for another two months before deciding that I should put my energy into my first social work placement at the Kaleidoscope Project in Kingston, Surrey.

The Kaleidoscope Project was opened in 1968 by the then Minister of John Bunyan Church, Eric Blakebrough, that provided a sanctuary for young homeless drug addicts where they would receive support and the hand of friendship. His book *No Quick Fix* is an important and fascinating account of the on-going spiritual journey of a local church that became experts in providing social and community services for those in desperate need. On my first day, as I walked into the project, I automatically realised—how could I forget?—that these users were the sorts of people that I had seen, even drank with at times, around various London pubs, clubs and parks. There always appears to be a stigma associated with those people who congregate in numbers usually consuming alcohol, sometimes smoking cannabis and whose appearance does not fit in with the social norm

When I noticed a small group of youngsters the other day drinking out of beer cans outside Waterloo Station I assumed that some of them were homeless due to the way they were dressed, and the state of their hair gave me the impression that they had been sleeping rough for some time. But when I went up to one of the group, a young girl, who was begging, she told me that six out of the eight people there were living in regular hostels in the West End that were provided by the local council. She came across as intelligent, articulate and was fully aware of her surroundings to the extent that we started up a meaningful conversation that covered subjects such as drugs, homelessness and politics. Emma explained frustratingly, ‘Me and three of my friends have various qualifications but were only able to find unskilled night work cleaning the floors of large London Hotels, which we had declined.’ The reason they had declined work, which could have given them some income at least, was that the council at the time would have taken away their hostel entitlement because of their income. What an absurd policy, that states when you earn so much money you then have to make your own accommodation arrangements, leaving potential vulnerable youngsters, if the work finishes, on the streets to fend for themselves. As Emma explained to me, ‘Due to the nature of hotel contract cleaning, it can last for as long as six months or as short as four weeks. If you start work, and have to leave council accommodation, then find yourself unemployed, you are back on the streets again, so what is the point?’

Emma was joined by two of her friends, Bill and Jake, who also lived in the hostel with her when they were not travelling around the country listening to musical concerts. Jake, also intelligent, explained, ‘The label given to us by various people is only a projection of their own thoughts and feelings and not based on reality.’ ‘Because we are dressed like this,’ Jake said with conviction, ‘most people think we are tramps or drug addicts, which is certainly not the case.’ He went on to say, looking me straight in the eyes, ‘None of us here have taken anything stronger than alcohol and cannabis.’ I thought to myself, why do policy makers continue to make life difficult for people, like the decent intelligent youngsters here who want to make something of their lives, yet hurdles are constantly put in their way?

After several of my cohort and I had met the various workers around the project, I was assigned a teacher who had been with Kaleidoscope for many years as volunteer and then employee. It was because of her and many other people's generosity that allowed Kaleidoscope to develop its services that would help many young alienated people back into mainstream society. During the first few weeks Sandra helped me find my way around the large project which was made up of a multi-story building for youngsters who were residents; facilities included a kitchen and large dining room, where a hot meal was provided every day, various offices for workers, and a general purpose meeting room. The Kaleidoscope interior was painted with several different bright colours which no doubt illumined the working culture there. So that we could meet most of the day project users, social work students worked first of all in the kitchen servery selling tea, coffee and food to the many people who came along mainly to receive their prescribed methadone; but some would also stay around to eat, for many, their only meal of the day. Regards methadone, the official state medication for heroin addicts, students would assist staff to give users their daily computer controlled amount which was prescribed by psychiatrists working at the project.

Around about this time I had anticipated that during the next two years, I had decided to stay on at Kingston for an extra year to finish the degree, I would experience many challenges to my inner resources, I decided to have an assessment for psychotherapy. Notwithstanding all my past problems, and there had been many, I was determined that this would be the opportunity for me to grow and develop into a much stronger person who in time, I hoped, would be able to take charge of his life. I had discussed the proposition of psychotherapy with my tutor who at first thought it was not such a good idea due to the nature of the work at Kaleidoscope, but after reflection she changed her mind, which did encourage me somewhat.

After visiting their crisis centre in North London, I embarked on three years of psychotherapy with Arbours. The Arbours Association was founded in 1970 providing sanctuary over the years for 'people in great emotional turmoil, without their having to be seen, called or treated as "mentally ill" ' (Sanctuary, 1995). Once a week after training at Kaleidoscope, thereafter at University, I would take the train from Kingston Station to Denmark Hill Station in South London where on each occasion I would meet with Clive, my psychotherapist, for fifty-minute sessions.

I found the daytime training, weekly psychotherapy sessions, and in addition, working in a new job two or three evenings a week in a residential home, very challenging indeed. There were many times when I was overwhelmed by anxiety, when I felt like I wanted to leave all my commitments behind, but I found the resilience supported by Clive to keep going. There were times when I arrived so anxious at Denmark Hill Station that I just had to unwind in the pub, which at the time was in the former station waiting room, before invariably arriving late for my psychotherapy session. I don't think Clive was that impressed, not, surprisingly, by my eccentric behaviour, but he never really stated anything to the contrary, although he skilfully reminded me of the next session.

Throughout my life I have had intense feelings that everything was about to fall apart in my life, leaving me with little but chaos on a grand scale. I can always remember, starting with my classroom experience many years ago, that I have this acute longing to be accepted by people just for who I am as a flawed human being. Many times over the years when I had been out with people I have had the impulse to ask them, 'Do you like me?', looking for the reassuring nod. Perhaps my life so far has been one long painful journey trying to find someone who wanted to spend some time with me unconditionally, but no doubt that applies to half of humanity.

After a few weeks of orientating themselves at Kaleidoscope, all social work students were expected to mentor one or two centre clients with their everyday lives supporting them to access various services or help them to adapt to certain changes they needed to make. The young woman I had worked with for several months came from a dysfunctional London family where her parents had been abusing her and her three siblings for years to the extent that the children were placed into the legal custody of the council. Daisy had herself, throughout the years abused various illegal drugs whereby on many occasions she had to be hospitalised for her own safety. Now in her early thirties, she had worked hard to minimise her drug taking and consequently was living on her own in a council owned flat, had a part-time job working in an office and had enrolled on an evening creative writing course. By the end of my training at Kaleidoscope, I had got to know Daisy well who in a few months had worked hard to move away from her previous chaotic life. Like so many people, including myself, whose lives had previously been fraught with complex problems, it is difficult, to be very honest, to know what can be done to help so many tragic individuals who have fallen through life's safety net. I greatly admire the amazing amount of motivation that is required by vulnerable people like Daisy to change the destructive conditions that once overwhelmed her to find some peace in life.

My social work training at Kaleidoscope came to an end for what was for me an incredibly moving experience. Other than learning the important professional competence of being able to communicate with other agencies to access various services for people, I was humbled by so many decent human beings on both sides of the fence who reminded me of the value of each individual life.

During the latter part of the first year of my social work course at Kingston University, due to the lack of money, I had to work as a part-time project worker in Croydon for The Mental After Care Association (MACA). Once again it was Anna, as she did at Safecare, who used to drive me to the large detached residential home, and after my shift completed, would drive me back home. She never complained about driving me at night sometimes through howling wind, driving rain or even in dense low lying fog. MACA had numerous residential homes around London where they supported people in the management of their mental health problems. Some of the older residents where I worked had been incarcerated in the large mental hospitals for many years, many of them forgotten by the world.

For example, one cold winter evening James told me a rather moving account of how he had been hospitalised at the early age of 18 having had a 'psychotic breakdown', but used to see his parents on brief visits only a few times. James, who had been in a mental hospital for about 40 years, had always thought, he said rather sadly to me, 'that my father, who was a successful architect, had been disappointed that his son had not gone to university and trained to be a lawyer or doctor'. Over a cup of tea I asked James, 'Looking back on your life, what do you think about your father's attitude to your problems, and did you ever discuss them with your parents?' 'Well Barry,' he said hesitantly, 'I was too ill to do anything with my life but my father never really accepted the extent of my mental illness.' He went on after lighting up another cigarette, 'In the mental hospital I had some good friends, even a girlfriend who I used to meet in the patients' café in the evening for a tea, but as we were segregated in those days in single sex wards, I was never allowed to visit her there.' He continued, 'I never wanted to leave the hospital, but they said I had to move into the community. I would love to move back to the hospital, because I am lonely here, and I don't like going to the post office to get my pension.' James expressed in no uncertain terms his dislike of the modern world. With tears in my eyes, I had to leave the room, making an excuse that something had to be sorted out elsewhere in the building.

Once again a truly moving, tragic story of one individual person whose sum total of life consisted of his old dusty medical notes citing different spurious diagnoses written by psychiatrists long since dead. James explained to me, as did other residents, that he smoked so much because in the large psychiatric hospitals a nurse or other worker would leave a group of patients to work on their own but after finishing some menial task all they could do was smoke until someone collected them. Many times since starting my social work course I had thought that I was not equipped to be a social worker because of my sympathies, which threatened to overwhelm me, for the many victims of punitive policies.

One of the more enjoyable activities in which any of the twenty residents could participate was working in the large Victorian garden that MACA had inherited when they purchased the house. Apparently still in existence are black and white photographs of the house when it had been owned by a wealthy tea merchant, showing a large number of employees working in the garden growing all manner of fresh vegetables for the master's many children to eat. At MACA the younger residents in particular were encouraged, with support of a project worker, to browse through gardening magazines or visit a nearby shop in Croydon to purchase various plants or seeds to plant in the garden. This encouragement was an attempt at counteracting the apathy brought about by ingesting strong medication on a regular basis, which can have the effect of reducing a resident's motivation. Many would sit smoking in front of the television all day accumulating weight on their expanding waistlines.

In spite of the fact that my professional, educational and therapy activities were all taking place at the same time, my relationship with Anna, my neighbour, was developing very well for both of us. For the first time in my life I was having regular contact with someone who was intelligent, kind and friendly, and with whom I was still in love with. Anna was born in Jutland, Denmark, has an older sister and younger brother who died several years ago from cancer. She had travelled to England with a friend when she was still a teenager primarily to learn English as part of her career development. After doing various short-term jobs, she had found a much sought after job as a secretary/translator at a Danish newspaper in London, with a view to becoming a journalist, and got married. At the time of her divorce Anna moved into the attractive, four-storey Edwardian house where she still lives. The house is imaginatively decorated and the walls are hung with lots of original paintings and drawings.

The one activity, which has subsequently developed into a passion, that Anna and I have enjoyed from the outset is local, national, even European walking although due to age creeping up on us we have both slowed down somewhat. Our lives consist not just of walking, however; we also have visited many London art exhibitions, watched numerous plays and listened to both operas and concerts. To attend live operas such as *The Marriage of Figaro*, *Aida*, *Madam Butterfly* and *La Boheme* is an unforgettable experience brought about due to Anna's generosity. Her intense passion for the Arts in general, but fine Art in particular, is something that has encouraged my deeper participation over the years.

We have held numerous enjoyable parties at Anna's comfortable home over the years for our various friends and families, especially those on the Danish side who regularly visit. I find nearly all the Danes rather adaptable, full of common sense and pragmatism; besides, contrary to what some people think, they have a good sense of humour. That Danish humour is understandable in the light of their culinary predicament. It must be problematic when you think about their preoccupation with having to cook different creative meals three hundred and sixty five days of the year from just one animal—the poor old pig!

There were also other parties that we held for our close British friends such as Martin, Maria, Daniel, Mick and Lucy and many others. On one occasion that I remember well, we celebrated my 50th birthday with various friends from City University, Kingston University and walking friends. That particular day, I thought to myself, after so many fruitless barren years, there were friends around to witness not just my birthday, but also my personal growth, and ultimately my life. Due to the reasons that I have highlighted elsewhere, at first I did not find it easy to attend events such as parties, where people are gathered around a usually small table enjoying themselves in different ways. Without the added confidence crutch of alcohol before those various gatherings, I would usually place myself on the periphery until such time that some alcohol at least had passed my lips to render me a part of the proceedings.

Many times while on holiday in Denmark, Anna and I have lived in an attractive summer house, a national enjoyment for many Danes, which was owned by a family member. Living in a summer house environment for two weeks gives you the much needed opportunity to be free of the everyday noise of vehicles, of ugly concrete high-rise buildings or the putrid smell of beef burger bars. Walking tracks here are devoid of the intrusion of street lighting.

At night everything was pitch black, yet the eyes adapt quickly to be able to experience, the first time for me without the intrusion of artificial light, trillions of stars in the sky above. It was a sheer delight to wake up early in the morning to a quiet breakfast outside on the veranda listening to the deep melodic sound of an old male pheasant that had been around for some time inspecting his territory.

Many times it was so delightful to have had various family members and friends visit us in the summer house, sometimes unannounced, for breakfast, lunch or dinner; sometimes they would stay overnight or even for a few days, and bring along a bottle of wine or two to share at dinner time. Summer house living is a special time for most Danish families as it gives them the opportunity to get away from their town life for a few weeks' holiday. A wonderful quality that I enjoy about Anna, something that incorporates everything I have said about her, is her infectious positive aptitude which is to get off her backside and do something about whatever situation she finds herself in—an ideal attitude to have when you are living in a summer house for two weeks.

CHAPTER SEVEN

MY FATHER DIES, WALKING HOLIDAYS AND FRIENDSHIPS

Our first walking holiday together was with Countrywide Holidays, a firm favourite with families, based within the beautiful Lakeland fells made famous by the late writer, cartographer and fell walker, Alfred Wainwright. Subsequently, AW, as he was known to countless numbers of walkers, became one of my heroes because of the immense effort he made to educate himself when growing up in deprived industrial Blackburn. That enabled him to move away to develop a successful career eventually becoming Borough Treasurer with Kendal Borough Council. During the seven days walking holiday Anna and I, along with twenty other walkers, lodged in a large attractive house where we had our own comfortable room but shared the showers and toilets. We both very much enjoyed the camaraderie among the walking group where in the mornings and evenings we would help with the washing up, cleaning and laying cutlery on the tables for the next meal. Whether at meals or walking the fells, fellow walkers told me stories of their many cherished experiences of walking holidays when they were young children with their families, when they would travel from home by train to various places around the country for two weeks of enjoyable walking.

Similar to other industrialised nations, where people worked physically hard for long hours in mines, factories and shipyards, for most British working-class families the idea of having a walking holiday in the countryside away from such polluting environments was a dream come true. Bert was one of those hardy souls that used to look forward, as he still does, to walking in the countryside, at first as a child with his family, and later, as he grew up, for he kept walking throughout his working life as a ship welder. 'Aye,' he said to me puffing on his pipe, 'them were the days packing walking clothes night before and up at 6 int morning ter take bus and train wid me parents of ter walk int countryside. Wonderful, great times them were with me mum and dad.'

While I had been listening to Bert's moving story, I noticed a tear or two making its way down his lined face. Another experienced walker who hails from the same area and had travelled with him on this holiday was his lifetime friend, Cyril. Now retired, both Bert and Cyril still walk with their many friends they have known for years, (some have now died), in the local ramblers' group. Other than walking, some of them like to meet at least once a week for a beer or attend the graves of their cherished friends. I asked Cyril about the times when as a child he and his family would go on walking holidays. 'Bludy marvellous, son, the healthiest thing yer can do for yerself,' he replied, adding, 'Me mum use ter make loads of sandwiches for us all at night and I use ter help er, bludy marvellous days them were. That's what them young people need ter day is walking; that would get rid of their weight problem and get 'em interested in countryside.' After reading so many interesting books on the subject of fell walking, it was for me personally a great moment, standing there on top of Great Gable, climbing my first fell in the footsteps of my hero, Alfred Wainwright.

After our first positive experiences of walking the fells with Countrywide Holidays, Anna and I have subsequently been on many more walking Ramblers' Holidays around Britain and Europe. In brief, they are the following: Grange-over-Sands in the south western Lake District, Church Stretton in the Shropshire Hills, the mountains in both Romania and Slovenia, the Harz Mountains in Germany, France in the heart of Provence, Krakow in Poland, Lake Iseo in Northern Italy, Mountains and Monasteries of Bulgaria, Christmas day on Samos and walking the Bay of Kotor in Montenegro.

Walking through the thick majestic alpine woods of Rila or Pirin Mountains in Bulgaria or the impressive Bucegi Mountains of Romania, where some places are still inhabited by bears and wolves, you come across shepherds, as we did, who live high up in very basic huts looking after their goats. When we came across them wearing thick homespun clothes and holding crooked staffs, they were most surprised. I was embarrassed when some of my cohort started taking photographs of them as if on a film set in Hollywood. As we had a local guide called Florin, as well as a British one, he was able to communicate with them explaining who we were and apologised for any intrusion. Florin had been told by the shepherds that they lived in the mountains for most of the time, only descending for several weeks in the year to buy goods for their long stay in sometimes very cold temperatures. Under the Romanian communist dictatorship of the late Nicolae Ceausescu, Florin, who was an active member of the Liberal party opposing him, was imprisoned, along with others, for their political views. During one of the many places we had visited in Romania, Florin took us to Victory Square in Bucharest, where many buildings were scarred by bullets, a place that witnessed the overthrow of their communist masters. In his delusions, Ceausescu had bulldozed thousands of houses and many churches so that he could build the House of Deputies which overlooks the city of Bucharest.

On our return to London I received a letter from Kingston University informing me that I had passed the first year of the Diploma in Social Work/Diploma in Higher Education course. I was so excited by the good news as it gave me further impetus to focus on the second year of my course. With great enthusiasm, I made the first day back at University, among my cohort, determined to make progress with my social work course. Lectures and coursework not surprising became more demanding, focusing on different theories and practices that students were expected to understand, assimilate and write about in detail in the various course essays throughout the intense second year. It is quite remarkable, understanding the nature of the course, that only a handful of students had left in the first year citing 'travelling, care for children and employment' as the main reasons. With the second academic year nearly half completed and having passed all my essays to date, leaving the important dissertation to write, I was facing my final placement to be carried out at MIND day centre in Beckenham, Kent.

MIND of course is the effective Mental Health Charity that champions the rights and development of people with mental health problems in Britain and they have many day centres around London. As MIND in Beckenham was my local centre, there were quite a few male faces I recognised there from using the local pub in Penge High Street. Most of the clients were from a working-class background, many with enduring mental health problems which stopped many of them from working. Similar to my first placement in Kingston, you were expected to assist with the everyday centre activities, also supporting those individuals with particular problems. I was impressed with the various courses that were available for centre users including art, writing and acting.

After a few weeks at MIND, I started supporting a middle-aged working class male who had throughout most of his adult life suffered from the various pernicious side effects of taking Benzodiazepine (BZ) medication, mainly valium. Similar to many other people who have been damaged by years of BZ abuse, Roger was getting little or no support from the medical profession. As I know all too well, users who have taken or who are currently taking BZ, friendly and supportive contact is vital if they are to have a chance to rebuild their shattered lives. That was the main reason why Roger was using the friendly and supportive culture at MIND, where he could at least find a sympathetic ear, cup of tea and warm shelter for a few hours from the outside world. However, he informed me that a lot of the time when he was not attending the MIND centre, he would frequent many different pubs around the area, also travelling further afield where he wasn't known. This sort of anonymous behaviour is not surprising to me as many users or former users, whether on BZ or not, do seek out another kind of chemical support to help them cope with the legacy of BZ. As mentioned above, that legacy can include panic attacks, confusion or a myriad other side effects or withdrawal problems. Many times, as I did, Roger himself travelled out many miles by public transport to pubs where he was not known, to consume large amounts of alcohol to relieve the various side effects or withdrawal problems of BZ. During the several months that he and I worked together it became clearer just how long he had been taking prescribed BZ, and the extent of the damage it had done not just to him but to other family members. It also, he informed me, inhibited his dwindling employment prospects over the years.

To be honest I enjoyed meeting with Roger on a regular basis but in my position there as a social work student there was very little I could do to change the predicament he was in. I did suggest to him—I had always been honest with him—that if he wished to carry on our work he could enter into counselling or psychotherapy which he might find useful in the long term but also painful with no guaranteed outcome. That was how we left things, with the ball in Roger's unenviable court hoping that he would someday embark on therapy, knowing that it is not a panacea for all ills. The day before my social work placement at MIND came to a close, Roger presented me with an attractive fountain pen set as a token gesture of our work together, recognising that we are both fallible individuals who are trying their best. Government, as I continue to write this book, wants to introduce a 'legal duty of candour' for all public workers whereby they will have a legal duty to tell the truth when things go wrong. One last word about my work with Roger is that I was so pleased to have acted as witness to his immense suffering, and bravery, to which his BZ prescribers are legally responsible.

My employment continued for another year at MACA in Croydon, working with some of the most difficult, demanding, vulnerable individuals in society. Whilst working one particular evening, a young man self-inflicted a terrible injury to his neck. Staff were made aware of the admission of this young man, from a psychiatric hospital, who had a history of self-harming that went back a number of years. We discussed the potential issues that could arise whereby continual vigilance should be employed by checking on him regularly. Around midnight I heard a shout from his room to which I immediately rushed to find, on opening his door, that he had slashed the side of his neck with a razor. While my colleague attended the young man trying to cover the wound, I phoned for the ambulance that arrived within minutes to give him medical attention and drove him off to the local A&E Department.

Apparently he was so skilled at knowing where to cut his neck without killing himself, something that he had tragically done on many occasions, one assumes, to get some personal attention to help him support his inner crisis. We never saw him again, as he was taken to another secure psychiatric hospital where he would receive the appropriate treatment that he so desperately needed. It was this tragic case, and others, that challenged my confidence once again in asking myself whether I really wanted to be a practising social worker.

It was not too late, I thought to myself, to go back to college to explain to my tutor my position that I no longer wanted to carry on with the social work course. After serious thought and after I had discussed the problem with Anna and others, and against my better judgement, I decided to continue at Kingston University. It was without doubt a major learning curve I had experienced working at Kaleidoscope, MIND and MACA with those unfortunate human beings who for various reasons are unable to live a normal life. Sometimes I saw people in states of great pain and suffering, who with the help of others, were trying to do something about the predicament they found themselves in. Also, there were many workers, volunteers, friends and families who did their best for the less fortunate sometimes beyond the call of duty. Whether I was going on to be a practising social worker or not, I didn't know, but what I had experienced as a paid worker, student and human observer will stay with me for the rest of my life.

I soon learnt with great excitement from Kingston University that I had passed my placement at MIND and subsequent exams, although I had to re-sit one exam, which had brought me my biggest success to date. I had also received top marks for my dissertation. This was in December 1997. I was over the moon that after all the hard work I had, at last, achieved professional status by joining the ranks of qualified social workers. Four weeks later at a student ceremony held at the Barbican Centre,

London, experiencing feelings of elation, and watched by Anna, who was among the two thousand people applauding me, I went up onto the stage to collect my Social Work/Higher Education Diplomas from the Vice Chancellor. It was the most exhilarating experience of my life yet. This success added further impetus to my emerging voice that had been suppressed all my adult life. Information from many different sources now began to flood my inner life, where my voice spoke for me in a more coherent fashion, mindful of the past, but excited about the future in which I had the potential for developing new ideas with people who I hoped would take me seriously as an individual.

Before I started to read for an extended third year in BA (Hons) in Community Care at Kingston University (my two diploma courses were originally for two years), all I wanted to do in my excitement was to phone my parents to inform them of my success. That same day after returning home with Anna from the Barbican, I sat down in my armchair and waited in anticipation, thinking about what I would say, as I eventually got through on the phone to my mother. I had not spoken to my mother for some considerable time. My feeling of elation of wanting to share my success soon dissipated when my mother, sobbing into the phone, informed me that my father had died in a residential home several months previously. The tears fell down my face, for I was so saddened to hear of my father's death, unable to conceive of that strong upright man ever dying. After the short painful telephone conversation with my mother, I promised to send her a photograph of me in a student gown holding my diploma. More importantly, I reassured her that I would visit within a few weeks. I thought long and hard, realising that not one of my siblings had the decency to inform me that my father was even living in a residential home and had died, and had been buried.

My father died in February1997 at the age of 82 years: He came from a working-class culture that was steeped in hard work, responsibility and stoicism where men repressed their emotions. After a mainly secure and uneventful young life as an only child, he falsified his age to seek out adventure in the British Army where he found himself being shipped to India amongst the heat, squalor and poverty of Bombay. Though he was not yet an adult in the eyes of the law, I admired my father leaving behind relative security to make such a monumental decision in joining the Army, as no doubt, life was tough.

Upon his return to London he did various jobs until meeting my mother, eventually moving to Runton and subsequently fathering 13 children between1936-59. As with many working-class men, I imagined that the only kind of power he ever had was over my mother, especially when it came to sex, as women in those days depended on nearly everything from their husbands. My father had always worked hard for the family, was never out of work and retired at the age of 73 when he had accumulated an additional hard-earned pension for himself and my mother so that they had a little extra in retirement. It appears that as the years went by he spent less time in the house working longer hours due, in part, to my mother's dominant personality which, I think, had always been a problem for him. He was a decent, kind, affable person who was never aggressive or sullen, and if he could, he would rather help someone than hinder them. My father was not, however, an effective role model, at least for me, but I suspect probably not also for my siblings. I would sincerely like to thank my father for everything he did for me, particularly in those difficult times when I was desperate and needed the warm welcoming support of my parents. I shall never forget him.

It was good news for both of my former student friends, Maria Fox and Martin Sidebottom, that they had both passed their philosophy degree courses at the City University. We made arrangements to meet for the first time in a year which would lead to other subsequent enjoyable meetings over the years to come. All four of us—another former City University student had joined us—met at Martin's first floor flat just two hundred yards from Putney railway station. The Edwardian house, similar to most of the houses in the road, had been converted into three attractive self-contained private flats which attracted the young educated people focused on successful careers. Martin was living in the flat with his girlfriend, a trainee solicitor in the West End, and desperate to find a job so that he could make a contribution towards their living costs.

'Well, it is so good to see us all here altogether for a drink after three years of hard slog at University. We deserved our degrees but of course we must remember that poor old Barry still has another year to go at Kingston University,' said Martin, laughing at me after taking a huge gulp of gin out of the glass he was holding. I replied, 'Thanks for reminding me my dear friend of twelve months hard graft in front of me.' Both Maria and Desmond, the fourth person there, agreed that by passing their degrees, it gave them both an advantage when it came to finding a better paid job—until Martin yelled, 'I don't want to find a fucking job not just yet!' This statement of Martin's was before he took another huge gulp of gin! His large masculine frame had not gone unnoticed by Maria who of course had seen enough of him at University over the past three years to know of his potential fitness.

I tried to take the mickey out of him by pointing at a photograph of him hanging on the ochre-coloured wall. 'Who's that ugly person there, Martin, who reminds me of spare ribs in bathing trunks?' 'Hey do you mind, that's me on the beach in Spain wearing my provocative shorts for all the sexy girls to ogle!' he told us all, full of confidence, as he smiled at Maria who had been rather quiet up to now. Since receiving her degree Maria had applied for several teaching jobs in Central London without success but she still had temporary work at her father's business to fall back on if she became short of money.

An hour later we walked down Putney High Street, then full of estate agents, charity shops and banks, and into Martin's local pub called The Bird in the Hand, just round the corner from Putney Bridge. The Edwardian pub had one large bar tastefully covered in light blue flock wallpaper with two light green transparent glass chandeliers hanging from the brilliant white ceiling. As we continued our heated discussion about work, Desmond rather hesitantly bought the first round of drinks back on a tray to where we were sitting. Martin thought that higher education was a bit of a con: 'You get into debt during your three-year course, work hard to pass your exams, then you find there are very few jobs around, so you sign on the dole for a mere pittance!' he said, half shouting the words at us. I had some sympathy with Martin's statement, although I was still at University with a whole year's study ahead of me, still convinced the care profession was a worthwhile job, though badly paid.

Desmond had applied unsuccessfully for many jobs, mostly in teaching but he would consider anything sensible that would give him enough income to pay his rent and buy food. 'I have had two failed interviews both for teacher vacancies with Hackney Council, but they said they will place me on their short list just in case a vacancy arises,' said Desmond, a little downcast, not really looking forward to the future. Martin brought another round of drinks back to the old tattered seats that we were sitting on just inside the main door. 'Fuck the work, I've had enough of sending out CVs and application forms to companies, never to hear from them again—it's waste of my time and resources,' said Martin, his face turning red with anger as he stood up to roll a cigarette.

So the various discussions ebbed and flowed around the subject of money, the god that most of us are chasing, which keeps our heads above water unless we fail and fall into the abyss. After a few more drinks we decided to call it a day, determined that one of us would get a job somewhere out there in the harsh world of capitalism where an uncharitable employer waits to suck out your marrow in return for a few pounds.

Martin moved from London, a place he never really enjoyed being, back to his hometown to try his luck there in finding a job he did not really want. Within a year he had tried three unskilled jobs working in warehouses packing plastic games for children, posting books to South America and clothes to poverty stricken families in Africa. Martin had even tried working for his father, but that job lasted no more than a few weeks when he tried to persuade his fellow workers to join a union to the great dismay of his father, who sacked him on the spot. The world of work was not for Martin at the time, if ever, as he was restless due to the fact that he wanted to travel around the world meeting people from different backgrounds to find out what made them tick. That is what reading philosophy for three years at University does to some people, including Martin—they become focused on trying to understand that certain group action doesn't necessarily lead to subscribed outcomes. He had that understandable desire to seek out knowledge.

At the same time he was writing a book based, I think, on philosophical value and belief which I did try to read but it was too intellectually heavy for me to understand. Around about this time he was still unemployed, back living with his family and kept phoning me so many times a day that eventually I had to keep my answer phone permanently switched off. During those times Martin's behaviour, to say the least, was rather odd.

It was around this time that Martin borrowed the money from his father to buy a ticket to India so that he could visit various towns and villages meeting as many spiritual people as possible who he thought could help him in his quest in finding the truth. In an excited and obsessive state he phoned me late one night from Delhi saying he had found God and all he wished for was to be a practising

Guru to help save those unfortunate inhabitants of the slums. The phone calls from Martin were incessant, both night and day, and bordering on the insane. Later there were no more messages from him for about two weeks, and I had assumed he had settled down somewhere amongst the local people who had accepted him, when one afternoon he phoned me from a psychiatric hospital in London saying he had been sectioned.

It transpired that he had been smoking very strong cannabis in the slums of Delhi, and for his own safety, had been hospitalised until they could put him on a flight to London where arrangements were made for him to receive medical treatment. When he had been stabilised he phoned me to explain that he had contracted drug induced psychosis. What is important is that he recovered and flew back to Delhi where he was going to live with an Indian woman and her children. After that I received several phone messages and postcards from him saying he was happy to stay there and would not be back as he hated capitalism. I hope Martin finds the peace he has so diligently looked for, whether that is living in a village family setting or walking round the slums helping the untouchables. I can visualise him wearing an orange robe over his large frame delivering spiritual teachings to the gathered many. All the best Martin!

The next time that I met Maria was at a leaving party she had arranged for her family, friends and colleagues to celebrate working as a sociology teacher for one year at a local College of Further Education. She was leaving as she had found a job teaching English to mature students in Bromley knowing that her family, who were successful people, expected her to take on more challenging and better paid teaching positions. During the evening Maria and I managed to chat for a few minutes about University, and I explained that Martin, after finding life tough at first, now found his feet on the ground and enjoyed living in India. I said sincerely to Maria, 'It is good to see you once more, it's been over a year and look what you have achieved in that time—well done!' 'Thank you so much, Barry,' was her genuine smiling response; she was nearly always positive about her life and also concerned for those around her.

It was not surprising when she remarked, 'I have been lucky when it comes to finding work—I think my face fits!' She would always undervalue her own achievements, even though she had done well when it came to the point of meticulous job research. Perhaps I was rather short-sighted when I had the opportunity to take her out for a meal together, yet for some reason I let the opportunity slip through my fingers, knowing that she could have opened doors for me. That lack of self-confidence was no doubt a reaction from my past experiences. It was at these times, when associating with people from a different background or mind-set, that I really had to keep reinforcing the idea that an intelligent voice, my voice, was emerging that could develop a new creative approach in my contact with people.

Over the next three years Maria held several dinner parties at different venues, though all of them were top class when it came to producing well-cooked delicious food for the many people that were always invited. As I have commented before, Maria was a super hostess, with a bubbly friendly confidence that helped her along the way to develop many friendships, to the point that over the years she became very popular. Anna and I were fortunate to have been invited to her parties where we met her attractive Australian mother, intelligent siblings and many of her friends and colleagues. On leaving one of her parties, the last time I was to see her, she came up to me with her usual broad smile all over her rosy cheeks to wish me well, saying. 'Thank you Barry, for your support at the City University. Also, I do hope you are successful in everything that you attempt. God Bless.'

During one of Maria's colourful parties, this particular one was in Kensington, I got into jovial conversation with one of her brother's theatre colleagues called Philip. We were discussing the merits of working when he asked me, 'What do you do for a living then, Barry?' 'I make rubber legs for the NHS,' was my alcohol-induced reply! 'That is a most unusual profession,' he said, looking rather confused by my statement.

My therapy sessions with Clive continued throughout the months although I would still miss one or two sessions from time to time due mainly to studying for my final year on the degree course at Kingston University. Clive was also a practising Buddhist, a fact I did not pick up on at first even though there were several Buddha figures in his hallway and therapy room. He demonstrated incredible skilful tolerance with me during the three years that I was in therapy with him, sometimes turning up early, late or smelling of alcohol, but most of the time I actually looked forward to seeing him. Also, after each therapy session had been completed, I would invariably make my way to the pub inside Denmark Hill Station for a few beers, moving onto another pub just up the hill, when the former one closed down a few months later. Even during this stage of my development, I was at times still impulsive which no doubt came from a past based on unthinking momentary craving. Regarding the actual therapy itself, I am not sure how successful it was notwithstanding that I was in therapy for three years but not really ascertaining that I had made any tangible changes to my life—but I am told this is how it is! Therefore, even if I have been able to make changes, progress or see things with more clarity, I do find it difficult actually to write down those things in an intellectual form. If pushed on the subject, there are two distinct ways of how I think therapy may have helped me to understand certain aspects of my life:

Therapy may have helped me understand why my parents allowed me to go out on my own, at all hours of the day and night at such a young age, to associate with mature manipulative men, who knew I was a vulnerable young boy with unmet needs—an ideal candidate to be sexually abused; that as a vulnerable young boy, my parents failed to understand that I had certain important needs that should have been fulfilled, but instead they increasingly left me alone with frustrations that developed into psychopathology problems. Furthermore, a substantial reason why I failed to flourish in certain areas of my life, as understood above, was the impact of an unstable relationship with my parents.

From an existential point of view, I can now try to understand how17 years of taking BZ had stunted my emotional development and damaged my cognitive recall.

Couple this with some of the powerful features of existential self-consciousness or self-reflection, which is a defining feature of all human beings; from a personal experience I only had, for a number of years, a rudimentary grasp of my conscious awareness. I tried to experience this existential awareness of myself of being alone in the world which sometimes provokes intense anxiety in relation to others who I assume are also alone. I also tried to analyse these experiences or anxieties, which are bound up in the concepts of freedom, isolation and responsibility, where for many years I was stuck within my own inner confines of utter confusion preoccupied with fantasy and observation, unable to set myself free.

CHAPTER EIGHT

BEING AWARDED MY DEGREE, CONTACT WITH MY MOTHER AND CHILDHOOD REFLECTIONS

Now in the final few months of my BA (Hons) degree course, the academic rigour started to gather momentum in carrying out research into various essays that had to be submitted on time, and also with one eye focused on the major piece of work underpinning the entire course, which is the Dissertation. As there was no third-year placement, it is therefore not surprising that the whole emphasis was on an intellectual and conceptual understanding of social work practices that we could encounter when qualified practitioners. About half of the original number of diploma students had decided to carry on with the degree but one or two, due to financial or family problems, did not finish the course.

It is not surprising that the subject for my Dissertation was BZ problems and also due to the fact that I had been awarded top marks for a similar Dissertation at the end of the second year. During the latter part of the third year, I met up with several of my cohort to discuss various ways of how we could approach our final piece of work which was due to be submitted within weeks. In the final stages I read many research papers, chapters from books and case studies, hoping they would give me sufficient knowledge to write my last piece of academic work, which I finally submitted with two days to spare. After all my cohort had submitted their Dissertations on time, most of us gathered together for the usual final drinks party in the student bar to celebrate, prematurely perhaps, three years of hard work, knowing that we still had to wait for a final piece of work to be marked. Three weeks later I was informed that my Dissertation had been given a pass. Although slightly disappointed with just a pass after all the graft I had put into the research, I had nonetheless gained my BA (Hons) Degree. After many years of frustration and disappointment living on the periphery of society, and my subsequent difficulty to adapt to a normal life, success had at last come my way—not that it would radically change my life. The hitherto conditioned intrusive dominant metaphorical voices that once held me back were by now losing their strong influence over me. I had been nurturing and influencing my inner life for some considerable time with more creative energy that I had enhanced particularly from academic work. This energy inspired me to speak with a louder, clearer yet informed voice.

Anna and I went to visit my mother for the first time in several months, since last visiting her after the death of my father, when I gave her a photograph of my diploma ceremony. I told my mother why I had not visited her before, explaining that I had been preoccupied with my education, working and therapy, which were all so important to me. My ageing mother was very pleased with my further success, obtaining my BA (Hons) degree, commenting with a half smiling face that 'your father would have been proud of the way you have worked so hard to achieve something'. That comment from her made me feel good about myself, knowing the tremendous effort I had made had paid dividends in helping me become the first in my family to achieve a University degree.

Three of us were sitting in the front room, discussing various things when my mind took me back to all those years ago when we were children causing mayhem throughout the house. We would have been shouting, fighting, and running around in the bedrooms, down the stairs and into the garden, knowing that if we were not careful mother was on hand to give us all a whack round the head or a severe ticking off. In the evenings when the noise had settled down somewhat there would be six vulnerable children sitting on the floor in the front room watching the black and white television mother had saved so hard to buy for us. We would sit there for several hours, in front of a warm coal fire, laughing and shouting at our cowboy heroes as they beat up the nasty Red Indians as my parents did their best to protect us from the vagaries of the outside world.

I conjured up in my mind's eye those cold early mornings when my dear old frustrated mother kept shouting at us to get out of bed as it was time to go to school. I was so thrilled when my mother bought me a new red coloured bicycle for my birthday and when my brother Bob took me proudly round the local roads teaching me how to ride it. It must have been very difficult for my overworked mother, with all those children to feed, to have bought a new bicycle for me knowing that my other siblings needed new or second-hand clothes to wear or certain bills had to be paid. It was quite amazing how she sorted out all the various needs that were crying out for her attention.

Sitting there with mother and Anna, my mind went back to those days in the late afternoon, having returned home from school, kids sitting at the table gobbling down mountains of chocolate-spread sandwiches, it reminded me of the biblical story 'of feeding the five thousand'. There were the fond memories of cleaning our soccer boots with dubbin after doing battle against another school team; and more fond memories of climbing trees in the wood at the back of our house, in Nonsuch Park and at the back of the local Chessington Road playing fields. Costing us sixpence each (6d), my siblings and I used to buy a fishing net attached to a bamboo cane which was sufficiently long to catch small fish some way out from the Hogsmill river bank where sometimes one of us would fall into the three feet of water. There were the unforgettable Sunday mornings, especially during the summer months, when six or seven children all at the same time would try to wash, dress and get downstairs to eat our porridge in minutes before my mother would, like a sergeant major, bellow at us to 'get in the fucking car!' Dickens might well have been proud of the Bradbury kids who all used the same face flannel to wash their faces, a cat's lick, put on anyone's clothes, not knowing who they belonged to and devouring their third helpings of food in seconds. Can you imagine the mayhem?

My mind returned to my mother and Anna sitting there with me in the front room, as I suddenly realised, with the passing of the years, how old my mother looked sitting there all alone with the marks of doing battle in life's arena etched all over her lined face. 'What is life like round here now, mum?' I asked her, wondering now that all her children had moved on. 'It's very quiet 'cos I am living on me own and especially since Dad died. Most of the families round here are young just like your Dad and I were all those years ago, when we moved from Badersea,' she recalled with obvious sadness. I tried to cast my mind back to those early days to visualise that morning when they all drove for the last time, from Battersea to Runton, to begin a new life in a new house of their own with a large garden for their forthcoming children. 'Who do you see nowadays mum?' I asked, hoping that at least some of her children, unlike me, still visited her. 'Quite a few come round 'ere from time to time, Bob, Susan and their children. 'Cos they're good to me, yer know, they takes me out for a meal on the Epsom Downs as well.' At that moment a feeling of guilt came over me when I thought of all that she had given to so many children, including me, and most of us now could not be bothered to visit her even for a few hours every month. What a scathing indictment, I thought, on modern materialistic selfish people who have nearly everything that my parents could only have dreamt about.

I made the excuse I wanted to use the toilet, but really, I had a strong desire to look round the house to see how different it was from the days when we were children now that it had been painted and decorated. As the years had gone by, the children had grown up and left home and my parents had become more affluent so that they could afford to have all the rooms professionally decorated. With thirteen children rampaging round the house, it had been near impossible, even if they had had the time, money or inclination to have made anything more than a rudimentary job of decorating anything in the house. From my early days, I can still remember that on one occasion my father, mother having asked him many times, painted the front room dark blue which gave it a foreboding appearance even on sunny days. Any colour paint will do, my father must have thought, as long as it covers the dirty walls scribbled on for many years by his gang of children.

My mind started wandering back again to the days when we were young, when there were at least seven children at home at any one time, when things were very difficult. It felt as if there was a never ending number of children, at all times of the day, coming and going which would have tried the patience of a saint. My father worked very hard to provide food for the family. No sooner had my mother cooked the food and put it on the table than it was gone—eaten in seconds by hungry children. My mother must have been under tremendous pressure trying to keep it all together. When I observe young mothers today trying to cope with just one child, I remember that there was my mother trying to socialize thirteen children; today such a situation would be totally impossible. At such times I feel so sad for her that she should have had to cope with such inhuman responsibilities. It is not surprising, but regrettable, that when trying to control the mayhem around her, she sometimes resorted to violent behaviour against many of my siblings and also against me. In hindsight it is also understandable that two of my younger brothers were sent to approved schools being in need of care and attention after stealing a few coppers from a local baker. I visited them on two separate occasions to see how they were developing but my instincts told me they should have been at home with their siblings playing games and sleeping in their own beds, instead of being locked up in a cruel outmoded Institution that did nothing worthwhile for working-class children.

My mother must have had a very unhappy life, yet, to my parents' credit, all thirteen children have grown up into adulthood, and other than two, all have had children and have done productive work although some of my siblings have done materially better than others. Due to having healthy supportive relationships themselves, most of my siblings have, to a greater or lesser extent, been able to move on from the past family problems to invest their energies into the well-being of their own children and grandchildren. What is undeniable is that my mother was invariably there when it came to defending her children no matter who was on the receiving end. I can vaguely remember when my mother marched to Hurst Road school to inform the Headmaster that she could only afford to buy jeans for her son (James, I believe): 'If that is not good 'nuff, then you buy 'im a pair of trousers or send 'im 'ome!' she roared at the flabbergasted Mr Nicholas. No more was heard on the subject.

Interestingly, when I walked out into the now forlorn looking garden it did not in any shape or form resemble the one we used to play in all those years ago. For example, when we were young children there was a small pool we could paddle or splash in, several damson and pear trees and a large slide that my father had made us. Now all that remains today is a garden with a green lawn with a hump on it reminding me of the Second World War Anderson shelter that used to be under the ground. I cast my eyes on a large wooden shed, originally a pigeon loft, down the bottom of the garden which was erected many years ago by my brother Lawrence and his friend to house their racing pigeons. On many occasions Lawrence and several of his friends, many Manchester City supporters like him, would trance down the garden to keep an eye on the breeding pigeons, repair the shed, yet still find time to smoke, drink bottles of cider and take the mickey out of each other. Incidentally, years later I saw Lawrence when he became a top level referee on the television, officiating as a linesman in front of a huge crowd at one of Manchester City's home football matches.

Before his death the shed had been used by my father to house his gardening tools; it was also a place where he could read his favourite amateur gardener magazine away from the world, or from mother, for a few hours, and enjoy a drink or two of his favourite Gordon's gin and tonic. For many years, until he became too old, my father had rented two vegetable plots, adjacent to his own garden, from the local council. Both plots produced an abundance of different vegetables for the table without fail every year. As my father told me on several occasions, smiling, 'After weeding the veg plots son, I get out the lavatory varnish (his nickname for alcohol) for a couple of hours, read the garden magazine and relax in the palace (shed) until I hear the sergeant-major (his nickname for mother) coming down the garden.' The very old shed which stands just outside the back door he erected many years ago for storing his tools he locked away from the prying eyes of his children, and in the latter years he put a freezer there for use in the household. As I looked at the old shed that day, which must have been fifty years old, there, still growing at the side of it, were the old remnants of mint that my father always used when preparing lamb for the Sunday roast. Little things like that are such a powerful reminder of our connection to the past when life appeared to be so slower and ordered, but perhaps that sort of sentiment is said by all passing generations.

Unfortunately when I was young there were some nasty family incidents that happened, and with great reluctance, I now recall some of them. The first of them was between one of my older brothers and my father which fortunately did not come to actually fighting each other. After a bitter row, my mother ordered my brother to pack his personal things and get out of the house immediately or she would phone the police. My brother left the house but came back ten minutes later to shoulder barge the front door in, breaking the door support and lock. He had intended to hit father who managed to escape from the house into the safe hands of the waiting police outside who then subsequently arrested my brother. The police told my brother to leave the house immediately or he would be arrested, which he complied with by getting in his car and driving away, not to be seen for years.

Another incident involved my mother and my older brother David. I was about twelve years of age and along with other siblings had been playing all afternoon in the back garden when our mother called us in for our tea. After about ten minutes my mother, for some unknown reason, started hitting my brother David around the head until his lip began to bleed. At this point my brother picked himself up from the floor and, not surprisingly, in an angry mood told mother to 'leave me alone'. She then told my brother, 'Don't fucking well talk to me like that, or you get another fucking dose!' My brother ran upstairs, got his few clothes together and within a few minutes left the house. To this day no one is really aware—how can we be?—of the pain and suffering David went through when he walked out of the front door not to be seen, understandably, until many years had passed. Can you also imagine the remorse that my mother must have felt when she realised what she had done to her young son but at the same time aware that there were many more young children she had to think about?

Wouldn't it have been wonderful if we could have enjoyed the pleasures of life with our parents knowing they loved and cared for us—perhaps they did—instead of the constant tension that divided and separated families, like ours, because of too many children? Most family problems around the world today are primarily the result of poverty where overburdened parents have too many children that they are unable to feed, clothe or educate. Most of this is allowed to go on unabated by religious leaders who tell those living in squalor to multiply. It is a lot better in the affluent West where there is some relative poverty, but according to the Save the Children Charity (2012) 'more than 3.6 million children in the UK are still living without basics. That's one child in four'.

Throughout the years I have often thought of that incident involving my mother and brother, when he would have been alone on the streets of London with no place to live, walking aimlessly around looking for someone to help him or scrounge enough money to buy a cup of tea. What made things worse for my brother was that he had a severe stammer, exacerbated by family members, including me, as we ridiculed him by calling him various derogatory names. I really admire my brother by the way he has handled things in his life, none more so than when he supported his then partner to bring up her three young children. All of those children, now mature people, are now doing well thanks in part to the human kindness demonstrated by my brother. After David's earlier experiences I am sure he had that human need to live in a family that loved him. It was many years later when I met Mick, a trainer where I used to work, who explained his young experiences of having a stammer, that I really started to understand how disabling the condition can be. More about my on-going enjoyable friendship with Mick later.

When David was around fifteen years old, I was several years younger, he explained to me one Saturday afternoon that we were going to steal money from a local bowling club in Epsom. After the two miles walk from Runton, we arrived at the posh middle-class bowling club, at the back of Epsom Hospital, where we were going to steal from. What must have been my first criminal instructions in knowing what to take from other people's pockets, David told me to follow him into the small bowling green changing room where we rifled coats and trousers of money, cigarette cases and lighters. With my heart thumping loudly, it felt like eternity until we eventually walked out of the changing rooms, down an alley and into Epsom Town Centre where we bought all manner of goodies including fish and chips, sweets, bottles of lemonade and comics. Afterwards David and I walked to a local park where he dished out the remainder of our ill-gotten gains; he handed over to me a new ten shilling note, some loose change, fifty cigarettes and a cigarette lighter. These new possessions of mine where beyond my wildest dreams and enabled me to buy new goodies for the next couple of weeks.

To be honest, I certainly enjoyed the thrill, at a young age, of illegally entering someone else's property with the intention of stealing anything I could. Considering my future criminal activities, some would argue that I am an ideal candidate for having the criminal gene test!

Sid is another sibling who had a hard time when he was young, but as he got older he grafted hard for himself as he saved the money to buy a lorry, contracting himself out to a haulage business. He married Sylvia, had a son and moved away from Runton to enjoy a better life in another part of the country. When Sid was young he was another one of my siblings who was sent to an approved school, but when he returned home he had to sleep in the bath as there was no other space available for him. I admire him and all my siblings for the way they fought for themselves to get something good out of their lives.

When I was about 10 years of age there was an ugly incident in the family kitchen involving my father and I, something that I have forgiven him for but can never forget. The vague memory I have of that Sunday afternoon was that I, as usual, was making lots of noise, probably being nasty to someone whereby I must have pushed my father's patience to the limit, when he punched my forehead, making it bleed profusely above my right eye.

That incident caused another almighty row between my parents until someone patched up my bleeding eye. Once again, can you imagine all those vulnerable children running and screaming around the house making an unbelievable noise, where the neighbours, on one side of the house, not surprisingly, moved frequently. Furthermore, at more times than not my mother would have been shouting at someone. Her bellowing could have been heard by neighbours one hundred yards away. From an outsider's view the pandemonium in our house must have made it seem like some kind of Victorian Workhouse much of the time.

When I was about thirty years of age and still living for varying lengths of time with my parents, my father, a local friend called Ivor and I dug up the old surface and put down a new concrete driveway at the front of the house so that my father's car had a stronger foundation to stand on. The three of us sometime later repeated something similar by digging up the old material, putting down a thicker concrete base round the back of the house which was used for tables and chairs during the summer parties. In fact, it was Colin, Ivor's older brother, when I first came out of prison in 1969, who got me involved in semi-professional football by taking me along to Whyeleafe FC. Colin was a very good goalkeeper in his time, I am reassuringly told; he played in the same school and district football teams as my brother James did.

As Anna and mother continued chatting, I sat there still reflecting on the past how football had for about three years, when I was 32-35 years old, played an important part of my social life—when I used to turn out for a public house football team in Runton. The Three Crowns pub attracted many young local working-class men, whose main aim was to get drunk and generally have a good time, sometimes at the expense of others, but there was very little crime committed. There were many characters who used to drink in the pub on a regular basis, and no doubt for some of them, it became their second home, especially characters like Chunky and Rotten Arse Dave. Chunky was about 24 years old, short, stocky and lived on the nearby Gibraltar Council Estate. He was preoccupied with the subject of masturbation, and after a few beers, usually appeared to have an erection for the rest of that evening. Apparently as a young boy he was a patient for several years in the local St Ebba's Hospital for people with mental disabilities.

It was not surprising that the Three Crowns attracted a particular client group, as it was a small dirty pub that badly needed redecorating to give it a new lease of life. The toilets were something that resembled Rowton Houses in their heyday. During the few years that I frequented the Three Crowns, there were at least three different managers who all had the same short term vision for the pub: let's get out of this hell hole sooner rather than later.

Some of the regulars and I took the initiative when we were determined to set up a Sunday football team which eventually played football in the Leatherhead and District League. Through our own efforts we bought a new football team outfit, several new footballs and first aid kit, but sadly after three matches someone stole nearly all the equipment. There was a rumour going round the pub that one of our midfield players had drunk the disinfectant, mixed with tonic water, one night under the heavy influence of cannabis. I played for the football team—we were called The Crowns—for three seasons, having done quite well during this time, though we were not championship material by any stretch of the imagination. Some of the lads used to turn up five minutes before a match still smoking, having just left a party or other, their rancid breaths smelling of alcohol and meat madras.

There was one distasteful individual who frequently used the pub. (He also played for the football team.) His sole aim was to con people out of their money. Several unsuspecting pub regulars including myself were conned out of many pounds of our own money when the holiday he was organising for us in Spain did not materialise. I am informed that this person now owns a large house which is worth a fortune, and has many people working for him. At the time it was rather short sighted of us not to have taken him to court.

I brought myself mentally back into the front room again with Anna and mother who were having a friendly chat together over a slice of chocolate cake bought recently, mother was at pains to inform us, at Tesco's in Epsom by her friend called Sybil, a local retired teacher. Long gone now were those days of the past, and all that I could hear in the house was a deafening ghostly silence whispering to me 'keep going forward', but I enjoyed meeting my mother again and it also gave me the opportunity to mentally visit past experiences, pleased that chapter was now closed.

Back to the present time of January1999, I made my way by train to the Barbican Centre to celebrate passing my degree along with my cohort. Anna had driven down to Surrey to collect my mother from her home in Runton so that they could both support me on the greatest day of my life so far. The University official called out my name and degree status, to the applause of several thousand people watching me in the auditorium. With anticipation I walked up the steps, wearing my gown and mortar board like some Dickensian character, onto the stage where I collected my degree from the smiling Vice Chancellor of Kingston University, Dr Peter Scott. During those few seconds of glory, walking the thirty steps or so onto the stage, receiving my degree and down a flight of steps, with acute anxiety I observed all those people out there, with their myriad experiences, witnessing my success.

When I met my mother and Anna, after the formalities had been completed, they were both so pleased at what I had achieved at the grand old age of 52 years. Subsequently my mother remarked rather uncharitably to three of my siblings that 'Barry's got plenty of time, he has got nothing else to do but get degrees'. That was the usual Bradbury reaction, I'm afraid to say, when one of us had done something that merited at least the words, 'Well done.' Anna had been very supportive during my various academic courses, to the extent that when I first started the access course it was she who taught me, after very much coaxing due to my lack of confidence, how to use an old Amstrad computer she had at the time. I soon realised that my six-year relationship with Anna had been the most productive and enjoyable period of my life to date.

CHAPTER NINE

REUNION WITH MY OLD SCHOOL FRIEND PETER UPTON. LILAC HOUSE AND OTHER EMPLOYMENT POSITIONS. RECAPITULATION: A REVIEW OF PAST PROBLEMS!

A few weeks later after my degree success and still glowing with self-worth, out of the blue came a letter from Peter Upton inviting me to a reunion party at his house in Brighton. Before the party, however, I had to focus on finding suitable employment now that my month-long period of relaxing from University life was over. First I brought my CV up to date, printed off many copies and took the train to the West End armed with a list of social work agencies walking from road to road, handing out my personal employment details and also registering at some of the agencies. As we usually over-hype things to get a favourable response, these agencies were no different, saying that they had plenty of work for me but they would at first have to circulate my CV to various employers around London. Two or three of the agencies were helpful in suggesting that I look in various professional social work magazines for up-to-date vacancies, go onto the Web to register with other agencies, local authorities; and it could be productive, one helpful worker thought, to try a mailshot to various private and independent social care providers. The growing unofficial consensus from the various agency workers I spoke to, in person or over the phone, was that a newly qualified inexperienced social worker, not surprisingly, nearly always found it difficult to find work. Furthermore, I thought to myself, no one had to spell this out. I had just turned 52 and so was rather mature to begin a full-time social work career, especially with a local authority. I came to the conclusion that my best bet, subsequently confirmed at an interview, would be that if I wanted to gather experience I should try working in a day centre or residential homes similar to what I had done previously with MACA in Croydon. Further interviews with three employers materialised for social work vacancies but they were all unsuccessful for reasons I did not ask but probably related to my age or inexperience or both.

At this stage I was subscribing to a weekly social care paper that had vacancies advertised for workers, more appropriate to my needs, that covered most of London, Surrey and Kent. After applying by CV for about thirty various social work/care, project worker and day worker vacancies, I was at long last offered an interview for a senior project worker job with a local charity in Surrey. I shall never forget the train journey from Anerley, where I had been living for six years, to Dorking, as I was accosted by a young gypsy woman carrying a young child strapped to her back. She explained to me, 'I have been thrown out of my bedsit three weeks ago for not paying the rent and I have nowhere to live with my young two-year-old son whose father is living in London but has disowned us.'

Imelda, that was her name, crying into a handkerchief, informed me, 'I have been living at Marble Arch in London for three years with Otto, my son's father, when one day he kicked us out of the flat with nowhere to go.' She continued in near perfect English, 'The local authority supplied me with the phone number of a private landlord, who I rented the bedsit from, but the pig threw us out with nowhere to live!' It appeared that she had been sleeping anywhere she could find in Central London, especially on friends' settees, which did surprise me somewhat because her very colourful red, dark green and yellow gypsy clothes were clean; also, her son's clothes looked tidy, and although he was young and vulnerable, I did not know whether he was in need of medical attention.

Here I was travelling by train trying to prepare myself for a job interview that I really needed after studying for four years to get in this position, determined to be successful, until this Romanian woman—that's what she told me—came onto the scene. But, I pondered to myself, these are the kind of people that I will be working with in most social work positions, so what is the problem? Start practising now, I thought. I had to draw a line, however, when she asked me, 'Can me and my son live with you? We would be good for you and I am good cook but we will go out during day to give you rest Baddy.' 'No. sorry, you can't live with me, definitely not,' I protested, 'but I will give you several phone numbers of places in London where you can rent an inexpensive bedsit for the two of you.' This I did as the train approached my destination, Dorking Station, where by now my main thoughts were concentrated on my impending interview with a charity just ten minutes' walk from the station.

I said goodbye to Imelda, wished her well and went on my way to find Blair House. As I made my way up a Beech-tree-lined street with large modern detached houses on either side, I noticed a two-storey grey concrete building probably built within the last few years but looking like a contender for the ugliest piece of architecture I have ever seen. I rang the front doorbell and within seconds a middle-aged woman, wearing a light blue suit, came to the door smiling. 'Good afternoon, Mr Merchant, please come in and follow me into the interviewing room over there,' she said. In the room was another white middle-aged woman, rather more attractive than her colleague, wearing a white top with dark green slacks. Smiling at me, she said in a soft voice, 'Hello Mr Merchant, please sit down. Would you like a glass of water before we start the interview?' I declined the water but asked for the window to be opened as it was rather stuffy with three people in a very small room, and not surprising, I felt rather anxious. With thoughts of my past uppermost in my mind, I reassured myself that I was confident enough to come across in the forthcoming interview as a mature, intelligent person with a voice of his own.

I could feel my neck becoming tense but felt reassured that I had explained about having dystonia on the application form. Mrs Gibbs, the attractive lady, started the interview by asking me about my previous employment, how I would handle certain situations that I found myself in, and my understanding of equal opportunities. The other interviewer, Miss Graham, asked me questions about mental health law, assessment of individual needs and how I would approach other social care agencies. The interview was over in less than an hour. Mrs Gibbs then explained to me that they still had several more people to interview but they would contact me within seven days.

I was so relieved that the interview was over as I am always self-conscious of spasms in my neck muscle when in close proximity to other people. That was the main reason of course why I did a lot of temporary work over the years, because I did not want to attend formal interviews where I felt claustrophobic; but those days, I firmly convinced myself, were long gone.

After fifteen minutes I arrived back at Dorking station, relaxed, to take the train back to Anerley when I noticed Imelda waving at me, with her son still strapped to her back, sitting on the same platform as I. She made her way to the end of the platform where I was sitting pretending to be reading a book when she said smiling, 'Baddy, how are you? I never thought I would see you again.' I replied, 'Hi Imelda, I did not expect to see you here again either. Why are you still here, and did you not phone those bedsit numbers I gave you earlier on?' She just looked at me for a few seconds, then said, 'I thought you gave them to me to get rid of me. Besides, I don't have any credit left on my mobile phone.' I explained to her that the time was nearly 4 p.m. which meant soon it would be too late to phone private landlords or hostels to get a bed for the night. 'Do you want me to phone around for you to arrange B&B for the night, Imelda?' 'Yes please, please,' she said, with such an anguished look on her small attractive face. After phoning several numbers, I arranged a B&B booking for a minimum of seven nights in Balham for her and her son. Also, I explained, she could also apply to the local council early tomorrow morning for money to cover their expenses. There was not a lot more I could do for her at this time even though I had great sympathy for the predicament she was in, but I did give her my mobile phone number just in case she needed support. The same question presented itself again, similar to one before, when trying to help Imelda—would I be sufficiently able to detach myself professionally from the emotionally charged problems I would experience later?

'Well done, mate, in gaining a degree for yourself, I knew you had it in you,' said Peter Upton enthusiastically during our first phone conversation for at least three years. During that time he had moved to Brighton with his girlfriend who had their baby son, called Joe, found a new job as a bricklayer working for a local building company and was buying a small terraced house. 'It was hard work Pete. I am so thrilled to have been given the opportunity to study at University; it would have been just a dream for me years ago.' 'Yes mate, I heard through the grapevine that you were at Uni doing your thing which did not surprise me really, because I have known you since we were kids at school when you were in the thick of things,' recalled Peter, reminiscing on our past. 'Thanks Pete, things have been tough for me over the years but I hope I've turned the corner.' We both agreed that we looked forward to meeting each other once again at Peter's forthcoming party in Brighton very soon.

With the rain bucketing down, I walked into East Croydon station like a drowned rat ready to be chopped up to mix with horse meat to feed the ever burgeoning dog fraternity in Britain. After waiting for ages in the growing queues, I eventually purchased my return ticket to Brighton, boarded the packed non-stop fast train, arriving some forty minutes later, more than ready to meet my long standing friends, some of whom I had not seen for a long time.

Ever since I was a young lad during my train spotting days, I have always been impressed by the legacy left by our Victorian ancestors who built British train stations such as Brighton. Most impressive about Brighton Station is the skilled professional architecture they used to erect many lengths of large heavy ornately designed steel to hold up the walls and roof which is now a grade 2 listed station attracting more than 7 million people each year. As I walked out of the busy ticket barrier, Pete was waiting for me outside W.H. Smith looking prosperously dressed in a smart dark green suit with matching shoes. We threw our arms round each other as only friends really can, both of us knowing, without saying a word, what the depth of our friendship really meant. It felt as though we had remained silent in each other's arms for ages, though in reality it was no more than a few seconds; but in that short time there was a reinforced connection that went back at least forty years to West Lane School.

'Hi, Barry, so good to see you after such a long time, you do look well,' Pete said with a tear in his eye. 'How are you, Pete! My God, you do look well yourself. At first I thought it was some film star standing there making an advertisement!' I ribbed Pete wearing his flash expensive suit. 'Yea, that's right Bow, I always tried to attract the girls by wearing decent gear. Anyway Bow, I am now over fifty years of age, married to Sarah and we have a baby boy called Joe named after his paternal grandfather who died only last year of cancer. You remember my old man don't cher, Bow? Lovely bloke, smoked, drank and gambled too much but was a grafter who looked after all the family?' 'I do Pete. Don't you remember when we were kids we knocked off his beer one evening?' It was so good to be in the presence of a really decent human being like Pete. 'Anyway, Bazzer, there is a good pub near where I live about two miles from here, so let's take that 6 Bus, it only takes twenty minutes.'

The pub, called the Bird in the Hand, was a large Edwardian building painted all light green on the outside with several blooming petunias flower baskets fixed to the wall, many rose and lavender tubs on the patio and a long garden, with borders full of various colourful flowers and customers sitting and chatting among themselves. Inside was equally friendly and inviting, with a mouth-watering aroma of curry coming from the kitchen. There were various sized wooden tables and chairs with colourful covers over them which in all gave one the impression of an establishment that was well run and an enjoyable place to visit. Pete bought two pints of ale for both of us before we were joined by a colleague of his called Dave who was a carpenter living not far from the pub. Both Dave and Pete had worked on several building contracts together mainly within the Brighton area, but one large contract had been in Osborne House, once the home of royalty but now a tourist attraction, on the Isle of Wight. Pete said if he had a few quid he would ensconce himself there as Lord of the Manor, a sentiment I shared as I had toured the huge house with Anna a few years previously.

Dave explained he had divorced his wife of ten years while living together in Dorset but moved to Brighton three years ago to start a new life. He had found a Housing Association flat in nearby Preston Park, worked for the same company as Pete did called Makostar, and regularly visited his children back home in Poole. He now felt settled and thought of Brighton as his adopted home.

'What do you do for a living, Barry?' asked Dave, who appeared to be interested in my friendship with Pete. 'At the moment I'm waiting for the result of a job interview I had recently for a senior project worker vacancy,' I said, not knowing what the future held for me. 'Have you been in that game very long?' Dave asked, since he knew someone in that profession. 'Not very long. I have applied for many jobs since I passed my BA degree at University so I am really hopeful that I get the job.' 'What have you done with your life so far, Barry?' Dave asked, probing away, trying to find out if I was genuine. 'For many years I found it convenient to work for private employment agencies where you can work for one week, one month or a year. Most of the contracts are well paid with no formal applications or interviews and you can make good money. I used to save my money from those contracts and then go travelling for a few months or whatever.' 'That's sounds good Barry, so what made you change that way of life and go to University?' Dave asked inquisitively. 'Well, after years of being on my own, mainly due to addiction to prescribed valium, and due to the insecure nature of the work, I decided to train for a profession.' With that the three of us drank up our beer to head for Peter's home some ten minutes away.

'Hi darling, meet Barry, the person I've told you so much about recently,' said Pete, kissing his wife at the same time.

We embraced each other as I said to his wife Sarah, 'Hi, Sarah, it is so good to see you after all this time has gone by. Congratulations on having a baby boy.' 'Thank you so much. We both love him to bits, don't we Pete?' 'We most certainly do sweetheart,' said a proud Pete smiling all over his tough yet attractive looking face. There stood Pete, Sarah and their lovely little baby all connected by an extraordinary energy circulating between them.

With that the internal door opened when in marched Nobby, his older brother Roger, John, Tony, Melvin, Chris, Billy, Ian, Philip, Alan and my old friend of yesteryear, Frank Davidson, whom I used to go scrumping apples with. I was dumbfounded for a few minutes as all these old familiar faces stood there looking at me as though it were only last week we were playing soccer or cricket or smoking fags on the playing fields at Hurst Road School. The tears started to flow as in a sudden gush we all at once started to hug each other with an intensity I've not done before or since. I was so overwhelmed meeting so many good friends on that occasion that the lasting effect on me has been enormous. There is very little more that I can remember about visiting Pete Upton that is intellectually relevant to this book.

After two more enjoyable days staying with Pete and his family, I returned to my small yet comfortable sparsely furnished studio flat in South London having the added bonus of my dear partner Anna living just feet away from me. On many occasions, I have spent much enjoyable time waking up in the morning cuddling Anna's attractive body, her soft blonde hair lightly touching my face as we lay on a soft pillow, calm as Greek lovers, thinking only of the moment. In fact throughout our on-going seventeen years relationship I have spent far more time in Anna's home than I have in my own.

Weekday activities would vary for us depending on work or other commitments, as unlike me, Anna has always worked, teaching adult literacy ever since I have known her. However during our relationship my activities have varied considerably from working for employment agencies, part-time and full-time care positions, six years at various educational establishments and working several years for a local authority. We would both look forward to our evenings and weekends together, where top of our list would be to go walking locally around various parks or woods, or go further afield walking along sections of the North Downs Way in Kent or Surrey or walks on another long distance path called The Greensand Way.

Another great passion of ours is working together in Anna's long garden which is full of various shrubs, plants and flowers. We have both spent many hours digging, planting, re-planting, feeding, mulching, scurrying, watering and have rearranged Anna's garden over the years to make it into a living creative environment. That is of course an on-going project which Anna is determined to keep developing into a haven for all wildlife to explore. Whenever I visit she has nearly always bought something new for her garden such as bark chips, summer bedding plants, compost or seeds for the herb garden. She loves, like me, the outdoors life where as a child with her family any free time was spent cycling, walking, swimming and spending time in the summerhouse her father bought so that his children could enjoy the wonders of nature.

Similar to when she was living in the USA with her own family, most of the early years in her London home were spent sleeping out in her garden amongst the wild and domestic animals that roamed in and out of her tent. With that in mind, given the opportunity, I would love to live full-time in a summerhouse even if it had just rudimentary living equipment so long as I could be among nature.

After returning home from Pete Upton's successful party, and aware that it had been four weeks since my project worker interview, I was thrilled to find out by word of mouth that I had been successful in getting the senior project worker vacancy in Dorking. Apparently due to an internal administration problem the charity had been unable to contact me to inform me of the outcome of my interview. Mrs Gibbs, the attractive woman who interviewed me, was most apologetic for the delay when she phoned to offer me the senior project worker vacancy and congratulate me on joining the charity. I was so thrilled to have been offered the job, along with the best salary I have earned to date, that Anna and I went out to a restaurant to celebrate my good fortune. Although the job wasn't a social work position within the new care programme itself, it was, however, a job that I had been educated and trained to carry out with all its attendant responsibilities.

I started the project worker vacancy one week later full of optimism when I was based in a small residential home for residents with enduring mental health problems in Leatherhead, Surrey. Most of the twenty residents had been in Lilac House residential home for at least ten years or more; a few had also been patients in one of the nearby mental hospitals that had fortunately closed down. The environment was similar to other residential homes that I have worked in where the majority of residents, made apathetic by medication, would sit in front of the television most of the day drinking tea until encouraged by staff to move around the house or go outside for a walk. When roused, most of the residents shuffled from the television room to the kitchen to make tea and shuffle back again. Only a few of the residents ever had any visitors on a regular basis who would bring sweets, flowers and clothes which encouraged them to dress up occasionally to leave the house on their own. Most of the residents had not been visited by family or friends for years, but the local Women's Institute, who were such kind people, did visit these individuals taking them various gifts. There was a small garden at the house where some of the younger residents would be encouraged to plant shrubs or dig over the earth supported by staff including myself. At every opportunity I used to encourage three young residents in particular to visit the local garden shop to buy their choice of flowers or shrubs and then plant them in the garden. In time other residents got involved as they walked down to the garden centre, supported by staff or not, to buy plants or flowers developing a little garden plot of their own. Lack of motivation is the eternal problem for patients in different kinds of institutional settings taking into consideration staff shortages and lack of funds for various activities.

My main senior project worker responsibilities were to support four residents with their own care plans which were put in place to help and support them with their everyday living activities such as healthy eating, personal hygiene, activities, interests, communication with family, visiting their doctors or dentists. At every opportunity we encouraged residents to help out around the house by cleaning their bedrooms, preparing the dining room or helping the staff to wash lunch/dinner utensils. All this co-operation goes to help improve the quality of life for those living in residential homes. On the whole my experience of working in residential homes have been a positive one for the individuals living there who appeared to be well supported and secure. Due to the nature of these places there is occasionally nasty incidents carried out by a very few disturbed individuals that upset the rest of the residents, but fortunately well trained staff should return things to normal.

Unfortunately one of the most unsavoury problems I did experience at Lilac House was with two members of staff who both worked there for many months. They had already been working there for about four months by the time I arrived in July 1999. In the afternoons staff hand over information to other colleagues who are finishing their workshift and communicate any problems, incidents etc., so they can act accordingly. Along with four other colleagues, I was just coming on shift when two of them, who were from Nigeria, started asking me various questions about the British benefits system as it transpired that ever since they had been resident in Britain both had been using false identification, including false insurance numbers, to claim various state benefits. Furthermore, during their employment at Lilac House they had both been using stolen security identification details. I was further shocked when they informed me of their first arrival into this country when they claimed a Nigerian friend had told them about the false identification scam which was being used by many Africans. I told them in no uncertain words that I had a duty to inform my manager immediately about the illegal position of two of his colleagues.

But there were also good enjoyable times for residents and staff at Lilac House when about every three months we used to have a party for the whole house. Furthermore, we used to celebrate every resident's birthday, giving them a party with a birthday cake, presents, playing music of their choice, and they were encouraged to invite family and friends along. One resident, Arnold, about fifty years old, had been at Lilac House for about ten years but prior to that had been in a mental hospital for several years, and was a very good singer indeed. At every opportunity, Christmas day, birthdays and parties, Arnold would love to stand in front of everyone singing country and western music of Hank Williams, Johnny Cash and his favourite Woody Guthrie. Apparently Arnold had been a very good semi-professional club singer before his mental illness had for many years taken hold of his life, yet there are those who remember him singing every day in the grounds of the local mental hospital. They say that on the days when he was singing, usually in his favourite orchard, many patients would be there to listen to his music instead of working in the occupational therapy unit. On a few occasions at Lilac House, he and I used to sing many Bob Dylan songs together to entertain the residents who thought that my singing was hilarious. Anyone could tell that I was out of my depth but we all enjoyed it.

After about eighteen months I left Lilac House, knowing that I had given my best. I had enjoyed working there and

I was especially fortunate to have met so many good people who had lived interesting yet varied lives. I had also learned some invaluable skills that I would take with me. As I had been able to save some money during the past year, I would take some time out from work to look around and walk those woods, meadows, downs, commons, byways and other obscure places that I had somewhat forgotten during the process of making money. That is the contradiction of the capitalist society we live under, working all the waking hours we can to buy everything we don't really need which leaves us in debt so we have to keep working to pay off the debt, leaving us little time for ourselves to wander, listen to the song thrush or just sit down on a fallen tree in a wood. It appears that most of humanity is subservient to the money god.

On this occasion, like many times throughout the years, I took the train to Hampton Court, once the home of Henry VIII, and walked across the Thames bridge and onto the Thames Path, a long-distance walk that starts in Gloucestershire and runs for 180 miles to the Thames Barrier. My personal journey on the Thames Path over the years has taken me from the Thames Barrier to Goring and Streatley, about 100 miles, so I still have many miles to tread if I want to reach the source of the river at Lyd Well in Gloucester. Passing Henry Tudor's magnificent Palace, I usually walked the three miles into the Royal Borough of Kingston passing on the way the huge grounds of Hampton Court on the left and Ravens Ait, a boating club on a small Island, on the right. As you pass the huge modern detached houses with large gardens on the other side of the Thames, Kingston Town comes into view with its Royal Charter, historic buildings and expensive modern flats. I have read that Kingston is the most sort-after place to live in London with its fast commuter trains, well built houses, grammar schools and extensive shopping precincts.

The Thames Path here crosses Kingston Bridge and drops down underneath the bridge where there is a conveniently placed pub called The Bishop out of Residence, a Young's Pub well known for selling quaffable bitters brewed by their own brewery. Over the years, especially when I was living in Runton and still on BZ, I would take the 406 bus into Kingston where I would use several of the pubs all day, including The Bishop out of Residence. Before the 12 hours per day drinking law, the pubs north of Kingston would close half an hour later than the pubs that I used on the south side, so on any one day there would usually be several men, including myself, rushing across Kingston Bridge to the nearest pub to get in at least one more beer.

Heading north towards Richmond the path passes some prime land with very expensive large detached houses and secured blocks of flats on it. I have always wondered how any person carrying out a legal job can possibly afford to live in such luxury when only down the road there are those living in relative poverty. Another half mile on and you come to Teddington Lock, next Eel Pie Island, the place where I went all those years ago to listen to various rock bands, take intoxicating mind-altering drugs and talk endless nonsense to others who weren't even listening. No doubt some of those unfortunate revellers of the former counter culture scene found their way back into Kingston and into the reassuring spiritual home of Eric Blakebrough's Kaleidoscope Project in Kingston.

Past the National Trust-owned Ham House, the place I loved to visit when I was inspired to learn about the first owner, Sir Thomas Vavasour, and his successors, the Dysart family. Also, a walk round the magnificently designed gardens is an experience not to be missed. Further on, passing rich meadowland that is occasionally flooded by the high tides, and into affluent Richmond Town with its grand buildings, High Street Banks, expensive coffee shops and Grand Theatre. Being in this town has always reminded me of those young ideological middle-class beatniks that I used to meet in various dives around Kingston, Twickenham and Richmond—many of whom I met in the 60's and 70's, and who had this sentimental idea about making love, dropping out and living in peace but with who, where and what for, they didn't say. The young middle-class bloke who took me home to his parents' great estate in Richmond after we had met at Eel Pie Island and was protesting against attending a bourgeois University is probably, by now, a Chairman of a multi-national bank.

Sometimes I would vary my local walks to lead inland away from the Thames where there is much delight to be had. For example at Richmond I would walk through the town, up Richmond Hill, past the large imposing beautiful red brick building of the Star and Garter Home for retired disabled ex-servicemen and into the park. Once here one can walk in many directions. I usually walked over to the Robin Hood Gate, next to the A3, as there is a road crossing that leads you on to Wimbledon Common. On the common there are several shady hidden quiet walks through the woods, of mainly deciduous trees, away from the Hooray Henry horse riders and speed crazed cyclists.

Most of these walks take you out to the Windmill Café, where you can now buy hand-fried chips or stone-baked bread, whatever that middle class jargon means, or re-join many of the quieter woodland walks that eventually take you out to the affluence of Wimbledon Village.

Back on the attractive Thames Path, which I have found to be one of the most interesting, enjoyable and quiet walks, especially between 1969-87, when things were very frustrating for me, as I was still addicted BZ. But there are many other reasons; I have highlighted some above as to why the Thames has become a true and trusted friend to me over the years. On some stretches of the Thames Path you can sit down to relax, read, write, draw, have a sandwich or just be in your own company without feeling threatened by anyone or anything.

From Richmond, I would walk into Putney, the starting point for the Cambridge and Oxford Boat Race, via many interesting places such as Syon Park, Old Deer Park, Kew Park, the Wetlands Centre and many more places that lead you on to Sir Joseph Bazalgette's well-constructed Putney Bridge taking the teeming London traffic. Directly below the Bridge on the south side, John Christie, of Rillington Place infamy, was arrested and subsequently hanged for murder, along with the tragic Timothy Evans who was also hanged but subsequently pardoned posthumously.

Many times I have ventured further along the path to Chelsea, passing along the way the mighty Buddhist pagoda in Battersea Park. Beyond this point you have to cross the bridge to the north side where the Thames Path for the next few miles consists of pavements. Depending on where I had started my Thames Path walk on any particular day, but if it was heading east from Kingston, I usually finished at Putney Bridge in time to go into the same pub that Martin, Maria and I would use many years later. Incidentally, several hundred yards down this road there is another Youngs pub; they own many pubs around this part of London, where twenty-five years ago I used to listen to the Small Faces rock band play with the irrepressible Steve Marriott singing.

I had tried unsuccessfully during the next few months to find a full-time job, anything that I thought could be suitable to earn a living, although primarily, I was waiting on the outcome of two social work applications I had recently made. As my savings started to dwindle, I made arrangements to visit an old friend, Alan Harper, who was the boss of Data employment agency in Epsom, whom I had worked for on numerous short-term contracts. We met in a nearby pub called the White Hart, once a favourite meeting place for Irish navvies in the 1960/70s, where we had a sandwich and beer to discuss any possible jobs that might suit me.

Alan was a shrewd operator of the first order who knew everyone by name, what was going on in their lives, how much money they were making, but was short-sighted when it came to putting his hand in his pocket to help out others. He was then about fifty years of age, had been in the Army for many years, owned three houses that he rented to racing lads, single though I did not think he was gay, just tight fisted. Alan and I parted on good terms with my employment situation unresolved yet optimistic now that I had some qualifications, experience and skills to demonstrate to a potential employer looking for a competent worker. I took the 468 bus—in those days it went to Chessington Zoo. As it was going through my old manor of Runton, I thought, I would drop in to visit my mother but then decided against that due to personal reasons; instead I visited the local pub in the village called The Parrot for a quick beer. The Parrot was a rather pretentious looking place not known for its friendliness, yet it pandered to the retired, rotund, ruddy looking former public servant-type whose usual order was half a bitter and a sandwich.

Into my second pint of beer, I was shocked when a ghost from the past walked through the door physically supported by a younger woman. It was Dennis, the man who had sexually abused me all those years ago in his home when I was very young and vulnerable. Although I was now nearly fifty-five years of age my mind immediately went back to his filthy bedsit full of male nude books, where he took off my clothes so that he could kiss my innocent body, then put my penis into his mouth until I had ejaculated. His manner then was like a rough wild animal prepared to do anything to satisfy his perverted sexuality. After those perversions he carried out on me he never once asked how I felt or would I like a drink or a wash; he was totally oblivious to any kind of human feeling or understanding. As I sat there in the corner of the bar, all I could do was stare at him without taking my eyes off his old lined face for a second until he recognised me, then gestured to his assistant that he wanted to sit the other side of the bar so that he was out of sight and sound from me.

Do not panic, I said to myself, stay calm. I thought it

would be productive to phone the police right then to explain to them what he had done to me when I was still a child. Then it might still be possible, even at his advancing age, (I estimated he was now about seventy-five years old), that the police, after enquires, could take him to court to answer for the illegal sexual acts he had performed on me. Also, I wondered how many other young boys he had sexually abused over the years and who were now suffering all these years later because he had not been brought to court. I did not contact the police to complain about the sexual abuse because I thought, who would believe an ex-convict and someone whose life up to now had been fraught with personal problems? Nor had I at this stage informed Anna that I had been abused by an older man who would now be known as a paedophile.

Furthermore, my parents obviously knew nothing about the pernicious sexual abuse that had been perpetrated on me at such a young age. My parents were responsible for my well-being during the times I was being abused, yet they failed to keep me safe and secure. Now that I have had many years to think about those sexual acts carried out on me by a paedophile, the gross defilement of my body carried out in the most disgusting manner possible, I realise how difficult it has been to have normal sexual relationships with women. This assertion has to a great extent been made possible by three years of painful yet rewarding psychotherapy sessions with Clive.

Furthermore, during my social work training and subsequent employment, I had encountered many difficult and demanding situations that at first I felt unwilling or unable to challenge due to being unsure of myself even though I was in a position of trust. Eventually though, I did build up enough confidence to deal with those personal problems head on, finding inner resources I didn't realise I had. All these experiences, and many more besides, I now realise were once unresolved problems that have kept me back from developing a worthwhile life due to insecurity which was probably based on guilt or fear.

Insecurity in my case includes inadequate protection, not being firmly supported or well-adjusted and beset by anxiety which have disabled me for nearly most of my life. The consequence has been unremitting frustration caused by tension, dissatisfaction from unresolved problems or unfulfilled needs.

It is important at this stage to recapitulate one more time, to compare and contrast the earlier summary: Once again I must try to understand the complexity of my younger life when considering how sexual abuse, and other incidents, may have harmed me. All that I would like to do is elucidate the number of problems I have had, as I understand them, stated here in a chronological order to see how one problem could have affected the succeeding one which may not necessarily be the case in someone else's judgement:

(1) I was accidentally electrocuted when about three years old and I did not receive any medical treatment or therapy. (2) I was sexually abused by three paedophiles at the age of about 12/13 years old. I assumed no one knew that this abuse was happening to me and certainly not my parents. (3) When I was about 16 years old, I was knocked unconscious and did not receive any medical treatment or therapy. I was responsible for burning my hands and after

hospital admission for skin grafts, I was, in 1968, sent to prison for 3 years at the age of twenty-one. (4) I contracted dystonia at the age of 20. With little knowledge of dystonia in the medical profession, it was often mistaken as a psychiatric condition. (5) Thereafter I took valium medication for 17 years. I became addicted to valium which caused me many years of isolation and alienation. The same GP, without ever asking me any questions regards side effects etc., continued to prescribe BZ for 17 years. All I had to do was phone his secretary and place an order for a month's supply of valium at 3 x 30 mg per day, easy as ordering a curry from a takeaway service. On several occasions, I sold a full unopened bottle of valium only to receive another full supply of valium next day from my GP with no questions asked. (6) Dependency on valium caused me mental health problems. (7) Today my dystonia has settled down considerably due to four monthly botulinum toxin injections. The side effects are minimal as they include mild, short lived, flu-like symptoms.

The consequences of being sexually abused as a young boy by three paedophiles, could be that I spent so much time on my own, confused, never really knowing or understanding where I actually belonged. To this very day, even though I have three very good trusting friends who I enjoy being with very much indeed, I do not identify with any particular group. It is not surprising, therefore, that my friend Sanghadeva has on more than one occasion so aptly called me 'a rather complex person'. I came to realise a few years ago, especially during the most difficult part of my life when things began to unfold, that I was preoccupied with observation and fantasy but not really understanding what it all meant, if anything at all. What adaptive role could that type of thinking have on any possible behaviour? Over the years I have come to the conclusion that a kind of silent defensive schism had developed for the purpose of helping me survive the subsequent onslaught, as on its own, my immature inner life would have been unable to cope with such overwhelming anxiety.

Another factor that must be considered is the important lethal legacy of drinking too much alcohol and taking prescribed BZ, which I took in great quantities, especially during the years from 1967-1983 when dependence was at its most disabling for me. It is probable that these two lethal substances when taken together during a long period of time had a detrimental effect on my mental health, but to what degree, it is impossible to know. The most enduring problem which I have been aware of for many years is my impulsive behaviour which at times has caused me great pain and affected the quality of my relationships with friends, partners, siblings and ordinary people. I have no idea where this behaviour comes from though it may have originated from my early abnormal socialisation. If that was the case, then it might explain my pattern of detachment from social relationships or lack of commitment to full-time productive employment. I have asked myself this question many times: Did the experience of the electric fire accident when I was still a young child exacerbate, bearing in mind I did not receive any medical or therapeutic treatment, all my other subsequent life experiences that followed?

To compensate me from being unsuccessful in applying for several social work jobs, Alan Harper phoned me from

Data Employment to offer me a temporary position as a stock controller working at a large Department Store in Central London. This was the first time I had ever been in the back of a large store where you were frisked by security staff every time you left or entered the building. It was like being in the bowels of the earth each time I had to walk the warren of tunnels that led to my place of work which was a large dark dirty room, very similar to the rest of the back of the building that the public never saw, unlike the glitzy front. The room itself was full of various races of people all sitting in front of stock control computers, similar to Orwell's Big Brother tele-screen room, which ran the whole huge Department operation. Tom, a tall Jamaican chap, introduced himself with a handshake that nearly wrenched my arm from its socket. ''Ere man, sit at this computer,' Tom said with a low deep calculating voice. 'The last person to use the computer 'ad to be fired brudder because she did not 'ave a clue 'ow to use it. She told me she was an experienced operator but 'fraid man she couldn't even turn the fuckin' ting on. Me thinks she was being shagged so much she didn't 'ave energy for work. Any way brudder that's why you are here to work this god for sackin machine,' as Tom sympathetically explained, looking at me with bloodshot eyes.

I really did not have much of a clue myself, although of course I told Tom I was an experienced computer operator, but you didn't have to be a budding Einstein to quickly learn the basics of one. Anyway, after I gave them the University spiel they appeared to be reassured of my competence but Tom alone nearly always had one eye on me after I told him we should thank the Greeks for introducing the first computer. Similar to most

Institutional survival you keep your nose clean, eyes peeled and ears tuned in to anything that was happening in the subculture of the building such as stealing goods, cheap clothes or food or drugs. At tea breaks or lunch breaks most employees would make their way to the overcrowded canteen below ground for a smoke, tea and one of the establishment's notoriously expensive bacon sandwiches that were guaranteed to give you diarrhoea within ten minutes of eating one. The war bunker, as the canteen was eloquently nicknamed, I observed within three days, was occupied by basically three different groups—internal apartheid I called it—who always sat apart from each other. There were the Jamaicans, about twenty of them, led by the ever smiling Tom who had been working there for about fifteen years, ten as a supervisor, and had emigrated to London as a young lad in the 1960s. They all loved playing cards, shouting inaudible words at each other most of the time and fond of asking the porter, who collected the dirty canteen crockery and cutlery, 'Jack, yer 'ad much pussy lately?' Another Jamaican, Leroy, who was about sixty years old, tall, well-built and no doubt institutionalised by the store culture, was always talking most poetically about his dear suffering wife of forty years, 'I gives 'er a good seeing to every mornin' brudder without fail. You gotta keep 'em well supplied with that old chap between yer legs, brudder.'

Another group of reprobates were the twenty or so white London Cockney's who mostly read the *Socialist Worker* newspaper hoping for the Revolution to start so that they could take over the Department Store's large money strong room to buy guns for the proletarian brothers. They were a good bunch of lads, but loved their beer after work in a local pub, not far from Oxford Street, where they used to dish out a lot of the day's contraband. One of them, Jimmy Scott, had served lots of time in prison, usually had watches, small clocks and lighters all over his body for sale and often used to ask me, 'Alwight Bow son, fancy anything cheap for the missus? Got some good watches, waterproof, bombproof, sledgehammer proof, even nuclear bombproof. Only a tenner each to you my son.' Jimmy's good friend was called Alfie. They were both born in the same street in Limehouse and both locked up together for six years on Dartmoor for robbery. Alfie, being a laugh a minute, was the local Trade Union representative for Shopworkers and a constant thorn in the side of management. As the Cockneys say in the East End of London, Alfie was a great spieler when it came to asking his immediate manager for overtime, better working conditions or even attending a funeral of a friend who didn't even exist.

The third group was made up of white working-class Cockney women and Indian Hindu women. The Hindus always brought their own delightfully aromatic cooked food with them to eat in the canteen, consisting of curry, rice and bread. Many of the Jamaicans or Londoners used to joke to the ladies saying, 'Why don't you eat our delicious bacon sarnies?' or 'You can't beat bubble and squeak,' or another rib would be, 'You haven't lived darlin' until you 'ad a bowl of Tubby Issac's jellied eels!' It was all taken in good fun by all concerned. It was in these types of easy-going working environments that I could relax and enjoy myself, earn a living at the same time with little stress on me, not being too preoccupied with my own personal problems.

I must say I enjoyed the six months that I worked in the Department Store until Alan Harper informed me that the contract had finished. He had no other work for me in the near future, but reassured me that new contracts were materialising all the time. Also by now in my middle fifties, I had to be realistic about the social work options that would be available to me in the future, realising my actual practical experience was limited. However, unlike the past where many things overwhelmed me, I was now undaunted by the various challenges that lay ahead of me knowing that I had put myself in a position where I could handle responsibility.

CHAPTER TEN

COUNTRYSIDE ALLIANCE. MY FRIENDSHIP WITH DANIEL: MANY YEARS OF CONTINUOUS WALKING TOGETHER

In September 2002, in spite of being aware of the pleasure that walking brings many people, over 400,000 people from the British countryside marched on Hyde Park to demonstrate against the forthcoming legislation that would enable walkers for the first time to roam over access and other land. The Countryside Alliance viewed their fellow countrymen as a threat to their way of life, holding aloft offensive placards, 'Let them roam in the Dome' and 'Roam in your own back garden!' It was not long before Government's Countryside and Rights of way Act would be enshrined in law, giving people for the first time in Britain the legal right to be able to walk on much more land such as downs, moors and commons that hitherto they had been excluded from by farmers and landowners. This new legislation represented the culmination of over one hundred years of successful lobbying and demonstrating by walking groups, and other affiliated groups, in an effort to walk over the land that many of their forebears had died defending yet had not been able to walk on themselves.

In Hyde Park that day I witnessed with my own eyes the superficial and short-sighted argument that many of the Countryside Alliance had demonstrated for in order to hang on to a way of life that in large part had always been financed by the British taxpayer. Where did they think the Common Agricultural Policy or Milk Marketing Board guaranteed funding, which made lots of farmers very rich, come from? What is irritating is that most of those low paid British taxpayers would probably never have the opportunity to walk on a countryside footpath. Most of the money that finds its way into the pockets of country coffers to keep it vibrant, comes from tourists and walkers such as myself. Cornwall, being one of my favourite walking counties, is full of attractive small villages offering comfortable B&B's on various sections of the Coast Path. It affords opportunity to visit interesting historic sites such as castles, churches, old tin mines and museums to name but a few, yet it is one of Britain's poorest areas and would not survive without tourism.

Also, I do appreciate that various parts of the West Country quite rightly receive financial support from the European Union which goes towards helping those people who richly deserve it as their forebears worked there for generations scratching out a hard living from the sea or land. Unfortunately many young people who are living or have lived in small towns or villages with their families around Cornwall and Devon have been made to move elsewhere, due to the professional classes buying second homes, which has made it financially impossible for them to remain there.

One important point about the development of Penzance,

and surrounding areas, which had grown from a parochial 19th century village to a thriving town today visited by large numbers of tourists every year, is that the area owes its growth, in part, to British Rail. But those Hyde Park protesters failed to understand that the major part of the West Country income is provided by outsiders.

After such a hectic and interesting day it was inevitable that I landed up in a pub near Marble Arch, some three hundred yards from Hyde Park, gasping for a few pints of nutrition. The pub, the Pearl Diver at the southern end of Edgware Road, was frequented by many Arabs who congregate nearby in coffee houses smoking very strong cigarettes smelling of horse excrement. The Victorian pub itself retains its original façade of lions, unicorns and powerful looking warriors encircling Greek Ionic columns that one might think could irritate the Muslim male customers—that's if they are aware of it. On the contrary, inside of the pub was pretty rank, conforming to the modern mentality fixed on most things plastic, although the bland styled ceiling was colourfully attractive with light blue/orange rectangular shapes.

I had been using the Pearl Diver for many years, probably since the days when I frequented the colourful bars of Soho, that place of many faces where even the pigeons take acid on a regular basis. I've also observed over the years that the Pearl Diver was also frequented, especially in the evenings, by young well-dressed gay males touting for work particularly with the Arabs in mind, who love the feminist camp behaviour of young white boys. On this particular occasion I sat down looking out onto the packed Edgware Road where thousands of chanting banner-carrying countryside supporters were making their way down to Marble Arch underground station where a young veiled female wearing training shoes stood trying to sell the Koran to them.

What a colourful, vibrant and multi-national city London is, I thought to myself, as the local one-armed paper seller uttered something in Cockney through the window that I could not understand. Having drunk four pints of my favourite 'real ale' called Red Dog, guaranteed to put you on the moon after six pints, I took the packed bus to Victoria station. This time, just like any other time, there was standing room only so I decided, on arriving at the station, to have another beer while the crowd thinned out. Incidentally, what irritates me is the constant spiel we get from pubs to call everything real—from places in Arran, Yorkshire, Norfolk, Wales, Devon, Cornwall, London, to name a few, that have this incessant desire to advertise 'real' ale, 'real' home cooked food, 'real fire' with logs. Only the other day I saw advertised on the South Downs, 'Bungalow for rent with authentic views over the Downs.' What were they selling all those years ago before they started advertising REAL with everything? The Victoria Station Pub I went into that day was one of those High street chain pubs that is well known for a pint of ale (they still use the word *real* but only for its beers), decent well cooked food, yet reassuringly without pop music.

Two hours later sitting on the train nearly inebriated among the well-dressed commuters, nearly all of them reading *The Metro*, I read that Victoria Beckham, that sage of the inner life, had passed her first O-level for flower arranging. On arrival at Penge East station, I tentatively made my way by foot some half mile to have another beer, this time in the Golden Lion in Penge High Street. Many years ago the Golden Lion used to be a popular local Cinema but was made obsolete with the development of the multi-national mega cinemas that now appear in most burgeoning affluent High streets and industrialised parks on the outskirts of City centres.

After buying a beer, I sat opposite a chap I had seen in this large skilfully decorated pub a few times before but I did not know his name or anything else about him except he was nearly always reading a paperback book. 'Hi there, how's it going, nice day,' I commented to the chap sitting opposite me who was wearing a rather thick beard which appeared to have several pieces of crisps lodged in it and a light blue shirt stained with so much beer on the front that it had changed colour to light brown. 'Yes, a very pleasant day indeed,' came the reply in a middle-class accent that had probably been developed, I thought, from one of the Oxbridge Institutions. Covertly looking at this chap, without being intrusive, I got a picture of him being some sort of University Professor of maths or physics.

'My name is Barry, nice to meet you. Are you a regular in here?' I thought I had better introduce myself otherwise he might think I am some sort of thick football supporter only interested in drinking beer with the sole intention of getting drunk so that I can make trouble. 'I'm Daniel,' was his uninterested response, peering over the top of his rather dirty glasses that were certainly in need of being put through a car wash. 'As a walker and interested in the politics of the countryside, I've been to Hyde park today to watch the powerful Countryside Alliance group demonstrate against the mass of humanity walking in the countryside and spoiling their way of life.' Daniel thought for a moment before responding. 'I enjoy walking myself and I am opposed to any person telling me that I can't walk anywhere in the countryside,' was his sharp focused reply. 'Would you like a beer, Daniel?' I offered, thinking to myself that by now I had drunk at least six pints of beer and was determined to have another. 'I will buy you one instead,' demanded Daniel, convincing me more than ever that he was not a teacher as I first thought but some kind of Government Official.

While he was at the bar buying the beer, I looked at the title of the book he was reading. *Stalin: A critical analysis of his leadership*. Bloody hell, what a heavy book to read, I thought, and conjectured that he must be a Communist. Daniel returned to our table with two pints of strong ale. It was reassuring to know he was an ale drinker like myself. I held up my glass. 'Cheers Daniel, all the best to you,' I said. His response was similar to mine. 'What do you do for a living?' I inquisitively asked as more drips from his glass of beer fell onto his stained shirt. 'I teach piano part-time at a London University and I also have a part-time job teaching piano in Sussex,' he half-heartedly responded, followed by, 'but I am fed up with both jobs.' Before he could ask me, I said, 'I trained as a social worker but although I'm unemployed at the moment, I'm optimistic about finding some work.' It was not a very convincing response. As I wanted to spend some time with Anna, I bade farewell to Daniel suggesting that we could meet the following week for a walk somewhere, to which he agreed, giving me his contact phone number.

Daniel and I did meet the following week in brilliant sunshine and walked a few miles on the Thames Path, passing attractive native trees covered in various coloured blossom, from Putney to Kingston. That enjoyable day became the first of many walks, both locally and nationally, that we would undertake together and where a warm friendship has developed. To mention a few of the National Trails we have walked together: Pembrokeshire Coast Path, Norfolk Coast Path, South West Coast Path, North Downs Way, South Downs Way, Pennine Way, Isle of Arran and the Isles of Islay and Jura. Due to my own personal problems I have had over the years enjoyed walking mainly on my own, as I still continue to, but I also look forward to walking with Daniel. That regular walking has developed into an enjoyable activity for me, as I hope it has for him, and is full of good camaraderie. Throughout the twelve years that I have known Daniel we have usually met once every week or two weeks depending on our other commitments.

One of our favourite walks is on the picturesque North Downs Way from Guildford to Box Hill Station which is about 15 miles when you include the station link to pick up the walk just off the A281. Regardless of the time of the year you walk this particular section, although it must be said it is particularly beautiful in summer, there is always so much different flora and fauna to experience. In springtime there are always so many different kinds of wild flowers in full bloom, including one of my favourites, the primrose that proliferates in ideal conditions on path edges next to deciduous woodland and woodland glades found in abundance on the North Downs Way. The terrain of this particular section of the North Downs Way is not difficult to walk so can be enjoyed by most people and is suitable for prams, and on some sections, electric motor scooters. After living most of my life in cities with excessive noise, smells and artificial light, I have throughout the years tried to retrain my awareness of and become more receptive to some of the different countryside sights, sounds and smells that abound on or around the different local or national trails.

On nearly every occasion when Daniel and I go walking we endeavour to do at least three things: To remain silent for as long as possible so we can take in the immediate experience of our environment; to sit down somewhere quiet, preferably on a fallen tree or log, to eat our sandwiches; and, after walking many miles, time and geography permitting, we always try to aim for a few pints of decent ale. Oh, what a sight we must have looked on many occasions, when alighting from the last coast train at East Croydon station, as two bedraggled figures, tired, muddy and listing like the Titanic after a few beers, made our way through the ticket barrier.

During the early years of our walking together, Daniel used to invariably contract what he eloquently called the 'Croydons' which was in actuality a sore crutch that made him walk like some out of work jockey. He now reassures me that the first article he buys when visiting his local shop is a large Johnson's baby powder. Mind you, there has been the odd occasions when Daniel has contracted the 'Plumpton's' and the 'Bromley's', or any other place where we have ended up, but fortunately such painful sights are becoming a rarity. On another walking occasion we got off the train at Leatherhead station, when we walked down the platform steps and onto the street below when Daniel asked, 'What's your next job going to be?' I said, spontaneously, 'Selling pegs and elephant's piss,' which became one of those standing jokes for a while.

In essence one of the main reasons I venture into a woodland setting, is that it is conducive to silence and peace. That's why I started taking longer walks when I contracted dystonia from the age of about twenty-two, as it gave me the opportunity to get away from stress, to develop various relaxation techniques and help me think how I might sort out my life at the time. To listen then, as I do now, to a robin singing its heart out on a branch just feet away from you is truly a wonderful and inspiring experience.

In a few of the social care positions I had, one of my main aims was to try to empower people by encouraging them to start walking in the garden, down the road or something more strenuous by walking to the local park. One or two went further when I took them by bus to Happy Valley, a large track of land near Coulsdon South Station; there we walked for several miles together, something they had not achieved before but they became sufficiently motivated to walk on their own when I left the job. Although I wasn't directly employed by the local authority to work with young people concerned, I suggested to colleagues involved with them, that walking over a period of several days or more carrying a heavy rucksack, cooking their own breakfasts, can especially motivate youngsters to help build a healthy self-esteem.

Other than our passions for nature, walking and the beer, Daniel's lifelong passion since he was a young boy has been to play the piano and subsequently to compose his own music. He explained to me that when he was young his strict yet supportive father gave him every opportunity to develop his piano playing. When he was a young boy and teenager he performed in many concerts on his own and also in duets with his lifelong friend Gordon. When they were teenagers they performed together in Bermuda. Later on in his early 30's Daniel spent two years in Hungary where he studied piano and composition, an experience he mostly enjoyed. From the outset of our friendship, Daniel has always invited me to both his public and private concerts in areas that include Enfield, Brighton, Pimlico, Kensington, Kew and Hatfield. In other concerts, Daniel and I have listened to other musicians perform his own work which he finds particularly pleasing. Daniel does have a good sense of humour, but is an intense, serious person which is reflected in a lot of his music and this is something I enjoy. No doubt one of the reasons why we have sustained a good friendship is because I am not a musician and know nothing about classical music apart from being aware that certain pieces sometimes move me to tears. But the main reason I enjoy Daniel's friendship is the enjoyable and challenging walking we achieve together. To sum that up, I shall quote one of the delightful sayings of Epicurus (341-270 BC): 'Friendship goes dancing round the world proclaiming to us all to awake to the praises of a happy life.'

CHAPTER ELEVEN

BEAUTY AND RELIGION: WORKING FOR AN ARTIST

As promised, Alan Harper from Data Employment did phone me three weeks later after my interesting employment had finished at the large Central London Department store. He phoned to inform me that he had an elderly American male client who had lived in Kensington for many years, after his partner had died, so I was to proceed, as they say, with caution. Alan and I made arrangements to meet Budd Kramer one afternoon in his attractive ochre-coloured Edwardian three-storey town house just off the main High Street. Sitting ensconced in luxury blue cord armchairs drinking red wine, Alan introduced me to Mr Kramer, explaining to him that I had trained as a social worker. He went on to inform Mr Kramer that I had other useful work experience relevant to someone like him who was aged 80 years and had had a stroke a few years ago which had affected the left side of his body. Mr Kramer asked me various questions relating to the helper vacancy, the official job title, placing a lot of emphasis not surprisingly on supporting him with practical skills not just around the house but also elsewhere such as driving him to the local supermarket. After three hours of questions, Mr Kramer must have been satisfied with the way I had presented myself because he asked me to start work for him the following Monday.

When I arrived at around 10 a.m. at the Kramer household, it was a chilly, windy January day, my 56th birthday. I observed that rubbish had been blown down the street and had congregated in a large heap down into his outside cellar. The trees were bare of leaves and no birds could be heard singing. I hoped this wasn't a sign of things to come. I rang the bell of the large wooden yellow coloured door which was opened by a tall slim African woman wearing pink gloves and holding a broom ready for action, I thought. 'Hello Barry, welcome, please come in—Budd is expecting you,' she said in near perfect English. She continued before I could say anything, 'My name is Ella and I work here three mornings a week as Mr Kramer's house cleaner. Would you like a coffee, Barry?' 'Yes please,' was my immediate response as I was feeling rather cold after standing around outside the house for only a few minutes.

At that moment Mr Kramer came walking into the kitchen. 'Hello my dear boy, how nice to see you once again,' he smiled. To lessen the tension he explained in his American-English middle-class accent that he thought he was a bit of a snob and hoped, therefore, that I didn't mind being called 'dear boy', which he thought was a term of endearment. I personally enjoyed being called 'dear boy' around the house yet it did have a ring of the Victorian upstairs-downstairs snobbery to it; but as long as I was being paid he could have called me rubber legs for all I really cared! Incidentally, my bedroom was downstairs in the basement, but due to the design of the house, it backed onto a most charming well stocked and maintained rear garden that became full of grey squirrels during the time the hazel nuts were growing.

Budd, as he insisted on being called, then proceeded to give me a tour of his beautifully decorated three-story house which took some time as he had a pronounced limp due to the stroke he had contracted when living with his gay partner Tony in Spain. He explained that his late partner had carried out various types of medical research around the world, leaving Budd to develop his own art work. When Budd had moved to New York as a young man to study fine art at University, he had first met Tony at an exhibition of the Impressionists' work in down-town Quigley's Art Gallery. After living together in New York for about one year, they bought a small farm with orchards and woods in Italy and lived there together for many years before moving to Spain.

There were creative oil, chalk, ink and crayon pictures of Budd's all round the house, but especially many more in his huge studio, the largest private studio, he claimed, in London. It was the size of the three floors of his house put together which left you wondering who used the place now that Budd was unable to use his painting hand. During the six months that I was employed by Budd, and with his direction, I enjoyed touching up several of his interesting pictures with paint or ink which was a process I found fascinating. He was an interesting chap with an enquiring intelligent mind even though disability must have been difficult for him, especially after a lifetime of producing his own creative work, to sell to anyone sufficiently interested in learning more about his inner life.

A typical day started with both of us having breakfast downstairs in the room next to where I slept, he listening to the radio which could have been heard one hundred yards away and me usually drinking lots of coffee to overcome the hangover from the night before. Afterwards we would have a brief discussion about what we would be eating for the evening meal, something that Budd very much looked forward to especially as he could participate in the actual cooking. During most mornings I used to go for a walk around the local area, and occasionally I would have coffee in nearby Battersea Park. At around 1 p.m. we would have lunch together which usually consisted of Budd's healthy eating regime of salad, pasta and one glass of red wine, but he always insisted, and I never resisted, that I have several glasses. 'My dear boy, you must have another glass of red wine if you so wish,' was his way of saying enjoy it, or perhaps what he was really trying to say was, you know where my bedroom is dear boy!

The downstairs evening meal was sometimes a bit of a pantomime as we were both the central figures trying to cook new dishes minus the cooking instructions. Sometimes we put in too much or too little salt; on one occasion we, or rather I, forgot to put in the main ingredient, called chicken, into the oven. We both burnt Budd's favourite dishes, especially roasted pigeon breasts in red wine sauce, fit afterwards for burnt offerings only, and on another occasion we checked the progress of the roast to find that we had not turned on the electric oven. One evening we must have had too much to drink for when we were washing up a particular sticky pan, I thought I heard Budd say rather excitedly, 'I'll hold it and you can scrub it.' No more will be said on that subject.

All the meals were had downstairs in a playful atmosphere, but when Budd had invited guests round we would dress the large oak dinner table with all his fine cutlery, crockery and glass. One such notable occasion cannot but spring to mind when a Father from the local Catholic community came round for an evening meal with us. Father Dermot was an interesting chap of around seventy years of age; he had lectured on theology for many years at Cambridge and at the same time had led church services for students. He had had several scholarly books published to great acclaim by his colleagues, the Catholic Church and secular commentators who had all concluded that his work was written for the development of higher spiritual endeavour. When I asked him if he would like a drink he responded cautiously by saying, 'Only a rather small gin and tonic. Thank you.' Dermot did not have any noticeable foibles like those of Budd's. After an hour of good humoured discussion I asked Father Dermot if he would like another drink. 'Yes, the same again please, that would be nice,' he responded. I must confess now by saying that I gave the good Father a rather large gin with very little tonic. Within fifteen minutes Father Dermot had requested another, this time saying with a little lack of mindfulness, 'Yes, that was a bloody good drink that was, Budd. I wouldn't say no to another.' He subsequently had three more drinks when Budd became suspicious that someone had been plying the Father with excessive amounts of alcohol that he had not requested. After strong coffee we put the sobered Father into a taxi to take him safely back home to his religious community.

CHAPTER TWELVE

MY MOTHER DIES

My mother had been admitted to Epsom hospital for observation, having not felt well with stomach pains for a few days. Anna and I took a large bunch of flowers with us to visit mother, hoping to brighten her up since she had told me long ago she did not like hospitals at all. It was not surprising she felt that way because from my mother's background you were always conscious of the workhouse being the next stop if you could not cope with everyday life. When we arrived at my mother's very clean bright hospital room, full of roses from well wishes, my sister-in-law Bernadette was there having a cup of tea with her. It was good to see her for I had not seen her or my brother Bob for some considerable time. 'How good to see you Bowser,' came her genuine smiling response. Bowser is yet another nickname I have been given over the years. I introduced Anna and told Bernadette what we had been doing with our lives during the past years and all that sort of meaningless information that people don't really want to hear but feel you are compelled to explain. After three weeks' rest my mother was allowed home on the proviso that she was supported by several of her local children and friends she had made after my father had died.

My sister Susan, another sibling whom I had not seen for ages, phoned me several weeks later to say that mother had fallen over again at home and had been admitted to St Helier Hospital for observations to see how her condition responded to treatment. I went to visit my mother on three separate occasions and on every occasion she looked well, although probably due to medication, she would intermittently fall asleep. On the fourth time I visited my mother, Susan was there, and though I had not seen her face-to-face for many years, she looked no different to the last time I saw her. She said that mother's problem was that she couldn't stop working, not surprisingly, perhaps; she kept bending down to pick up something unimportant and would then fall over, cutting her head. The last time that happened she hit her head on the television, had fallen onto the floor and, being unable to phone for the ambulance, had slept all night on the floor.

Susan had attended the three local schools that I had, met her husband on holiday, got married and had worked hard to buy a comfortable home, bring up two children who had by now moved on and so consequently she had more time for herself. It was rather odd though, for as I sat in front of my sister, I thought to myself, I don't really know her at all, which was the similar experience I had with my other siblings. Other than reciting all their first names, I don't even know where most of my siblings live yet alone trying to understand their lives, their loves, likes and dislikes that most families, I assume, are informed about. There are at least thirty nephews and nieces in my family but I have met no more than half of them. The point being that you have to spend time with someone if you want to get to know them well.

My mother's medical condition deteriorated to the extent that St Helier Hospital phoned me early one Sunday morning to say that as my mother was near to death, I had best come to the hospital immediately. By the time I had arrived she had passed away from the life she held onto with all her immense tenacity. My mother, who was a gallant warrior to the end, died on 25 April 2004: What can I say about her that does justice to her life and is a true reflection on who she was and the immense responsibility she carried on her shoulders throughout her difficult, demanding and unhappy life? From what I understood of her background, my mother came from a decent secure working-class family where hard work was always the order of the day. Both her parents did their best to provide for their children during the ugly upheaval of the First World War when times were very difficult and resources very scarce indeed.

After working at two unskilled jobs in the local button factory not far from where she lived, my mother, like other young working-class women of her generation, was expected to marry young and have a family. She was only eighteen years old when she married my father and had their first child less than a year later. She went on to have another twelve children which must have been a considerable physical and emotional burden for her; trying to provide food and clothes alone would have preoccupied all her waking life. Looking at various old black and white family photographs recently, I thought that all my siblings appeared well fed, tidy and clean. What a monumental effort that must have been for my mother when you consider that she washed nearly everything by hand—only the bed sheets were sent to the laundry—using an old clapped out mangle to extract most of the water from the clothes. It is due credit to my mother that she managed the family household with the minimal resources she had at her disposal.

It is, therefore, not surprising that the heavy responsible burden of providing for thirteen children took its toll on her. I have observed many mothers over the years, both professionally and personally, who were unable to cope, due to many different problems, with even one or two children. Yet my mother with immense strength of character showed much determination to look after her own children. No doubt her dominant personality helped her control the chaotic home environment full of screaming children. Sometimes, not surprisingly, she was unable to cope with the overwhelming stress of looking after so many vulnerable children, to the extent that it was inevitable she used physical and emotional abuse on them. The tragic consequence of an insecure family life has been detrimental to some of my siblings' relationships, including myself. Unless one has vast resources it is near impossible to socialise thirteen children in a way that provides the opportunity for them to grow and develop their individual lives although most of my siblings did just that.

It is important to remember that my mother was an individual in her own right as well as being a grandmother, sister, niece, aunt and daughter. It never occurred to me when I was a young immature person, that my mother or father had any other kind of identity of their own beyond being a providing parent. As such she got very little out of her life, and since the day she married until my father died, my mother had never spent one whole day alone on her own. Sometimes I'm sure I treated my mother no better than an unpaid servant, assuming that she would always be there to cook my meals and wash my clothes. For that I am truly sorry to my mother for such an immature attitude towards an individual person, who like most people, started her life full of dreams and expectations, hoping that by moving with her new young husband to Runton things would turn out well for them. Unlike today's family culture, where people understandably move on due to many different reasons, my parents remained together throughout those difficult years until the end of their lives. Both of my parents will not be forgotten as the family purchased between them a large seat which is in the public grounds of Bourne Hall, Ewell Village, overlooking a lake full of various water birds. Like my father, I shall never forget my mother as she gave so much and received so little.

So that we could have a permanent reminder of our past way of life, a friend and I made a video of various parts of Runton as it took in some of our earliest experiences. We visited our first two schools, West Lane infant and junior schools, the latter having being sold for private residence. Interestingly my friend, some forty-five years later, could still find his initials that he inscribed when he was a pupil on one of the old Victorian brick walls at West Lane academy 'for rogues'. When we arrived at my old home, I was shocked to see how the house had deteriorated since my mother's death. It was now empty and ghost like with large weeds growing up through the concrete that my father and I had laid many years before. My friend who had been videoing the proceedings, and has been a good friend of my youngest sibling Lawrence since they were teenagers, commented on the small size of the rooms and thought it impossible that so many children could have fitted into such a small area to eat and play. I had one more brief glance at the garden, looked at my father's rather old dilapidated shed and stopped at the front of the house to look through the curtained window, for the last time, to observe the right-hand corner of the empty front room where my dear mother used to sit. All was silent.

CHAPTER THIRTEEN

FURTHER ACADEMIC SUCCESS, PATROLLING THE STREETS OF SURREY, FRIENDSHIP WITH MICK AND MY BROTHER MARTIN DIES

Other than working at two part-time social care jobs in Surrey, during the previous two years before my mother's death I had been researching for a Master of Science (MSc) degree at the Institute of Psychiatry in South London. Many years prior to the MSc course proceeding at the Institute, I had been an outpatient attending the Neurology clinic where people with dystonia were sent, some considered to have a psychiatric illness, in those desperate days when I was unable to function. The incompetent medical diagnoses that were made in those days was a scathing indictment of their woefully inadequate training. For example, it was understandable that doctors had asked me whether I was still taking my medication and whether it helped my dystonia; but they never enquired about the state of my emaciated body or whether I had a job or whether I had a place to live, which are all relevant questions that can affect your overall neurological well-being. But they would argue that is the responsibility of social workers to find out, not doctors. The only thing I did receive was the same old clapped out information. It was no different to the blind leading the blind.

The first year at the Institute of Psychiatry I regularly attended lectures, read and wrote various essays which in time would lead to the Advanced Award in Social Work award. I did not find the overall content of this course particularly inspiring which is probably the reason why I falsified one of the course elements although there were several visiting lecturers who I did find interesting, but assumed some of them did not take social workers that seriously. That is not to say that AASW courses or similar are not relevant, they are an important source of on-going professional development for social workers of all backgrounds.

I enjoyed the second year at the Institute of Psychiatry where I studied for the MSc degree in Mental Health Social Work. My research thesis entailed collating information sent in to me from over one hundred questionnaires completed by those individual volunteers who had been involved in the failed BZ Litigation during the 1990s. In the questionnaires there were various questions that focused on the individuals' personal experience of taking BZ; more importantly, I wanted to find out how many of them had received or were offered non-medical treatment such as psychotherapy. The results were quite shocking, but not surprising, which demonstrated that very few research volunteers were actually offered any other non-medical treatment by their BZ prescriber. My MSc thesis results were similar to other medical and non-medical BZ research that had been carried out, before and after, my research.

There was a short shoddy oral exam where four people squeezed into my tutor's small, cramped room. To this very day I am still very disappointed that I wasn't given a reason as to why I did not receive a viva voce, notwithstanding that the BZ issue has been a personal, as well as a huge professional, problem that the present Government say they are going to sort out. Furthermore my MSc research took me many months to write, understandably, during which I read many sources on the subject. After discussing the complex issues with users or former users of BZ, not those involved with my thesis, whose invaluable experiences informed some of my work, I was unhappy that no respect was shown to their invaluable input. There was a suggestion that the reason why I wasn't allowed a viva voce was because some of my references were not up to date!

I did, however, enjoy using the extensive library to research my thesis, and as a student, being able to attend some of the interesting public debates that covered various mental health issues. With the right conditions I had been able to work hard so that I could pass my MSc degree, which would have been only a dream years ago when I was struggling to find any kind of coherent voice of my own.

With Anna in support, I deservedly received my MSc degree certificate from the Vice Chancellor, Graeme Davies, and acknowledged by the large audience, at the Royal Festival Hall in October 2004. 'I have done quite well,' I thought to myself as I stood at the Festival bar looking at my reflection, dressed in mortar board and black gown, in the large glass mirror opposite.

After MSc success, I took another leap forward by progressively taking more responsibility towards a personal life that can enjoy the everyday experiences most people of a younger age have long since integrated into their own personal lives. Those conditions I needed to change my life around are the qualities that education can deliver: books can offer limitless possibilities of learning that can develop into knowledge that can set you free. The new understanding I now have of myself tries to focus, with faltering steps, on a creative vision of human endeavour.

After going through a formal application and two interviews, I eventually found myself employment as a community worker with a local authority in Surrey working specifically with vulnerable adults who had various drug and alcohol problems but generally patrolling the streets. This was a new scheme, funded by the Labour Government, to help local communities take back control of their streets. One of my first duties, supported by an experienced senior colleague, was to appear in the magistrate's court to give evidence against a local well known drug abuser who had been charged with criminal damage, smashing a large pane of glass belonging to Tesco's. As he was found guilty—it was the drug abuser's twentieth criminal conviction—the magistrates decided that a custodial sentence would be inappropriate and decided instead to make an order whereby he would spend a stipulated number of months in a drug rehabilitation unit.

I mention this court case of a drug abuser found guilty of criminal damage because it highlights the ever-growing problem throughout Britain which successive governments have tried to resolve by introducing a number of costly measures that have ultimately failed. The answer to the ever-growing illegal drug abuse problem in Britain is a rather complex one to tackle, bearing in mind that many different agencies have tried in their own way to address it without success. Decriminalising drugs has been debated for some considerable time but even in those countries where it has been tried, illegal drugs, gangs and profit still exist.

Other than patrolling the streets with a colleague where we acted as the 'eyes and ears' of the community reporting crime or anti-social behaviour to police or other agencies, we also attended weekly tenants and residents association (TRA) meetings. At those meetings, sometimes attended by police and other agencies, local people had the opportunity to discuss various problems that sometimes besieged their otherwise well-run and clean estates. On one occasion I stood up to give an outline of what our job entailed, explaining that as community workers we can be contacted by various means of communication, including walking into our Estate office to report anything of concern. At that point Muriel, the TRA chairperson and champion of the downtrodden, jumped up to undermine me by shouting, 'You fuckin' lot are never there when we need yer, are they Bert?' Bert was a white male, aged about seventy with silver hair growing over his ears which made him look like some over-aged beatnik. 'Yus, that's right me dear Muriel, they are never around when fings are 'appening on our Estate,' he mumbled. This sort of argument continued all afternoon until Jack, a former Desert Rat, intervened to say he was getting hungry for his dinner and wanted to call it a day. 'The 'ol girl has me dinner ready soon, bubble and squeak it is, so let's all fuck orf home,' was Jack's response. This employment, similar to all the others I've had, was another step along life's highway, as I tried to understand during the time I earned my living, the nature of the human predicament.

Whilst working for this local authority it was my good fortune that I met Mick who used to visit our office in the capacity of contract trainer where he would lead courses relevant to the development of our work as community workers. When I got to know Mick he explained to me that when he was a young lad stammering had prevented him from doing many things that might otherwise have enabled him to move on with his life. Further interesting information that Mick informed me about stammering gave me more understanding into my brother David's own disabling condition. Throughout the years, to his credit, Mick has overcome his own limitations by meeting other working-class people who were self-taught and who encouraged him to educate himself. This self-education over the years has encouraged him to be employed as a teacher so that he can help other students realise their own potential.

Since 2005 Mick, Daniel and I have developed a regular walking group going out for local or longer walks of five or more days around the country. As I highlighted above on my walks with Daniel, Mick has joined us on several of our challenging yet immensely interesting long-distance walks, including Pembrokeshire Coast Path, Isle of Arran and the South West Coast Path in both Cornwall and Devon.

During our first night on rain-soaked Arran we arranged a B&B, not far from the ferry, in a large Victorian house with several gardens full of shrubs, especially large multi-coloured rhododendrons. Mick and Daniel shared a twin bedroom, as they usually do but apologised to each other for smelly feet, and I was given a double room on my own due to sleep problems I've had for the last three years. The three of us were drinking tea in my bedroom, looking at pornography on the television, when the rather austere looking Scottish landlady knocked on the door. 'Come in!' I shouted, and she opened the door to be confronted by me sitting on the bed wearing only my Marks & Spencer multi-coloured pants. She looked rather sheepishly at me. 'Sorry for the intrusion, but I'm afraid you will have to move to another bedroom tomorrow due to a couple needing this room,' she said, trying to close the door quickly as I still sat there like a Dorothy Perkins mannequin. She probably thought, why can't those decadent Sassenachs ever refrain from such disgusting behaviour! I'm afraid thereafter I had no choice but to nickname her the 'Arran Beast'.

Some months later my eldest brother Martin died of cancer, aged 70, on the 8th August 2006 in Pathos, Cyprus. We held a memorial service for him on 8th September 2006 at All Saints Church, Runton, which was well attended by two of his sons, several of his siblings and also two friends from his Army days in the East Surrey Regiment. It was a wonderful warm turn out for a kind, friendly person who was greatly liked and valued by most people. The whole congregation sang several hymns including Martin's favourite 'Morning has Broken', followed by a brief moving account of his life by his son Stephen. Afterwards there was an enjoyable reception in the Hall next door where for the first time in years I met a few siblings, uncles, aunts, nieces, nephews, cousins and acquaintances.

On 23-26 November 2006, two siblings and I flew out to Cyprus to spend a few days with Martin's wife to visit his final resting place, a small grave several miles from Pathos. After working hard all his life, he retired with his wife to Pathos where they bought a beautiful house in a quiet road inhabited by several other Britons, but he did return to London occasionally to earn some money working with his friends. I shall miss his good humour.

CHAPTER FOURTEEN

WISHHART CATERING, MY EMPLOYMENT TRIBUNAL AND VOLUNTARY WORK

After leaving the decent job I had as a community worker in Surrey, I never stayed anywhere very long, Alan Harper once again helped me out by placing me with a catering company supplying services to horse racing tracks around the South of England. My first day at Wishhart Catering of Kingston was about meeting my new colleagues in convivial surroundings in a plush new Hotel not far from Sandown Racetrack. After all the new employees had congregated in the large well-furnished hall, Mr Greening, the Chief Executive, sitting on the stage, rose to his feet to explain why we had all been invited to today's meeting, being careful to point out that he hoped we would all become an integral part of Wishhart Catering.

The next day, along with six other colleagues, we drove down to Plumpton Races taking with us enough catering supplies, we hoped, for a two-day meeting held in that beautiful part of Sussex, a mile from the foothills of the South Downs. The first race had started, a three-mile steeplechase, when three men around my age approached the Silver Stand Bar. I was delegated the job as barman before racing. I realised that one of the three was Jimmy Hughes who I recognised from all those years ago in Epsom. He also recognised me immediately. 'Be fecken Jesus, how are you, Barry?' he asked, smiling still with an unmistakeable broad Dublin accent. 'Hi Jim, so good to see you after so many years. How is the rest of the Hughes gang?' 'They're all well be Jesus, though I don't see any of them a great deal. They're all still after the crack so they are.' I pulled their three pints of Guinness, said goodbye to Jim and carried on serving the ever-growing line of waiting punters when Jim returned to the bar to hand me a betting slip with his contact phone number on it. Unfortunately I lost the slip of paper he gave me so we did not meet again.

Looking back on those times when I associated with the Hughes family, and others in a similar position, I wonder now if I wasted my time or did I benefit from those experiences? Many years later, it is very difficult to know, but one thing is for sure, I certainly enjoyed myself at the time going around with characters such as Jimmy Hughes or Larry the Louse. I wonder whatever happened to Larry who disappeared one day from Epsom never to be seen again. Like many thousands of Irishmen who ventured forth to earn their fortune either in the USA or Britain, most ended up grafting on motorway construction but a few like Larry preferred to chance their luck walking the open byways. I should imagine he is long dead but when I am walking on a quiet out of the way track or sitting down in a lush flower meadow to eat my sandwiches, I sometimes think of all those hardy individual souls such as Larry who didn't want to live the household life, but instead took their chances elsewhere.

Par for the course, as they say. I only lasted working for Wishhart Catering for three months but they were a decent employer and above all else I enjoyed the thrill of driving round the countryside, visiting different, especially small race tracks, which demonstrates that I'm basically still a drifter at heart. Similar jobs to the one I had at Wishhart Catering are ideal for those people who don't like a regular place of work, instead preferring to be on the road meeting different people who visit the large number of race tracks around the country.

After the Wishhart job had finished, I worked several years until early 2008, my longest employment ever, as a neighbourhood warden for a London Local Authority. Due to the constraints placed upon me, I am unable or unwilling to state any details beyond the following: I ceased my employment due to a forthcoming employment tribunal action that I had taken out against my former employer which I subsequently lost. I was the first warden to successfully apply to the council for back pay they had failed to pay me at the time. The £825 was subsequently paid in full. That paved the way for all my colleagues to successfully receive their back pay. This important point was confirmed in the Tribunal Judge findings. Regards my legal fees of £500, that was paid for in full by financial donations from my former colleagues and anonymous well-wishers for which I am very grateful.

Besides having a legitimate claim against my former employer, I had also been unofficially warned by two council employees, one a former trade union official and the other a former manager, that I would not be re-employed due to my sickness record. At the time the council were re-assessing all the wardens for their jobs and one of the main criteria they used was based on an individual's sick record. By fair means or foul, the council wanted to get rid of those employees deemed to be 'trouble makers' whose only *raison d'être* for speaking up was to voice concern about the various practises which they understood to be detrimental to local service users.

'What the fuck are you doing here, Bazzer?' came a loud booming sound from someone to the side of me. When I looked it was my old mate Pete Upton smiling at me like a Cheshire cat. He was wearing his building overalls and holding a large trowel in his hand. I walked over to him. 'Hi, Pete, how is it going?' I smiled and arrogantly spurted out, 'I'm doing contract work again for a new Agency from Putney I registered with a few months ago. I've got a job as a porter, something Einstein would have been proud of.' 'Good to see you, Barry. What's an educated man like you working here for?' Pete provocatively asked. 'Well, Pete, there was no other work available so I had no choice but to take this poxy job.'

Pete, along with his two colleagues, had started knocking down a large wall outside the stores where I was working, to rebuild it with reinforcing rods as the last one had cracked. I thought about what Pete Upton had said to me about working hard for all those years to educate myself only to end up in a very lowly job working in factory stores with other men who did not even get the opportunity to go to University. As I was getting on in years I was not in a position where I could choose. What can you do under the capitalist system where the only *raison d'être* for existence, it appears, is to make money so that you can

keep the wolf away from the door.
These are the times when I feel like putting on my boots, rucksack and hit the byways of Britain where at least I can get some fresh air, exercise and be surrounded by a healthy environment. It is either tragic or admirable, I oscillate on the subject, when you think that a person grafts hard all his life, for forty or fifty years, to buy or rent a home that he will never own. On retirement most will only exist for a few years and then die probably in debt not having had any real enjoyment out of life. Isn't it absurd that most working-class people have never really had the opportunity to walk over the beautiful British countryside, the place their forebears died protecting during various conflicts and where most of it is still owned by families that originated from Norman times?

After that rant against the inherited landowning elite, today we have a new challenge for those pampered poltroons from the working class super rich. The new god today is money epitomised by the vast amounts paid to sports people such as Wayne Rooney. In Britain today we have the celebrity super class of film stars, bankers, insurance brokers, sports personnel and many others whose only spurious claim to fame is a large pair of breasts or having sex with many famous or infamous partners.

Meanwhile I'm now well over 60 years of age and as a volunteer I am trying to help those people, like the many good people who helped me over the years, to improve their quality of life. Over the years I've volunteered for Amnesty International, a great organisation that supports prisoners of conscience around the world from State violence. When I first visited their London office early in the early 1980s, I was so reassured and confident that there were individuals prepared to stick their necks out for other people so that they may be free to speak out against oppression wherever it may be.

Documented above is the great work that Victims of Tranquillisers did for other less fortunate people—another example of what can be achieved when people co-operate together. I was so privileged to have volunteered for VOT as I learnt so much from Reg Peart and all those other countless individual heroes whose lives really moved me beyond words. I shall never forget any of those BZ users.

The Dystonia Society has been a very supportive organisation for me, and no doubt for many others, over the years. They have arranged countless meetings where members, families and friends can meet each other in an environment of support and goodwill. Regardless of where you live there are now local dystonia support groups around the country where group meetings are held on a regular basis. For those who need personal support or require up-to-date information, the Dystonia Society has an effective helpline during office hours. Other times there are also helpful volunteer contacts you can phone or email for support. In 2010, I did voluntary work at the Dystonia Society based at their London office for a year, where I generally helped out with whatever needed doing from making tea, answering the phone, mailing post and so on.

In the last few years I have been an active member of the National Pensioners Convention that represents over eleven million older people, although only a fraction of that number are actually members; nonetheless, we are now the largest single group in Britain. I have attended various protests but my main voluntary work is writing to my constituency MP, Government Ministers and others, highlighting pensioner poverty issues hoping it has an impact on future policy. On a limited budget the paid staff and volunteers do a fantastic amount of work by bringing to the attention of politicians, media and public the financial predicament many older people find themselves in today after a lifetime of working.

CHAPTER FIFTEEN

MEETING MY FORMER TUTOR, ACTIVITIES WITH ANNA, FRIENDSHIPS AND MEDICAL MISDIAGNOSES

On one large demonstration in which I participated not long ago, which was against draconian Government policy cuts, there, to my delight, I came across my former Tutor at City University, Dr John Cowley. John, who is a short, placid, intelligent man, had worked at the City University for some considerable time, and his main teaching subject was in Sociology having obtained his Doctorate studying Marx's scientific materialism. As his tutor group was made up of mostly mature students, I think John took us under his wing by explaining the nature of University life and to be aware of those lecturers, if given the chance, who would try to intellectually beat us up. That day on the demonstration in Hyde Park he explained to me that he was trying to get his latest book published but so far had been unsuccessful. I know that over the years John has put a lot of his time and energy into developing neighbourhood activities and helps manage a shop for local people where they can meet, have tea, buy inexpensive clothes and generally keep in touch with each other. The nature of his research over the years has been to study the behaviour of organised human groups. I'm so pleased I met John Cowley at University, because I learnt, among other things, that due to inherent power within groups, the individual's position in that process is not fixed.

The one fulfilling area in my life today is still the pleasure I receive from my relationship with Anna who is good fun and intelligent to be with. Over a period of many years we have continued walking, visited various Art exhibitions, sometimes accompanied by her Danish friends, visited the Theatre, Opera and many more other enjoyable activities. I often wonder what I have done to deserve such great fortune. Over the years I have met two of her closest friends, Peter and Ingeborg, when both have travelled to visit Anna in London, and being in love with the arts themselves, they have visited many art exhibitions, theatres and cinemas. Anna has known Peter for over fifty years, having first met him in London when she was young yet determined to make a good life for herself. Peter is tall, intelligent, affable, a former lecturer and an obsessive collector of various books, videos, and DVDs. It is true to say that whenever Peter visits Anna in London, I am usually unable to pick his large case off the floor due to the enormous number of books therein. Ingeborg, Peter's partner, is also an intelligent, articulate woman who has taught languages at her local college over the years. As both of them are now retired, they have the opportunity to get more involved with various local activities but what they enjoy doing most of all, I believe, other than spending time with their families, is to travel to different countries.

Only last May 2012, Anna and I travelled to Aarhus, which is in Jutland and is Denmark's second largest City, to visit

Peter and Ingeborg for several days. Although I have travelled to many places in Denmark before, Aarhus had not been one of them. I found it a fascinating place, where the old part of the city is juxtaposed with a new modern 21st century city. For example, our hosts showed us round the large harbour that is now being re-developed by building modern blocks of apartments for the young Danes. During the last 50 years the Danish economy has grown considerably to give its people a comfortable lifestyle supported by an effective benefits system. We stayed in Ingeborg's well-decorated spacious flat which overlooks a quadrangle where residents can meet, grow vegetables and fruit and hang out their washing without interference. I am told that Denmark used to build a lot of its apartment blocks with the same kind of resident community spirit in mind, especially during the height of industrialisation, when people could grow fresh food for themselves.

Regards some of Anna's other British friends, at first I used to feel very unsure of myself, probably anxious, mindful of what they did, or had done, for a living which would have been a profession or rank superior in every way to the employment positions I had held. Most of these people Anna has known for over forty years when she was first married to her then husband. But after a while, I became self-assured in the company of these decent people who showed me the utmost respect, and communication became more open and interesting between us. I was fascinated to know where they had grown up, what motivated them to embark on a particular course of learning and how their professional status had developed over the years. But if you are not born within a particular class or background then your life chances could be rather limited from the outset. For example, it would have been quite legitimate to have predicted, from our working class background, what Peter Upton and I would probably have done for a living. Nonetheless over time I have spent some enjoyable time with some of the people I have referred to above whose hospitality I very much appreciate.

Once again I state that friendships constitute the one area of my life that I find gives me great satisfaction and is something I have craved for a great deal of my life. It is a wonderfully reassuring feeling that the people you spend time with take you seriously as an individual, unlike my earlier life where I was undermined by so many different people, including some of my siblings, which consequently affected my self-esteem. Friendship, not mates or acquaintances, is something I have been consciously aware of since my days at the Croydon Buddhist Centre. In my friendships I try to be honest and open although I've realised you must keep working at them otherwise they will stagnate.

Although I worked very hard at various educational establishments during the six years I studied to pass my qualifications, I would be less than disingenuous if I did not state that I was really disappointed with the nature of the social work/care jobs I had. Having sorted out some of my own problems at the time, I no doubt rushed into social work naively thinking I could save or at least help others from the same fate. I did find social care work somewhat rewarding, but only to a limited extent although as I have already mentioned, I learnt a lot about human problems and the good decent people, from varying backgrounds, who do their best to support others. If I had given myself more time to think about my next move after passing the Access course, or had sought professional advice, then my employment outcomes might have been different. However, environmental work interests me very much and I did attend two horticultural colleges belatedly, where I was offered two-year diploma courses in land management, but by this stage I was, if not too old, then I certainly did not have the resources to have paid my way.

As medical misdiagnoses continues into the 21st century, all I can really say on the subject is this: If you can, then stay away from doctors unless you have a minor medical problem that is relatively straightforward to treat. Otherwise, do not unquestioningly take their medication and certainly not over long periods of time unless you are sure it is beneficial to your health. You can get support from family, friends and many organisations who will help you with emotional or other needs. As individuals we have developed skills, experience and empathy to help each other in acute crisis, therefore, there is no need to always run for the medical machinery to treat our problems. Swallowing lots of different pills for long periods of time will not necessarily improve your well-being. Stay physically close to that person who is suffering from stress or anxiety or depression, even hold them, act as a witness to their suffering, and in time things will improve. Please remember, doctors themselves don't really know if their pills work or not; for them it is a question of suck it and see.

CHAPTER SIXTEEN

MY MOVE TO WOODINGDEAN, POLICE INVESTIGATION AND COUNSELLING

In June 2011 at the age of sixty-five, I decided to move to Woodingdean which is on the fringes of the attractive South Downs not four miles east of Brighton in Sussex. Why did I want to move fifty miles away, after seventeen years of on-going support and friendship that I was receiving from my partner Anna in London? It was without doubt the most difficult and heart-wrenching decision I have ever had to make in my entire life. The main reason why I had continued to live next door to Anna was that in time we considered, that at some stage, we could live together for the rest of our lives. But due to Anna's on-going complex financial arrangements it was impossible at this moment in time. Furthermore, I had recently phoned a housing charity based in Brighton on the off chance to see if they had any accommodation vacancies, to be told by the manager that a bungalow had just become available—notwithstanding that the same manager had previously offered me the opportunity of a tenancy three years before; so out of respect, I travelled a week later to inspect the bungalow, deciding the next day over the phone to accept their offer.

A secondary consideration as to why I wanted to move away from the tenancy I had for 17 years was because I did not enjoy living in a multi-occupied house where tenants, and sometimes their drunken friends, would come and go any time of the day or night making unreasonable noises that used to wake me up at a time when I was trying to establish myself in social work. That anti-social behaviour continued intermittently for several years after. Many times throughout my tenancy when I've been woken in the early morning by unreasonable noise, I could fortunately go next door to sleep in Anna's house. For the first six years in my flat there was no loud noise at all but when the three older female tenants died, (those who had been living there when I first arrived), things changed considerably. If my long enjoyable relationship with Anna had not lasted, I had several opportunities over the years where I could easily have moved away although I am grateful to my former Landlord for giving me the tenancy to the flat all those years ago when I was homeless.

I found a local remover in London who transported all my worldly goods, not very much I can assure you, down to Woodingdean where I moved into my well-decorated comfortable terraced bungalow on 6th June 2011, feeling that I had done the right thing, knowing that there was no return to my previous flat. The removers placed all my chattels and goods in the middle of the lounge/diner/sitting room or whatever it is called and asked me to sign something (which I did hoping it wasn't my life savings!), before leaving when I gave both the removers £10 each. That was it! I was left on my own desperately looking at all this stuff on the floor wondering where it was all going to fit, or rather, I was anticipating some of my new neighbours coming in to give me support, but not realising at the time that the average age was about 80 years.

Having erased that idea from my mind, I opened the smart looking sliding doors that opened out onto a small stone slab patio. Brilliant, I thought—the right size for late night drinking parties or early morning breakfasts where I would be bombarded by low flying gulls trying to shit over the toast! Beyond the patio is the communal lawn and each tenant has a small patch of flower border that they can either maintain themselves or have the weekly gardener do it with no added cost. After a couple of hours during which time I had contemplated phoning the Samaritans, my mood lifted when I thought of the sexy black senior magistrate who I used to visit in Marylebone—but then realised that by now she must be as old and ugly as I am! Reality dawned when Anna phoned me to ask how the move went: did I have any food and if not, there was a very good Indian takeaway, she kindly informed me, just ten minutes away in the village. 'Thank you sweetheart,' I murmured to Anna, 'I was thinking of going into Brighton for a curry!'

Over the next week or so I managed to find a home for all the stuff on my bungalow floor that had accumulated over the years bought from various places like Oxfam, Scope, the Heart Foundation and many more well-deserving charitable organisations. When I think about it, after sixty-five years on this earth, all I have to my name is a small amount of savings and a few chattels and goods that altogether are worth no more than £100. It reminds me of the time when I had once worked on large Council Estates in South London looking after the well-being of a particular group of older clients who had worked all their lives, many of them over fifty years, yet owned very little.

One client, Cecil, aged about 85, had lived a colourful life, joining the Merchant Navy when he was 14 so that he 'could see the world, otherwise, me son, poor people like me didn't have a chance to do anyfink,' as he ruefully remarked. After leaving the Merchant Navy, Cecil worked for the next fifty years for a large London building company, first as a labourer, then worked his way up to a supervisor , saying 'that was a decent job that was son, workin' in and arund London all my workin' life.' When I first met Cecil he was cleaning his path after a covering of snow fell the night before. He asked my colleague and me in for tea, apologising for the dirty state of his small flat that he had occupied on his own for the last forty years. Although he had worked all his life, Cecil possessed very little furniture and most of that was old cheap stuff he had bought from a local second-hand shop.

Back in Woodingdean my life is settling down to a routine. There are six other tenants, including Clive whom I had first met some twenty-years ago when I was his lodger for a short while at his home near Croydon. When he sold his house he moved to a Housing Association owned flat in Crystal Palace where he lived for several years. When my relationship with Linda had finished I was subsequently offered a flat with the same Housing Association, a consequence of Clive putting my name forward. Similarly here in Woodingdean, it was Clive several years ago who first gave my details to the manager, where I was subsequently offered accommodation, but I declined for personal reasons at the time. So I owe a gratitude of thanks to him for his support in helping me obtain the small attractive bungalow which I now occupy.

It was during my four monthly botulinum injections in March 2012, at the National Hospital in London, that the consultant mentioned, not for the first time, myoclonus dystonia. He went on to explain that the jerks I have are possible myoclonus originating from when I was younger. The consultant wrote to my GP explaining this rare condition, suggesting a regular supply of medication to be worthwhile when the jerks flare up. According to a Dystonia Society leaflet on the subject: 'Myoclonus dystonia is a rare condition where myoclonus (sudden 'electric-shock'-like jerks of the muscles) and dystonia occur in combination. This type of dystonia typically starts in childhood, and usually affects the neck, trunk and arms. The jerking movements and the dystonia may improve when alcohol is taken.'

Although I have not had the opportunity to discuss myoclonus dystonia in depth with the consultant, I have considered, on many occasions, that the condition could have been linked to being electrocuted at a young age. However, with the passing of the years, it is now virtually impossible to ascertain if that was the case or not. As I have mentioned earlier in the book, I realised from the earliest days with dystonia that it was alcohol responsive. Furthermore, I have also read that myoclonus dystonia can be associated with childhood psychiatric disturbance which is reasonable to suggest in my case when considering my early disturbed background and subsequent personal underdevelopment.

At first I have had very little structure in my everyday life outside of where I am living here in Woodingdean. However, the one major area of interest in all my adult life has been walking, which was a factor in moving down to the South Coast. Over the years Daniel, Mick and I have walked the whole 100-mile length of the South Downs Way from Eastbourne to Winchester which passes through some outstanding scenery. During the first few months walking not only afforded me the opportunity to get lots of exercise on the large expanse of the beautiful South Downs but it also gave me the time I needed to think about my past problems which at times felt insurmountable. Furthermore, I now have the time, unlike before, where I was mindful of having to take the train back to London, to walk leisurely around the Downs taking in the abundance of different colourful wild flowers growing there. The long warm summer days on the Downs, which is my real home, are truly magical and inspiring as on most weekdays one doesn't meet other people except for the odd walker or cyclist.

When I am not on the Downs or at home, I am strongly influenced by the gravitational pull to take the local bus some four miles into Central Brighton to be amongst other human beings. Having visited Brighton for many years—my first visit was when my mother's shouting embarrassed us on the beach—I was quite familiar with the town centre but areas further afield less so. The influence of the gravitational pull attracted me to start using various pubs, bars and coffee shops that I had not previously known. These places, I hoped, might be the kind of decadent places used by similar characters I had associated with during my life. In most of those morally reprehensible environments that I had frequented over the years, there were various characters such as transvestites, gays, the mentally ill, drug addicts, alcoholics, tramps, petty thieves and many more individuals who for one reason or other, like me, tended not to fit in.

During my many forays into these places, I found that most of these people are situated in the Kemp Town area. I would usually take up my usual stance by putting space between me and most of the other drinkers until I felt assured that there was no danger. This lifelong preoccupation with space probably means, until I am confident that another person does not want to undermine or humiliate me, I remain wary of their motives. As lonely or isolated as I have felt during my short time in Woodingdean, I still find it incredibly difficult, not to meet, but to sustain social contacts. On many occasions over the past year or so I have met some apparently friendly decent people whose only motive, it appeared, was to have a chat over a beer and sometimes offer their contact details.

After I am sufficiently confident about a particular person, I then exchange personal details, although I don't do that every time, explaining that I will contact them at some time. This has happened at least on three or four occasions when I have been offered personal contact details of someone, then later deciding to delete it from my phone or throw away the written identity of that person. Sometime later maybe one, two or three months have passed when I return to that same place hoping the person is still around to talk with. Sometimes people are sympathetic but that doesn't last until they decide not to acknowledge my presence at all which I find at various times painful or even alienating. Those are confusing experiences, like numerous others throughout my life, when it is very difficult to find my authentic voice among a maelstrom of many others all fighting each other to be given the opportunity to speak out.

What I do find reassuring, however, is when I see the familiar friendly faces of Anna, Mick, Daniel and Lucy, Mick's wife, who have all visited me down here on different occasions. Whenever possible we all go out walking somewhere or other around the Downs; afterwards we usually stop for a drink and a meal.

Only last July 2012, Daniel and I went walking for five days on the South West Coast path covering nearly thirty miles by taking in the areas of Gwithian, St Ives and Morvah as we inched our way round this beautiful, inspiring and challenging 630 miles from Somerset to Dorset—ever optimistic that we can finish the longest walk in England before our legs pack up on us.

Recently, Daniel, my friend and walking partner for about twelve years now, and I had a most enjoyable walk on the attractive South Downs. We walked the two miles from Hassocks Station, where we met, to the top of the Downs to pick up the South Downs Way near Clayton Windmills. We then headed south on the Sussex Border path, a long-distance track that winds its way round Sussex, to the A27 passing along the way the Chattri Indian War Memorial, and as we walked we had views of the beautiful expanse of the open Downs. We continued walking on the Sussex Border path, this time heading north until we reached Devil's Dyke, a deep dry valley, where we changed direction to head south, once again, three miles over the downs to Mile Oak where we took our bus into Brighton. When we got off the bus, anticipating a few cool beers, Daniel came out with one of his characteristic jokes, saying 'it appears I've got the Mile Oaks'—no doubt referring to a sore crutch. 'More Johnsons baby powder?' I wryly reminded Daniel.

In early October 2012, Anna, Daniel and I returned from an intensively enjoyable seven-day walking trip in the small mountainous country of Montenegro. Having seceded from Serbia after the Balkans conflict, prosperity is returning slowly to a country that is determined to be in charge of its own destiny. Our hotel was set in the beautiful Bay of Kotor, southern Europe's deepest bay, with wonderfully enticing walks in the hills behind the local town and also across the bay including Lovcen National Park. Our Ramblers guide, ably assisted by a local guide, took us out every day on different, challenging and enjoyable walks that surrounded the Bay of Kotor. Without doubt that was one of my most enjoyable walking holidays with Ramblers.

Over the years it has been Ramblers Holidays, amongst many other activities, that has contributed to my personal development, especially in trying to make my voice stronger within a group of individuals I have not previously seen. Although I still find it very difficult to interact with some people, Ramblers Holidays has given me the opportunity to become more confident and assertive in the company of mainly successful middle-class professional groups. There have been times when I have been argumentative with some walkers, and I apologise to those particular individuals who have thought me unreasonable, but on the whole I think I have managed myself well. It is important to remember that these walking groups attract certain individuals who are usually over the age of sixty, successful, assertive and who know what they want out of their holidays. These walkers are intelligent but they are not always right or correct when they assert their opinions or ideas, which means at times I have to challenge people who are able, most of the time, to skilfully argue their case. In the past, due to being constantly undermined by various people, I would have been too sensitive to have had the confidence to challenge assertive intelligent people. These experiences have given me the opportunity to become a stronger person within a demanding setting, that in the past I have found very difficult, to find a strong enough voice to make myself heard above the noise of my family life.

From the depth of my heart I would like to thank all those individuals, especially my parents, who tried to support me during those darkest days when I was overwhelmed by conditions that I found insurmountable. My parents provided a home for me, at important times, when I was unable to venture too far into what I thought was a hostile world. After spending several days away travelling around, they would unquestioningly provide me with the sustenance to survive: warm bed, hot wholesome food and clean clothes when I returned. That allowed me the time to try to sort things out, but on your own, with the nature of the problems I had, it was an uphill task especially when you consider I suffered from a lifelong chronic insecurity. Of course my parents didn't know what was happening to me, nor could they offer any help with my many problems, but neither could the doctors who caused the medical addiction problems in the first place. It has never been my intention of playing the victim game, far from it, as I was responsible for myself. However, I can forgive but cannot forget that at times my parents were irresponsible and negligent and failed to look after vulnerable children when they most needed love, warmth and security.

One has to consider the inadequate or irresponsible way I tried to sort out my own personal problems. Though my former GP was responsible for prescribing BZ over 17 years, I should, however, have taken responsibility for drinking excess alcohol; that, at times, was frankly reckless, even though moderate amounts did benefit dystonia. Furthermore, it is unknown what part alcohol played, if any, in the management of myoclonus dystonia, especially as it is now considered to be a child onset condition. The selling of my BZ prescriptions was irresponsible and illegal and I would like to apologise for my immature behaviour. I may also have made unjustifiable medical demands on various hospital A&E departments, but trying to find more than mere shelter for the night can be subsequently understood from the point of view of a vulnerable, confused young man, as I then was, desperately seeking help. But, I did of course, waste valuable limited resources that hospitals can ill afford to lose and have always desperately needed to provide effective services for an ever-growing country. Once again I do sincerely apologise to all those well trained professionals who showed me no less than human understanding and kindness.

Finally it has only been in the last two years or so that I have had the confidence or courage to try and explain to my friends the various incidents that happened to me during my life. That process had been painful yet cathartic which gave me the courage to write this book about myself. In writing this book I have been mindful that none of my siblings will be aware of all or most of its contents.

Suffice to say Brighton and Surrey police forces have worked with me making investigations into the sexual assault allegations that I have made against the two paedophiles. Those investigations are complete (January 2013) as both men are now deceased. My sincere thanks go to both police forces.

The Brighton sexual assault centre, victim support and mankind counselling service have all been most helpful and supportive. Thank you all so much.

My story continues...